W9-BNQ-710

More Advance Praise for *Secrets of the Moneylab*

"*Secrets of the Moneylab* is an entertaining introduction to the economic principles of risk, choice, trust, and consumer behavior."

> —Preston McAfee, vice president and research fellow at
> Yahoo! Research and author of *Competitive Solutions*

"This is a well-written book that clearly articulates the value that experimental economics brings to businesses."

> —Bernardo Huberman, senior HP fellow and director of
> the Social Computing Lab at HP Labs

"Chen and Krakovsky superbly introduce the underlying behaviors of human decision making. Whether you're a novice or a guru, *Secrets of the Moneylab* has something to offer."

> —Feryal Erhun, assistant professor, management science
> and engineering, Stanford University

"This is a brilliant book. It shows you how to apply powerful behavioral economics methods to revolutionize the way you run your business. It is a must-read for any scientifically minded manager."

> —Teck-Hua Ho, William Halford Jr. Family Professor of Marketing,
> Haas School of Business, University of California, Berkeley

SECRETS OF THE
MONEYLAB

HOW BEHAVIORAL ECONOMICS
CAN IMPROVE YOUR BUSINESS

Kay-Yut Chen
and Marina Krakovsky

PORTFOLIO / PENGUIN

PORTFOLIO PENGUIN
Published by the Penguin Group
Penguin Group (USA) Inc., 375 Hudson Street, New York, New York 10014, U.S.A.
Penguin Group (Canada), 90 Eglinton Avenue East, Suite 700, Toronto,
Ontario, Canada M4P 2Y3 (a division of Pearson Penguin Canada Inc.)
Penguin Books Ltd, 80 Strand, London WC2R 0RL, England
Penguin Ireland, 25 St Stephen's Green, Dublin 2, Ireland (a division of Penguin Books Ltd)
Penguin Books Australia Ltd, 250 Camberwell Road, Camberwell,
Victoria 3124, Australia (a division of Pearson Australia Group Pty Ltd)
Penguin Books India Pvt Ltd, 11 Community Centre,
Panchsheel Park, New Delhi—110 017, India
Penguin Group (NZ), 67 Apollo Drive, Rosedale, North Shore 0632,
New Zealand (a division of Pearson New Zealand Ltd)
Penguin Books (South Africa) (Pty) Ltd, 24 Sturdee Avenue,
Rosebank, Johannesburg 2196, South Africa

Penguin Books Ltd, Registered Offices:
80 Strand, London WC2R 0RL, England

First published in 2010 by Portfolio Penguin,
a member of Penguin Group (USA) Inc.

1   3   5   7   9   10   8   6   4   2

Library of Congress Cataloging-in-Publication Data

Chen, Kay-Yut.
Secrets of the moneylab : how behavioral economics can improve your business / Kay-Yut Chen
and Marina Krakovsky.
p. cm.
Includes bibliographical references and index.
ISBN 978-1-59184-354-2
1. Economics—Psychological aspects.   2. Success in business.   I. Krakovsky, Marina.   II. Title.
HB74.P8C44 2010
658.4'032—dc22
2010017339

Printed in the United States of America
Set in Fairfield LH
Designed by Vicky Hartman

To our parents,

without whom nothing would be possible:

Fong-Ching Chen and Ngar-Sheung Lam Chen

and

Rina and Gennady Krakovsky

CONTENTS

· · · · · · · · · · · · ·

Foreword   ix

INTRODUCTION   1

1.   CAPITALIZING ON UNCERTAINTY   11

2.   FAIR'S FAIR   39

3.   WHAT GOES AROUND: RECIPROCITY   63

4.   CROSSING THE BOUNDS OF REASON: RATIONALITY   86

5.   REPUTATION, REPUTATION, REPUTATION   117

6.   IN WHOM WE TRUST   146

7.   PLAYING TO THE RULES OF THE GAME   172

8.   PREDICTING THE UNPREDICTABLE   188

CONCLUSION   214

Acknowledgments   217

Notes   219

Index   241

Foreword

Secrets of the Moneylab reads like a collection of short stories. It is also excellent economics. This is no coincidence. The economist and the novelist have the same basic problem. They both must describe what motivates people and how they interact, and they need to wrap it up with an interesting conclusion.

A somewhat recent development in economics, beginning in earnest some thirty or forty years ago, has been the incorporation of lab experiments. Kay-Yut is a leading experimental economist at Hewlett-Packard. Economic experiments—some his own, many from others—are a source of Kay-Yut and Marina's stories. As the authors explain, such experiments give managers a tremendously useful tool. When they have an idea, they need not try it out in the outside world; instead they can test it in the company's "Moneylab." Think of the savings—if all our bad ideas could be discarded after inexpensive trial runs.

Just as important, Hewlett-Packard has given Kay-Yut access to its business culture. And we see this practical orientation everywhere in *Secrets of the Moneylab*. The "results" of the Moneylab experiments are not their only important use. The questions they pose are also very valuable.

I confess that I especially like this book because of my own personal method for doing economics. This is my personal secret (not a secret of the Moneylab). My method, especially for listening to seminars, is this: while the seminar speaker is presenting the mathematical model, I try to tell my own corresponding story. I people it with Richard, Sue, and Mary, and reach my own conclusions, not from the mathematics, but from my imagination. This method leads, surprisingly often, to conclusions that are not obvious from the math—but are valid just the same.

But that takes us back to why *Secrets of the Moneylab* is such a good book. In situation after situation, it presents the basic economics in stories. And because we all think most naturally via stories, this is economics that really gets at the truth. You, the reader, will see where and when the economics of *Secrets of the Moneylab* apply because you can ask your own questions regarding how you think Richard, Sue, and Mary will actually interact with one another.

And you will also have a lot of fun. *Secrets of the Moneylab* is economics at its best: a sequence of beautiful stories.

—George A. Akerlof, Nobel Prize–winning economist and author of
Animal Spirits and *Identity Economics*

Introduction

Several years ago, Marina heard that Hewlett-Packard was looking for people to participate in "economic experiments." Something intriguing was happening in her own backyard, and by the sound of it had been going on for years, yet she knew nothing about it. Marina's personal curiosity added to the universal lure of easy money, so she signed up. Before long she was at HP Labs in Palo Alto, with a dozen or so other participants in what looked like a corporate classroom: a gray, windowless room with rows of desktop computers facing a large whiteboard. Once she and the other guests were seated at their terminals, a hyperkinetic man dressed like a math professor began pacing the front of the room. He scribbled an exchange rate on the whiteboard (1,500 experimental dollars = $1 U.S.) and gave brief instructions before setting the research participants to work.

Each participant would play the role of either buyer or seller, interacting with the others through the networked computers. Buyers would order goods from the sellers and pay for them, while sellers would receive payment and choose how much to actually ship. At the end of each period, buyers and sellers would see who'd fulfilled which orders. Given this information, buyers would choose whom to do business with in the next period; sellers, meanwhile, would decide how to proceed themselves. At the end of the game, the money earned during the experiment would convert to U.S. dollars: Marina and the others would earn real cash in proportion to how well they'd played.

The game lasted about two hours. Everyone played in silence, and couldn't so much as send instant messages to each other. Instead, they could communicate only through the buying and selling choices they entered into their computers. Yet they could see so much: which sellers shipped as promised and which ones cheated, how this information seemed to affect future buying decisions, and, in the last bidding period, who stayed honest when honesty no longer paid. They were seeing something of the essence of human nature at work.

When the game was over, a research assistant entered the room with a cashbox in hand and counted out each player's winnings. Marina received about $75.[1]

She wanted to know more: what did any of this have to do with HP's business? What she'd known about HP Labs was what most people in Silicon Valley knew—that its research led to the development of inkjet printing, one of the company's most profitable offerings. But what was a company known for its computers, printers, and calculators doing paying people to play these games?

As a reporter, Marina carried a license to ask nosy questions. When she approached the man who'd run the experiment, he handed her his card: "Kay-Yut Chen, Principal Scientist, Decision Technology Dept."[2]

Kay-Yut, it turned out, wasn't just running that day's experiment—he had started the whole lab, right after finishing his PhD in economics at Caltech. Not only that. HP's lab was the first-ever experimental economics laboratory inside a corporation. That made Kay-Yut one of a kind; he'd been featured in *Newsweek,* and Marina went on to write about his work in *Scientific American* and Portfolio.com.[3]

Learning from Mistakes the Easy Way

The premise of using economic experiments in a company is simple: to make good decisions about major business processes, test them out in the safety of a lab. Without such testing, an HP marketing manager told Marina, "You could waste millions of dollars implementing a program that isn't good." Indeed, that's what would have happened had the manager not asked Kay-Yut to test the idea of rewarding retailers for being among the top three in sales of HP products. On the surface, some healthy competition between the likes of Walmart, Best Buy, and the many other HP vendors seems intuitively appealing; in fact, winner-take-all sales contests are popular in many other industries. But Kay-Yut's experiments, like the buyer-seller game Marina tried, had shown that this incentive would backfire in two ways. In the experiments, most participants playing retailers, seeing that they had little or no chance to win, gave up at the outset. The sure winners, on the other hand, had no incentive to do any better, since they were likely to get the bonus anyway.[4]

Because of these test results, HP scrapped the idea, keeping their existing incentive program, which simply rewarded retailers according to how much business they brought in, in place. That wasn't just because the new program had fared poorly in the lab. Had the programs been equivalent—indeed, even if the new program had offered marginally better results than the old one—it still might never have gotten the green light. Any major change carries hefty costs, such as training and legal review. By telling you exactly how much better one program or policy is than another, experiments help managers decide which changes are worth the expense.

But why even go through the trouble of running an experiment—why not just use a spreadsheet to see which program will make you more money? Managers do this all the time. For example, to compare two incentive programs, a manager might set up a formula to calculate total revenues based on each program—and plug in guesstimates for the relevant variables. The manager might assume, for example, that a winner-take-all program will boost revenues among the top three performers by 5 percent—and then have the spreadsheet calculate total revenues and ultimate profits. And if the assumptions are right, then the spreadsheet will give the right answer, much as a mortgage calculator will correctly tell you which of two mortgages will cost you less over the life of a loan. But what if your assumptions are wrong and your guesstimate is off—what if the program doesn't boost revenues by even 1 percent? Then the spreadsheet won't work, by the immutable law of Garbage In, Garbage Out.

So, to know how people will really respond to incentives—to see how they'll actually think and behave, not how you guess they will—you need to test your assumptions. And rather than testing these the hard way, by rolling out a plan and seeing how it does in the real world, you can run an experiment.

The idea of testing business ideas and confining your mistakes to the lab is so obvious when you hear it that you may wonder, as Marina did, why more companies don't do it. In fact, those on the cutting edge do. Some, like Google and Yahoo!, use in-house labs for fine-tuning keyword auction rules and other advertising programs; others, including eBay, Ford, and Hitachi, have enlisted experimental economists on a consulting basis. A couple of companies, Capital One and Harrah's, have become well-known in the business press for running field experiments, testing out new marketing programs on small samples of actual and prospective customers before rolling out the most effective programs company-wide.[5] And some lesser-known companies use randomized tests to help online retailers see which Web page designs will lead to the most purchases.[6]

But on the whole, experiments are still a highly unusual way of making decisions in business. When the University of Chicago's Booth School of Business premiered a class called "Using Experiments in Firms" in 2008, it was the first of its kind. The teachers were two economists who'd never taught at the business school—Steven Levitt (of *Freakonomics* fame) and John List (who conducts clever field experiments to see, for example, why car mechanics price-discriminate against people in wheelchairs). In most companies, says List, "the level of experimentation is abysmal."[7]

Anybody who's worked in a company knows this, yet it's remarkable given how far experimental economics as a whole has come. As an academic field, experimental economics has been around for several decades, and in 2002 two pioneering experimentalists, economist Vernon Smith and psychologist Daniel Kahneman, shared the Nobel Prize in Economics. Today there are well over a hundred economics labs around the world, not including labs running experiments in related fields such as experimental psychology, management science (or operations research), and marketing science.[8] Even government agencies, not usually the most forward-thinking of organizations, have turned to experimental economists to improve policy decisions, such as how best to sell broadcast spectrum rights or how best to grant rights to use tracks on a public railroad.[9] But businesses, which should care more than anyone about maximizing profits, have largely ignored the experimental approach.

Some of the reasons make sense. Unlike basic academic experiments, ones that use a simple, highly stylized game to look at just one aspect of human behavior, the kinds of experiments run by Kay-Yut and his counterparts at other companies often incorporate the myriad important details of an actual business setting. For example, in an experiment we'll look at later about the effects of different Minimum Advertised Price policies, HP simultaneously took into account many variables, such as the differing goals of the company's many retailers (from e-commerce partners who care mainly about market share to big-box retailers who try to maximize quarterly profits), relationships between sales of different products, and product life cycles (from introduction to phaseout). Designing an experiment like that takes not just experimental know-how, but also a deep knowledge of the business. Equally daunting, it takes time and attention, something managers busy fighting the fire du jour don't have.

In the end, the biggest obstacle to adopting experimental techniques may be simple inertia: it's easier to just keep doing things the way they've always been done, especially if your competitors aren't threatening to outpace you in their methods. If something ain't broke, why fix it?

But following tradition doesn't always yield the best possible results. Even so-called best practices may have better alternatives—and only by trying these alternatives do better practices ever emerge. For example, a long-standing tradition in the airline industry is to schedule flights through hubs, such as O'Hare, JFK, and LAX. This hub-and-spoke system makes it possible to offer many more routes with the same number of planes, so major national airlines have gone along with it at least as far back as the 1980s, when the government stopped regulating which cities the airlines must serve.

For all its efficiency, the hub-and-spoke system creates congestion and delays, and forces travelers between smaller cities (like El Paso, Texas, and Fresno, California) to take two or more connecting flights.

But since every player was subjected to this, the airlines hadn't had to change their ways. And by going unchallenged for many years, the practice of flying planes through the world's busiest airports remained a "best practice."

Southwest Airlines founder and former CEO Herb Kelleher saw an opportunity to break with this tradition. After all, passengers prefer direct flights and hate delays. What's more, delays are costly for the airlines themselves. By abandoning the hub-and-spoke model, Southwest became the most profitable airline in history. As Kelleher would say, "Those airplanes aren't making any money while they're sitting on the ground."[10] In part by flying into smaller, less congested airports, he was able to offer a seemingly impossible combination: better service at lower prices.

But the lesson here isn't to be like Kelleher. His point-to-point strategy, like Southwest's many other innovations, could have easily backfired, in which case nobody would be writing books about "Southwest Airlines' crazy recipe for business and personal success." The idea is simply that by always following established best practices, a person or organization will never find out if something else might work better. To innovate and distinguish yourself from the pack—and to surpass your own personal best— you must take some risks, and to make these risks less risky, you can test out your ideas, keeping what works and abandoning what doesn't.

The experimental approach is just starting to catch on. The movement, which began in economics and psychology departments (and went on to become standard practice in both), has made its way to leading business schools—including Wharton, Harvard, Stanford, MIT's Sloan School—where researchers have used experiments to better understand how people lend and invest money (the field of "behavioral finance"), how managers make efficient use of resources ("behavioral operations management"), how people act in groups ("organizational behavior"), and how shoppers choose what to buy ("consumer behavior"). From the business schools, which teach the next generation of business leaders, the next step is application in firms, as the early-adopting companies are already showing.

Still, not every company will start its own experimental economics lab, and not every business decision merits the cost—especially in time—of designing and running such carefully controlled tests. Sometimes, you have to make the best decision you can with the information you already have. Yet your current knowledge may not be enough; for most people, that knowledge comes from a messy mix of habit and intuition, conventional wisdom, personal experience, and anecdotal data about what seems to have worked for others—not the most evidence-based way to do business.

Fortunately, you don't have to choose between running the kinds of experiments HP does or simply flying by the seat of your pants. That's because plenty of decisions can benefit from the many insights already gleaned from the research. For example, the HP buyer-seller experiment Marina participated in is part of a larger body of experiments on reputation. These experiments reveal broader truths about how reputation works and how people use information about reputations to make business decisions. Whether you're running a large organization or simply managing your own career, you'd be wise to learn from them.

As you'll see throughout the book, the same is true for the vast body of research done by economists and other social scientists working in universities. Their experimental investigations into people's sense of fairness and reciprocity, attitudes toward risk and trust, the human tendency to game the system, novel methods of prediction—all these areas of research and more offer new, scientifically grounded ways of thinking about the forces that drive human behavior in business.

The most brilliant businesspeople already have a good feel for many of these principles, though they can't always articulate them. The distinguished economist Charlie Plott, a mentor and sometime collaborator of Kay-Yut, happens to be an avid fisherman—and he compares a great businessperson to a fish in a stream. "The fish knows how to operate so as to catch a fly. It can move through the water in an energy-minimizing way, position itself, and strike effectively. But the fish can't understand hydrodynamics. Like the fish, the businessman is good at doing what he does. That doesn't mean he understands the principles that govern what he's doing." This lack of insight into why what you're doing works, Plott suggests, comes from being too immersed. Or, as Plott puts it, "To understand the science you need to be outside the water."

But what if you're already great at what you do, fortunate to have excellent business sense—why should you bother learning formal principles like the ones we lay out? And why should you listen to the advice of eggheads with little firsthand experience running a business? For the same reason seasoned business leaders like Mark Hurd of HP and Meg Whitman, formerly of eBay, have. Here a sports analogy helps: every top athlete, despite natural talent and years of practice, needs a coach.[11] And not just to push the athlete, but to improve form and make a great technique even better. In a sense, that's what Kay-Yut and his colleagues have done for the business leaders who turn to them, and it's what this book aims to do for you.

About Our Approach

This book draws on several decades of experimental research in business, psychology, and economics. Although the experimental approach is at the heart of this book, we don't limit ourselves to tightly controlled lab studies, which, as you'll see in later chapters, have their own limitations. Where possible, we bring in field experiments but, like lab studies, these are sometimes impossible to run, for either ethical or practical reasons; so we cite dozens of findings from other scientific ways of knowing, particularly so-called natural experiments, such as those on the effects of hygiene report cards on restaurant revenues. And though we're skeptical of stories and cherry-picked examples as a form of evidence—just as you're right to be—memorable anecdotes are an excellent way to illustrate a point; that's why we use them throughout the book. Likewise, though experiments can't always answer *why* people do what they do, people are curious about such things, so we often offer plausible (if sometimes speculative) explanations, citing evidence when it's available. In general, we believe that the more you understand and remember about how people make business decisions, the better your own decisions in dealing with others will be.

What happens when you don't have a good grasp of human economic behavior? If you're chairman of the Federal Reserve Board, the result can be national disaster. During the 1990s boom, Alan Greenspan famously mentioned "irrational exuberance" as a cause for escalating stock prices;

after the financial meltdown, Greenspan admitted before Congress that the meltdown—unprecedented in his long and distinguished career—shocked him into seeing a fundamental flaw in his understanding of how the world works.

Your own decisions may never have the kind of impact (for good or ill) that a central banker's would—and this book isn't about government policy anyway. But whomever you're dealing with—whether it be your rivals, your boss, your customers, your suppliers, or your employees—knowing more about what drives human behavior will help you make better use of the power you do have.

How to Read This Book

We start by exploring what makes people tick. Traditional thinking in economics, and even in the business world, has been that people are essentially greedy, selfishly driven by the desire for personal profit above all else. There's obviously some truth to this, but over the past two or three decades new research has told a more complex story, as we show in chapters 1, 2, and 3. Chapter 1 focuses on something most people *don't* want yet that constantly hovers above us all: uncertainty. We show how much people are willing to pay to reduce uncertainty—and help you see ways to profit from reducing uncertainty without going into the insurance business. Chapter 2 takes you through the research on fairness around the world. We also look at several other important values (or what economists call "social preferences") that consistently drive human behavior when money enters the picture. Chapter 3 turns to another major motivator: we look at the business and philanthropic implications of the powerful human urge to reciprocate, as well as the ways an over-reliance on financial incentives can disrupt other motives.

Once you understand what people want, how do you know what they'll actually do? That's the question we tackle in chapters 4 through 7. Chapter 4 shows the limits of our ability to optimize for what we want. Since people will never perform as optimally as machines, we show how to nudge your partners' decisions closer to the optimal level. Chapters

5 and 6 are twins, both dealing with how people cope with one type of uncertainty: uncertainty about other people's behavior. Reputation is one way to deal with this type of uncertainty, and it's the focus of chapter 5. We show the economic value of a reputation and lay out the many ways you can capitalize on a good one. We also disentangle several often-confused aspects of reputation and offer caveats about what reputation can and can't predict. Chapter 6 extends the discussion of coping with people's unpredictability through a broader discussion of trust; we introduce the Trust Game and show what it reveals about developing trusting, wealth-creating relationships with others. And we go beyond the Trust Game to show several scientifically grounded ways of proving yourself trustworthy and deciding whom to trust.

Chapter 7 deals with what people do in situations where rules are important. People may be selfish or altruistic, and limited in their ability to maximize for whatever goals they have, but whatever system you set up, many will try to game it, often subverting the system's actual intent. Focusing on systems with timing rules—from negotiations and auctions to compensation schemes and penalty systems—we show the systematic ways people game them and offer advice for avoiding similar pitfalls as you make up the rules for your own systems.

In chapter 8 we delve into a hot topic in business experiments: predicting the seemingly unpredictable. We discuss the ins and outs of "crowd wisdom" prediction markets, from the just-for-fun Hollywood Stock Exchange to internal markets in HP and other companies. We also introduce other ways to make business predictions and reduce the costs of uncertainty.

In the final chapter, we leave you with some ideas about how to start applying the many principles you've learned throughout the book.

Through *Secrets of the Moneylab,* we hope to inspire a fresh way of looking at the world, as if through the eyes of an economist. You may never run a controlled experiment or even hire an outside expert to do it for you, but we hope you'll at least begin to question all-or-nothing thinking, seek data to challenge your hunches, track distributions and not just averages, watch hidden costs, question one-size-fits-all advice, and harness the big power of small changes.

1

··············

Capitalizing on Uncertainty

In 1754, Giacomo Casanova tested his luck in a Venetian gambling house. Gambling was nothing new to Casanova, who since his student days had experienced both winning streaks and devastating losses, including a stint in debtors prison. But this time the legendary libertine was playing for high personal stakes: one of his lovers, a well-born nun who in his autobiography he discreetly calls M— M—, wanted to leave the convent. Trying to raise money for her escape, Casanova played faro, a roulette-like card game in which winning a bet on the color of the card drawn doubles your money.

To beat the casino, Casanova used a betting strategy called the "martingale." The strategy is simple: you start with a small bet, and if you win, start again by betting the same amount. If you lose, double your previous bet, and keep going until you win. The idea is that you're bound to win eventually—and when you do, you'll not only cover your losses, but also come out ahead of where you started. For example, suppose you start with a $5 bet. If you lose $5, you double your bet, and if you lose that $10 bet, you bet $20, and so on until you win. Suppose you lose the first four bets, and win the fifth, getting $80. The $80 win covers your first four losses, which total $75 ($5+$10+$20+$40), and leaves you $5 ahead of where you began.

For Casanova, the martingale strategy worked well for several days in a row. Soon enough, though, his fortune turned, and the martingale couldn't reverse it once his money ran out. The couple sold MM's diamonds, but through more gambling quickly lost the proceeds from that sale. In the end, Casanova writes, "There was no more talk of her escaping from the convent, for we had nothing to live on!"[1] Rather than besting the casino, he'd lost his shirt.

There's something compelling about the martingale—and the many other progressive betting strategies devised since. The idea that reds and blacks, or wins and losses, tend to even out appeals to our sense of how the world works. And it's tempting to think you can turn uncertainty into certainty by applying skill to win a game of chance. But as Casanova's example shows, faith in the martingale reveals a misunderstanding of how chance actually works. It's true that reds and blacks tend to balance out in the long run—that's the Law of Large Numbers. But it's not true that they balance out in a short time. In a deck of fifty-two cards, for example, getting seven reds in a row is not uncommon, though people find it remarkable when it happens. In fact, although the chance of getting seven reds in a row at any specific point—say, at the beginning of the deck—is low, the chance of such a run *somewhere* in the deck is about 1 in 3, and with more decks the probability rises.

If you had infinite wealth and no limits on how much to wager, the martingale would work. (Of course, if you had infinite wealth, you wouldn't be trying to win more.) But casinos have table limits. For example, a table with a $5 minimum bet might have a maximum bet of $500. If you keep doubling your initial bet, you'll come up against the table limit after seven losing bets (the seventh bet being $320), so even if you could be sure the eighth bet will be a winner, you won't be able to use the martingale to recoup your losses (which by this time amount to $635) because the most the casino will let you bet is $500. Thus the casino tends to win even in a game without a house edge.[2]

What's more, without a table limit (and with no house edge), the casino would still beat a progressive betting strategy because everybody has a personal limit. You may empty your savings account, max out your credit cards, and pawn your jewelry—but sooner or later you'll hit your personal limit. The casino, on the other hand, while not infinitely wealthy, is much better capitalized than you are. A few bad bets may wipe you out, but a few players' big wins won't wipe the casino out. Able to cope with the swings of uncertainty, the casino always wins in the end: through the Law of Large Numbers, the casino transforms uncertainty into certainty.

This is not a chapter about the casino business. Nor is it about lotteries, stock markets, or the insurance industry. But we use examples from all these fields because they're a simple way to illustrate important lessons about uncertainty and people's attitudes toward it. Though uncertainty can be unsettling, if you understand how it works you'll be able to make money from it as surely as the casinos and insurance companies do.

Risk Avoider—Who, Me?

Are you a risk taker, or do you try to avoid risks? If you're at one of the extremes, the answer is easy. Do you love to bet on a long shot in the hope of a big payoff? Then you're a risk taker. If, on the other hand, you'd rather play it safe, sticking with what little you've got instead of risking it for whatever's behind Door #2, well, you get the picture. But most of us lie between these two extremes. Luckily, there are ways to get at your risk attitude—to tell not only which way you lean, but pretty closely how much. One way to do this is through a simple experiment, designed by economists Charles Holt and Susan Laury,[3] in which you choose which of two lotteries to play in. For example, suppose you see this choice:

Option A	Option B
1/10 of $2.00, 9/10 of $1.60	1/10 of $3.85, 9/10 of $0.10

If you choose Option A, you have a 10 percent chance of winning $2.00 and a 90 percent chance of winning $1.60. If you choose Option B, on the other hand, you have a 10 percent chance of winning $3.85, and a 90 percent chance of winning $0.10.

Notice that the spread in Option B is much wider than in Option A: even though the upside in B is much higher (in percentage terms) than in A, the downside is much lower, too. Option B, therefore, is a much bigger gamble than A. If real money is on the line, do you take the safe bet of A (in which case you'll win at least $1.60 but definitely no more than $2.00) or do you prefer the riskier Option B (with a high chance of $0.10, but the possibility of winning $3.85)?

Given these payoffs,[4] very few people would choose B—you'd have to be a pretty big risk taker to do so.

But what happens when the odds change? Look at the rest of the table:

Option A	Option B
2/10 of $2.00, 8/10 of $1.60	2/10 of $3.85, 8/10 of $0.10
3/10 of $2.00, 7/10 of $1.60	3/10 of $3.85, 7/10 of $0.10
4/10 of $2.00, 6/10 of $1.60	4/10 of $3.85, 6/10 of $0.10
5/10 of $2.00, 5/10 of $1.60	5/10 of $3.85, 5/10 of $0.10
6/10 of $2.00, 4/10 of $1.60	6/10 of $3.85, 4/10 of $0.10
7/10 of $2.00, 3/10 of $1.60	7/10 of $3.85, 3/10 of $0.10
8/10 of $2.00, 2/10 of $1.60	8/10 of $3.85, 2/10 of $0.10
9/10 of $2.00, 1/10 of $1.60	9/10 of $3.85, 1/10 of $0.10
10/10 of $2.00, 0/10 of $1.60	10/10 of $3.85, 0/10 of $0.10

As you move down the rows, the chances of the bigger payoffs increase in both Option A and Option B. Put another way, the lower you are in the table, the higher your chance of winning $2.00 (if you choose A) and $3.85 (if you choose B). For example, at the very bottom, choosing A means you'll win $2.00 for sure, whereas choosing B means you'll win $3.85 for sure. Therefore, Option B should seem more and more attractive the lower you are in the table—to the point where everyone should choose B in the last row.

As you choose between Option A and B in each row, do you find yourself switching from A to B at some point? Most people do because Option B becomes increasingly less risky and more attractive. But precisely *where* you make that switch differs from person to person. Where you make that switch also gives a good measure of your attitude toward uncertainty—your risk attitude.

Specifically, if you've been choosing A but, in the row with 50-50 odds, you switch to B, you're *risk-neutral*. This means you care only about your expected payoff, not the range of variation. We can tell this because in the previous row, Option A had a slightly higher expected payoff than Option B—the difference in expected payoffs was $0.16; but in the row with equal chances of the big payoffs ($2.00 or $3.85) and the low payoffs ($1.60 or $0.10), it's Option B that has a slightly higher expected payoff. Therefore, if you care only about the expected payoff, you'll choose Option B only once you reach this row, and you'll continue to choose Option B in every row after that. A person who cares only about her expected payoff and not about variation is risk-neutral.

Most people are *not* risk-neutral—they're risk-averse. In the table, they continue to choose Option A, with its narrower variation, even when the expected payoff from this choice is lower than the expected payoff from Option B.[5] They prefer the bird in the hand even when there's a decent chance of catching the two in the bush. The further down in the table you go before switching to B, the more risk-averse you are. Put another way, the greater your risk aversion, the more you are willing to give up to reduce variations in the outcome.

Some people are neither risk-averse nor risk-neutral: they're risk-loving, actively looking for high variations even if, on average, they're making a little less. But like the risk-neutral, these people are rare, and you'd be wise to assume most people are risk-averse.

The stakes presented in our table are very low, so you might wonder how well they predict people's actual behavior. What happens when the stakes are higher? It turns out, according to more experiments by Holt and Laury, that higher stakes actually increase risk aversion. This is also what happened in experiments in China, where the low cost of living enabled researchers to offer participants huge payoffs—three times their monthly earnings. Here, too, participants acted very risk-averse, needing much higher expected payoffs to justify a gamble.[6]

You might also argue that the real world is much more complicated than a choice of two lotteries; for one thing, real-world problems rarely present themselves as neat rows in a table with clearly stated odds and spreads. But risk aversion can make sense of some otherwise puzzling behavior in the real world. For example, years ago Kay-Yut collaborated with a researcher at Ford Motor Company to study car lease contracts.[7] The experiments found that, in a game where participants were given the option to buy a hypothetical leased car at the end of the contract or opt for another used car, these consumers held on to their leased cars more often than standard economic theory would predict. In effect, they were willing to pay more to hold on to the car they had been leasing. There are several possible explanations for this behavior, but the researchers believe risk aversion explains it best: there's always some uncertainty about a used car, so even if a leased car is more expensive than another used car, it's a known quantity, so consumers are willing to pay a higher price.

Now let's look at a more complicated case, studied in a series of experiments by Kay-Yut and Charlie Plott. To understand the type of situation these experiments investigated, imagine that you're an art dealer bidding on a van Gogh. You've got a client lined up and ready to buy the painting from you for $1 million. But to make the sale you have to first win the auction. Here's where the uncertainty comes in, because this isn't an ordinary English auction, the type where potential buyers keep bidding the price up as they're outbid by rival buyers. In the English auction, winning is a matter of just outbidding the next-highest bidder: for example, if bidding stops at $750,000, and bidding is in increments of $1,000, you need to bid only $751,000 to win the auction, and there's no reason to bid more. But the auction you're participating in is different: it's a "sealed-bid, first-price" auction, which has its own rules. In this type of auction, each bidder submits a single secret bid (a sealed bid) to the auctioneer, who then picks the highest bid (the first price). If the highest bid was yours, you pay exactly that amount and the auction ends. If somebody else's bid was the highest, that person wins the auction. Nobody has a second chance to outbid the competition.[8]

The rules of a sealed-bid, first-price auction create a lot of uncertainty: how do you know what to bid given that you don't know how much others will be bidding? One way to reduce this uncertainty is to bid high, because the higher you bid, the more likely you'll be to win the auction. But there's a trade-off: the more you bid, the smaller your profit.

For example, if you bid $900,000, your profit is $100,000 (that is, the $1 million your client will pay you minus your cost); this profit is only half of what it would be if you win with a bid of $800,000—but bidding $900,000 gives you a better chance of winning the auction. Thus, risk-averse art dealers will trade off some of the profit by bidding close to their buyers' sale price; better a lower profit, they figure, than the risk of no profit at all. In the long run, playing it safe like this yields lower profits (lower expected value) but, as with any risk-averse strategy, the payoffs are more steady.

This may seem like an arcane and very specific situation—after all, it's not every day you will be bidding on an auction item to resell, let alone in this particular type of auction. But look at it this way: versions of the sealed-bid, first-price auction appear in various guises all the time. When you're making an offer on a house knowing only the asking price, you're in effect participating in this type of auction—which explains why houses in hot real-estate markets often sell for far more than the asking price. And when your company is bidding in an RFP (Request for Proposal), you're competing with other bidders not knowing how much they'll bid. Similarly, when you're asked to name a price for your service, you often don't know how much the buyer is willing to pay—so by naming a high price, you increase your profit but risk having the customer buy less from you (or losing the buyer altogether). Uncertainty is all around you.

In these experiments, Kay-Yut and Charlie Plott used participants' bids to calculate their risk attitude. Just as in the lottery-choice studies, most people were risk-averse.[9] Even so, there was a wide range of risk aversion—some people bid a little more than they needed to, while others bid much more than that. Interestingly, the actual bids were based not only on each participant's own level of risk aversion but also on his or her belief (right or wrong) that the other players with whom they're competing are also risk-averse. But people have a hard time knowing how risk-averse their rivals are—another level of uncertainty—and, as this study showed through the pattern of overbidding, people can be wrong.

People aren't always risk-averse, however—not only are some people risk-loving or risk-neutral, but even those who act risk-averse in some situations don't act risk-averse in others. For example, one study compared first-price auctions with English clock auctions, the type where the price keeps dropping at a steady rate. The English clock auction also has a level of uncertainty, since participants don't know how low the price will drop before a rival snaps up the item. Nonetheless, for reasons not yet understood, the study found that whereas people acted risk-averse in the first-price auction, they acted risk-loving in the English clock auction.[10] Another study, this one analyzing households' insurance deductibles, found that households show more risk aversion in their homeowner's policies than in their auto policies.[11]

Most economists would say that it's not wrong to be risk-averse (or risk-loving)—that the attitude toward risk is merely a preference. What matters is whether your risk attitude is appropriate to your economic environment. For example, those of us with steady jobs and retirement savings (and especially those with a trust fund and a paid-off mortgage) might scoff at the idea of renting furniture. Rent-to-own contracts are a terrible deal, charging, in effect, an exorbitant interest rate for the renter's option to stop payment any time. But among the poor, who are in constant danger of losing work, settling a hefty medical bill, or paying to fix their clunker, such contracts seem relatively attractive. They're a reasonable risk-averse strategy against this kind of economic uncertainty.[12]

In some situations, some people are so risk-averse that they're completely off the charts. A trio of behavioral economists began with two Barnes & Noble gift certificates, one for $50 and the other for $100.[13] How much would participants in the experiment pay for each of these—and how much would they pay for a chance to win one or the other? For example, how much would *you* pay for a lottery ticket giving you a 50 percent chance of winning a $100 gift certificate and a 50 percent chance of winning a consolation prize of a $50 gift certificate?

The economists—Uri Gneezy, John List, and George Wu—found results that are hard to believe. By all rights, you'd expect people to choose a price for the lottery ticket somewhere between the price they'd pay for the $50 certificate and what they'd pay for the $100 certificate. (In fact, perfectly risk-neutral people should pick a price that's exactly in the middle, since the payoffs of $50 and $100 are equally likely.) What did people offer to pay instead?

Before we reveal the answer, we should make clear that the people answering the question about the lottery ticket were not the same ones answering the questions about buying an individual gift certificate.[14] Nonetheless, the participants in all the groups were randomly selected, so on average their answers should be consistent. People in the $50 group were willing, on average, to pay $26.10 for the $50 certificate, so researchers can assume that the people in the lottery group would have been willing to pay roughly that much had they been asked that question.

Here's where it gets weird: the people in the lottery group—the ones choosing a price for the chance to win either a $50 certificate or a $100 certificate—said they'd be willing to pay, on average, only $16.12 (with a median price of only $5). This seems mind-boggling: if you know that the worst you'll do in the lottery is win a $50 prize (but equally likely a $100 one), why would you pay less for this than for the sure chance to win a $50 prize, no more, no less?

Another behavioral economist, Uri Simonsohn, used experiments to test several possible explanations for this effect.[15] Could it be that participants were simply not understanding the instructions? That turned out not to be the case. Simonsohn also speculated that the puzzle might be explained by comparison: by seeing both possible prizes, the people in the lottery condition might have devalued the $50 prize, something people bidding on the sure bet of $50 wouldn't be in a position to do. But this hypothesis didn't pan out, either. Simonsohn concluded, therefore, that many people must simply have a distaste for uncertainty. They're averse not to the prospect of a downside, but to *uncertainty itself.*

In truth, this so-called Uncertainty Effect still has us scratching our heads. These relatively recent findings still call for, as the scientific cliché goes, further research. There's one thing, though, we can be fairly certain of: uncertainty sometimes makes people do strange things. While it makes sense for people to insure themselves against catastrophic events—fire, death, and the like—experts argue that it's a waste of money to pay for insurance against small uncertainties. Yet people often do just that, buying notoriously overpriced extended warranties on inexpensive appliances. Why should someone spend a quarter to a third of the price of, say, a camera or a laptop to extend the warranty? Part of the reason is consumers' lack of information about a product's failure rate—a high level of uncertainty about a fairly inconsequential event. Some researchers have also found that people are likelier to buy an extended warranty when they're in a good mood, happiness making people risk-averse with respect to losses.[16] (Although a good mood leads people to be risk-loving when there's a potential upside, that same good mood makes them risk-averse when there's a chance of losing what they started with.)[17] And Simonsohn believes the Uncertainty Effect may play a role: if you really hate uncertainty, you'll pay more than is sensible to reduce it. It's a fact whose business implications we'll explore throughout the chapter, but first let's turn to the question of why uncertainty is so troubling to many.

Variance Can Kill

Nassim Nicholas Taleb, the former derivatives trader best known for writing *The Black Swan* and *Fooled by Randomness,* has a favorite saying: "Never cross a river because it is on average 4 feet deep." Why? Because the average tells you only half the story—it says nothing about the spread, the variations on the high or low side. In some places, the river may be only two inches deep, but elsewhere it may well be ten to twenty feet deep, deep enough to drown a nonswimmer. And even if you know the range of variation—that the river's depth varies from two inches to twenty feet—you can't be sure about the depth of any one spot. People don't like this uncertainty. It's scary. It would be much safer to know that the river is four feet everywhere, like a flat-bottomed swimming pool.[18]

This vivid example captures a lot of what you need to know about risk aversion. First, it explains why you need to consider variance, not just average. Second, it suggests why humans have a tendency to be risk-averse, since those who care only about the average are less likely to survive.[19] Third, it shows that our aversion to uncertainty isn't limited to uncertainty about money: there are lots of other kinds of uncertainty that we don't like—and, as the following example illustrates, uncertainty can be bad on both the high end and the low end of a distribution.

Suppose you're running a restaurant with an average lunch crowd of two hundred customers. It's the perfect number: you've got just enough tables to seat all these customers. But suppose that some days you get as few as one hundred customers, and other days there are three hundred. Now you've got problems on both sides of the average: on the slow days your revenues are down by half—but you're still paying rent for the space, you're still paying your chef and your servers, and, as if that weren't enough, some of your perishable ingredients are going to waste. It would be nice if these losses were offset by the busy days, but since you really can only seat two hundred diners, you have to turn one hundred away every time. Not only are you losing potential revenue, you may be alienating customers, some of whom may walk out to discover a great new restaurant down the street.

Of course, variations in the upside aren't always bad. Depending on the nature of your business, you may be better able to absorb the highs and perhaps offset the lows. If you're shipping products out of your garage, for example, it doesn't matter as much if your order numbers fluctuate from day to day. Still, given the same average, most of us would prefer a constant, uniform flow to cycles of feast or famine. This is why many people would rather forgo a higher average—a higher expected value—in exchange for steadier payouts. This aversion to risk is not unreasonable, and it's the prime reason most people prefer a steady paycheck even if they know that, in the long run, they could earn more being self-employed.[20] It's also why lawyers generally prefer to settle a dispute, even at a lower payoff, than go to trial, which incurs costs that may never be offset by a verdict in their favor.[21]

So, given a choice, most people would prefer less risk to more risk. For example, in the lottery-choice studies, about two-thirds of participants act risk-averse even when the stakes are low, less than $4; as the stakes get higher, the fraction of people who act risk-averse only rises.

Because people usually don't like risk, they try to reduce risk in one of several ways: avoiding it altogether, learning more about the risks involved, pooling risk, or transferring it to somebody else. Avoiding risk altogether is generally a bad idea because without risk there's no reward. Learning more about risks—for example, by getting a more precise range of next quarter's demand, by running a background check on a job applicant, or by finding out which client is likely to stiff you—is an excellent idea. In fact, several of our chapters deal with ways to look before you leap, particularly the chapters on reputation and trust and the one on predicting the unpredictable. This chapter, therefore, focuses on the other two strategies for coping with risk aversion: risk pooling (or risk spreading) and risk transfer.

Safety in Numbers: Risk Pooling and Risk Spreading

Unlike an individual, a large employer is better able to weather inevitable ups and downs—very much like the casino in our opening story. For example, a self-employed taxi driver might have some busy days and other days when he's sitting idle—not because of seasonal fluctuations or other predictable events, but just because of random variation from day to day. Another solo taxi driver will have the same problem, but because the day-to-day variation is random, he might be busy on the other driver's slow days and idle while the other driver can't keep up with demand. A taxi company, on the other hand, is much less likely to have 100 percent of its workforce sitting idle (or struggling to keep up with demand): although the company, too, faces random variation, it's able to even out the ups and downs as the total number of calls to the dispatcher is spread out among the various drivers. The more drivers there are, the more these ups and downs cancel each other out, reducing the total variance. This is one way the owner of the cab company is able to profit from its size alone: by assuming the risk from the risk-averse employee, the employer can pay the driver less than if the driver worked for himself.

From the point of view of the individuals, they are pooling their risk; from the point of view of the group or organization or, more generally, an owner of any portfolio, they are spreading the risk out. Someone holding a portfolio of multiple stocks is more diversified than someone owning one stock, and someone managing multiple suppliers (or catering to multiple customers) is more diversified than someone reliant on one supplier (or customer).

The general idea of pooling the risk to reduce a heavy impact applies to many other situations. It's how insurance companies can consistently turn a profit despite not knowing whose house will burn down and which policyholder will need cancer treatments. It's one reason lawyers band together in firms and doctors form group practices. And it explains why efficient companies cope with inventory uncertainty the way they do. One way they do this is through centralized warehousing: Amazon, for example, pools the demand risk from across its customer base into just a few warehouses, thus getting a leg up on large retail chains (such as Borders), each of whose stores must absorb its own inventory risk by stocking a certain number of copies of each title in each store. For a manufacturer of complex products, such as cars or computers, one way to use risk pooling in managing inventory is to use standard parts across multiple products—and to delay customization until the last possible moment. HP, for example, must produce slightly different printers for different European countries—but orders for, say, Danish printers, are much less predictable than orders for printers for Europe as a whole. Therefore, keeping all these different printers in stock (though it reduces backlog risk) would greatly increase inventory risk, the risk that some of these printers will never sell. Instead of stocking all the different printers, then, HP's European distribution center pools the inventory risk by keeping plenty of standard printers on hand, waiting until actual orders come in before attaching specific power cords and language-specific manuals to create products for each country.[22]

Notice that risk pooling (or its flip side, risk spreading) isn't the same as hedging: hedging involves balancing out one type of risk with another that tends to swing in the opposite direction, like offsetting the risk of investing in the stock market by also buying bonds. But risk pooling doesn't rely on hedging: with risk pooling, *even two or more equally risky items* manage to be less risky than one alone.[23] A classic example is using two separate planes to fly the president and the vice president of the United States. Some companies, including HP, do the same thing when their executives fly. But although the likelihood of both execs dying is much lower with two separate planes, spreading the risk across two planes also carries a cost: the likelihood of at least one of two planes crashing is *almost twice* the likelihood of the only plane crashing.[24]

The same logic holds for projects, suppliers, and customers: if you put all your faith in one deal and the deal falls through, you're through, but if you spread your bets among several deals, then no single deal will doom you. For example, when the recession hit, many self-employed individuals actually had more job security than people employed by large companies: even though there was a risk that any given company would go under or slash its budget (thus making it risky to be employed by a single company), by spreading the risk among multiple clients the self-employed were less likely to be hit by total loss of work. One Canadian entrepreneur, who had decided to leave a banking job to start a Montessori school, put it this way: "You know that at any time you can be given a pink slip, especially in this economy—so with this unrest and having the rug pulled from underneath us has made it easier to take a risk, and the risk that's associated with becoming self-employed is actually less than putting all your eggs in one basket."[25]

But notice that this is true only of the uncertainty about losing all your work; the uncertainty we talked about earlier—sporadic income from week to week—is still higher for the self-employed than for the person drawing a steady paycheck.

Many other situations involve multiple types of uncertainty. For example, a company like Amazon or Netflix must decide how many warehouses to have. Having one centralized warehouse pools inventory risk, thus making it less likely that the store will be out of stock or will have to carry too many of one item; on the other hand, the centralized warehouse increases the impact of another type of risk: a calamity on the one warehouse, such as a fire or road closure. The key to managing sources of uncertainty is to pinpoint all of them. Then you can assign probabilities, dollar values, and other relevant numbers to them; these numbers will help you figure out which type or types you most want to avoid. In chapter 4, on rationality, we give an example of how Kay-Yut tackled this type of risk problem at HP.

Transferring Risk

We've said that insurance companies profit from pooling risk. But for them to acquire the many policyholders necessary for risk pooling to be effective, individuals must be willing to transfer the risk to the insurance company—so willing that they will pay a premium to do so.

Here's how it works. An insurance company collects risks from many clients and earns money by charging these clients a *risk premium*. A large auto insurer, for example, has millions of policyholders and, because of the Law of Large Numbers, every year it covers losses from a fairly certain number of accidents. Although it is highly unpredictable whether a particular policyholder will get into an auto accident or how costly a particular accident will be, the total number of claims the insurer has to service (and the total cost of these claims) is predictable. Insurance companies use complicated formulas to calculate how much each policyholder should pay each year, but the basic principle is simple: the expected payout (on average) plus a risk premium. If the chance of getting into an accident is 10 percent per year, for example, the insurer charges 10 percent of the average cost of an accident—plus a risk premium. Added together, the risk premium is the profit the insurer is going to make[26] and comes directly from the premium checks you write every year. People may not relish writing such checks, since they get nothing tangible or fun for their money, but risk aversion makes them willing to do it; they are, as insurance salespeople say, buying peace of mind.

Insurance companies aren't the only ones in the business of assuming risk and charging a premium for it. Almost all retailers do this, at least to some extent. In a standard retail agreement a manufacturer sells to a retailer who resells the goods at a markup to the end customer; the markup comes in part from the fact that the retailer assumes the risk that some of the inventory won't sell or that it'll sell at a loss during a clearance sale. And by assuming more risk than their competitors, some retailers are able to negotiate better prices with their suppliers. For example, Men's Wearhouse sells the same clothes as department stores like Nordstrom and Macy's, but for 20 to 30 percent less. The company's president, George Zimmer, is able to profitably underprice the competition because he buys at a discount, and he's able to get that discount by taking on two related risks that competitors don't: ordering on a nonreturnable basis and placing orders as much as a year in advance.[27] By selling at a steep discount to Zimmer, the wholesalers are, in effect, paying him a risk premium to reduce the uncertainty of demand.

We don't know why Zimmer is willing to take on this kind of risk while his competitors aren't. Perhaps he knows his customers' tastes better than either his suppliers or his competitors do; if that's the case, his risk is lower than it is for his suppliers—so the price break more than makes up for the risk he takes on. We do know something similar works for Amazon, which buys most of its titles on a nonreturnable basis. This is an anomaly in publishing, which typically works on consignment—but by ordering with the promise that it won't return books to the publisher or distributor, Amazon can buy books at 50 percent less than the competition. And it can do so almost risk-free because of its just-in-time inventory system: through its deft order handling, including the use of customers' preorders, Amazon doesn't need to place an order with a publisher until its own customers have ordered the book.[28] The more you know, the more profitable is the risk premium you charge others.

Making Money from Risk: Insurance in Disguise

Most of us aren't in the insurance business. But we can all use the principles of insurance to profit from other people's risk aversion.

Guarantees are one way to do this. Consider this outrageous claim from the grocery chain Trader Joe's: "We tried it! We liked it! If you don't, bring it back for a full refund, no questions asked." How can Trader Joe's possibly know whether you like soy-ginger dressing, gnocchi in gorgonzola sauce, white bean hummus, or the hundreds of other gourmet products they carry—let alone guarantee you'll like their store-brand versions of these products? In one sense, they can't—any more than a watchmaker can know for certain that a given wristwatch will keep on ticking throughout its warranty period. But Trader Joe's doesn't need to know for certain, though its internal vetting leaves it reasonably confident that most of its customers will like most of the products they buy. And if Trader Joe's knows more about the quality of its own products than would-be shoppers do, then the store's job is to get customers to just try the products. "You can afford to be adventurous without breaking the bank," the Trader Joe's Web site says, referring to both their affordable exotic fare and the risk-free return policy.

That's the theory, anyway. But does Trader Joe's liberal returns policy pay off? That's an empirical question that can't be answered by looking at the company's bottom line alone. After all, it's possible the grocer is succeeding despite this policy, and might actually be better off with limited returns. It's possible—but not likely. To see why, let's look at a study of a different retailer.

The study, which analyzed sales at a mail-order clothing company, looked at the question of how much customers value the option to return a product they'd ordered but ultimately didn't want. The researchers found, perhaps not surprisingly, that different customers place a different value on this option. More interestingly, they found that the value of this option depends on the type of product. The option to return men's tops, for example, is worth only about $3 per purchase. But the option to return a pair of women's shoes is worth quite a bit more—more than $15 per purchase. We can speculate about why that is. The sizing of men's shirts is fairly standard, so if you know you wear 16 × 34, chances are the shirt you order will at least fit. Indeed, the return rate for men's tops in this study was 14 percent. But the rate of returns for women's footwear was more than twice as high. Shoes have to be tried on for good fit, and the wider array of colors in women's shoes leaves more room for error when it comes to matching a shoe with a dress. (For men, ordering a light blue shirt to go with a pair of black slacks doesn't carry the same risk.) In any case, the economic analysis showed that the store's return policy increased average purchase rates of women's shoes by more than 50 percent.[29] If the store didn't have such a liberal return policy, they'd have to lower the price of women's shoes from $50 to $35 to convince people to buy as many pairs.

Because of customers' risk aversion, liberal return policies can be very effective at generating revenue. In light of this analysis, we can see why shoe retailer Zappos.com offers a 365-day return policy (though, as we'll see later, 365 days might be too much of a good thing). Or why Trader Joe's offers money back on any item in the store. The policies serve as an insurance policy, encouraging customers to buy more and perhaps even to pay more for the same items without the insurance.

The return policies are far from costless, though. Items that are returned often can't be resold—or, at the very least, must be sold at a discount. Stores must also bear the sheer logistical cost of handling returns. The optimal return policy must figure out the best trade-off between all these costs and the benefits of a generous return policy. But there's a simple way to think about the trade-off, one that takes risk aversion into account. As we've seen with men's shirts versus women's shoes, the benefits of liberal returns are lower for some types of products than others because of the different levels of buyers' uncertainty involved. We can draw the same comparison between clothes tried on in the store and those ordered through the Internet, or a computer whose specs you can read about before buying and a lamp you have to see in your living room before you're sure it's right for you. Accordingly, many retailers have different return policies for different types of products, with return policies for electronics being among the most restrictive. Amazon.com has twenty-nine different product-specific return policies.[30]

You don't have to be a big-time retailer to offer guarantees or some version of them. Agents working strictly on commission or lawyers charging on a contingency basis can all attract risk-averse clients and, at the same time, signal their confidence in their own ability. Such arrangements are more customary in some industries than others, of course. But just because such a guarantee isn't common in your field doesn't mean you shouldn't consider it; its very uniqueness may offer you a competitive edge. For example, when Domino's Pizza began guaranteeing pizza delivery within thirty minutes, it was the first pizza chain to make that promise, and many attribute its becoming the country's largest pizza-delivery company in the 1980s to just that. (Unfortunately, the company apparently didn't consider one serious risk to this guarantee: reckless driving by its delivery people. After a jury awarded $78 million to a woman struck by a speeding Domino's driver, the company gave up the thirty-minute pledge.)

Several sports teams have used "playoff-or-payoff guarantees" to boost sales of season tickets. Fans are understandably wary of spending several thousand dollars a seat without knowing if their team will reach the postseason, especially if the team has been on a losing streak. Play-off-or-payoff guarantees, which have been offered by the NBA's Atlanta Hawks and the NHL's Florida Panthers, among others, allay these concerns by offering ticket holders a rebate if their team doesn't reach the playoffs. These clever guarantees have boosted ticket sales and made price hikes more palatable. For example, in the year the Florida Panthers offered a 5 percent rebate if the team didn't reach the playoffs, season ticket renewals were up by 11 percent.[31] We're guessing these guarantees are especially effective because fans of a particular sport are choosing whether to buy tickets at all; because each sport usually fields only one team per city, that team has a local monopoly—and doesn't face competition from others offering similar guarantees.

A New York City hotel offers a quirky example of differentiating yourself through a guarantee. An otherwise unremarkable place to stay in midtown Manhattan, and needing to compete with brand-name rivals in the same neighborhood, the Benjamin Hotel is the only one to offer a "sleep guarantee." According to its Web site, "We guarantee that you will receive a good night's sleep during your stay with us or we will provide you with a refund." (This isn't just a marketing gimmick—the hotel has a "sleep concierge," a menu of pillow types to choose from, and other amenities to show that it takes good sleep seriously.)

One type of unusual guarantee was made possible through unusual insurance: Tourism Victoria's "Sunshine Guaranteed" promotion. Victoria, British Columbia, is a sunny place, especially in the summers. In 2009, to encourage travel in April and May, the city's tourism trade group promised visitors booking at least a two-night stay $500 back if it rained more than 1.25 centimeters (about half an inch) during their stay.[32] This promotion made visits during a typically slow season more attractive, and Tourism Victoria was able to make the promise by buying weather insurance through WeatherBill.com. Here, tourists were transferring risk to Tourism Victoria, which in turn transferred risk to WeatherBill .com.

There are many other ways to transfer risks. Free samples or free trials are one way to do this. (Free trials are especially popular with information products—like software downloads, cable service, electronic book chapters, and the like—where the trials cost little or nothing extra to the manufacturer.)

Also consider the consignment agreement. The word "consignment" may bring to mind images of musty secondhand shops, but consignment is a standard arrangement across a range of industries—including art and antiques, book publishing, sometimes even electronics. Unlike the standard retail agreement, in which the retailer buys inventory and thus assumes the inventory risk from the wholesaler, a consignment agreement has the wholesaler owning the inventory until it sells and thus keeping the risk that it doesn't sell. The consignment store takes a commission on items that sell and doesn't have to worry about the possibility that some or all won't sell. This may not sound like a good deal to the wholesaler, but that all depends on the size of the commission. If the owner of the store is risk-averse, she should be willing to take a lower commission than the markup on a retailer agreement. For the wholesaler, a consignment deal may be the only way to get a particular store to carry his products. For example, some fashion boutiques, like Albertine in New York City, sell interesting but lesser-known designers' clothes on consignment; this practice enables the boutique owner to try new things with low risk and enables the designer to get into a store that might not otherwise carry her work.[33]

You can also profit from risk aversion in hiring. For example, when a car dealership in New Mexico wanted to attract a better class of salesperson, they began offering a salary-only compensation option. According to the dealership's general manager for sales, "We felt the stable family person who is looking for some kind of insurance would apply," even though the salary was only $2,000/month. This manager's insight was that for people who had never tried sales—and didn't know if they'd be good at it—a commission-only system would seem too risky. It would be so risky that applicants would pay a risk premium (in the form of a lower paycheck) to avoid it. And the plan paid off: "The idea of a salary made them willing to try something new. They are stable family people and don't have the greedy salesman image," says the sales manager. Once they learned more about their own ability to sell cars, they sorted themselves into two groups, with good salespeople switching to a commission-based compensation plan, through which they could earn more.[34]

Once you have a workforce, you might be able to apply the idea of risk transfer to get these employees to aim for the stars. The idea, which has been explored at HP Labs, is to get risk-averse workers to take on potentially profitable risks by letting them buy insurance against the outcomes they fear.[35] For example, many managers prefer to play it safe rather than to risk a demotion or the loss of a bonus if their risky plans don't pan out. But if most managers avoid risks, the organization won't enjoy many successes, either. The solution might be for a large organization to pool the risk and absorb the occasional calamity, just as an insurance company does. By offering "decision insurance," an organization can change employees' behavior in the same way that a retailer's return policy changes shoppers' behavior. At this point, the idea is still tentative: not only has it not been put into practice, it hasn't yet been proven to work in the lab. The main challenge is balancing the rewards of risk taking against the possibility that people who are protected from the downsides of risk will take too many foolhardy risks. (We've seen this "moral hazard" problem—which we'll have much more to say about later—on Wall Street. Executives who take huge risks stand to earn huge bonuses if all goes well—but don't lose any of their own money if their risks are unsuccessful.) Yet innovative companies have found ways to encourage profitable risk-taking. The most famous example is Google, with its "20 percent time" policy of letting engineers spend one day a week pursuing creative Google-related projects without pressure to show results. Most of these projects don't go anywhere, but the handful that do (like GoogleNews) make the other risks worth it.

What if you're the one who's feeling risk-averse in a particular situation? In that case, think of ways you can reduce the risk rather than avoiding the situation altogether. For example, when a Russian magazine approached Marina about writing a long article, she was wary. Even though she knew the editor's reputation for treating writers well and got the impression that the company publishing the magazine was a solid one, she didn't have a lot of trust in Russia's volatile business environment—or in her power to enforce a contract in a Russian court. She considered turning down the assignment, but, with nothing to lose, instead asked the editor for part of her fee to be paid up front. Though author advances of this sort are the norm in book publishing, they're almost unheard of in the magazine world, but Marina offered to take a somewhat lower fee in exchange for this advance. The editor found a way to push this unusual arrangement through the system, so before Marina began work she received a chunk of her payment. Of course, there remained the chance that the magazine might fold before the final fee was paid, but the advance reassured Marina that, even in this worst-case scenario, she wouldn't be left with nothing. By reducing the potential downside and enabling Marina to take on a meaty project she would have otherwise turned down, the advance created a middle ground between taking on too much risk on the one hand and no upside at all on the other.

From the editor's point of view, the advance entailed some risk for the magazine—the risk that the writer would just take the money and run. On the other hand, not budging on the advance would entail the risk of losing the editor's first choice of writer for this assignment. Also, magazines are in a far better position than writers to pool risk—not only are magazines better capitalized than individual writers, but a typical magazine assigns more articles each year than a typical writer produces—so the occasional deadbeat writer affects the magazine's bottom line less than a deadbeat magazine affects a writer's income. Finally, the editor must have known that, even without reputation on the line, unless the full fee were paid up front, most people would like to stick around for the remainder of the fee. Marina's willingness to take a fee cut in exchange for this risk transfer—in essence, paying a risk premium—probably helped, as well.

What we're saying is that you don't have to have the negotiating clout of Amazon or the Men's Wearhouse to put down risk as an issue in negotiations. If you're asked to take on risk, the other party should pay some price. Similarly, if the price must be kept constant, you can try to shift the balance of risk accordingly—though, as we'll see, your market power will affect your success at doing this.

Beware Moral Hazard and Adverse Selection

We hope these examples make risk transfer sound attractive, and perhaps you're already imagining ways you can take advantage of risk aversion. But you need to be careful because risk transfer isn't just a shift in risk from one party to another—it can actually increase the total amount of risk.

That's because of moral hazard. If someone is insured against risk—whether through traditional insurance or some other form of risk transfer—that person has less incentive to prevent the risky outcome. A classic example is the car owner who's more likely to park in an unsafe neighborhood or just to drive more recklessly once he's insured. One study found that "no-fault insurance"—the type that pays regardless of who's to blame for the accident—goes hand in hand with higher rates of fatal accidents.[36] Moral hazard happens in other businesses, too. Zappos .com's generous policy leads people to buy lots of shoes—over $1 billion worth in 2008—but it also leads to lots of returns. Some people order multiple pairs in different sizes so they can try them on at home, knowing they won't have to pay any shipping costs or restocking fees for returning them. That leads to a return rate that's three times higher than in brick-and-mortar stores.[37] In 2008, all the returns left the company with net sales of only $635 million,[38] which may sound like a lot until you consider the operating costs, which left a profit margin of only $10.7 million. Had the rate of returns been even a little higher, the company would have ended up in the red.

Insurance companies have a couple of ways to deal with moral hazard. For one thing, they typically charge a deductible, so the driver thinks twice before taking an avoidable risk. For another, they often raise premiums for drivers with worsening records. The principle in both cases is the same: instead of a complete risk transfer, the insured and the insurer share risks, so that accidents become less costly for the insurer and more expensive for the insured. When that happens with auto insurance, the result is that people drive more safely.[39] In a retail business such as Zappos, the analogue could be to charge customers a restocking fee or have them pay for their own shipping. Or Zappos could allow returns for any reason—but restrict the policy to fewer than 365 days. (How long does it really take to try on a pair of shoes?)

You can use the principle of risk sharing in many other business settings to ward off moral hazard. If you pay your salespeople a fixed salary, for example, you're insuring them against poor sales—but by doing so, you also reduce their incentive to work hard to make those sales. That's why commissions are a part of most sales compensation schemes. On the other hand, they're rarely the whole package: because good salespeople have options, they will generally choose to work for an employer that offers at least some fixed compensation. In fact, paying no fixed salary should be a red flag to would-be employees: just as paying salespeople only a fixed salary reduces the incentive to sell, so paying salespeople strictly on commission creates a moral hazard for their employers, who have less incentive to make a saleable product.

Another example of risk sharing occurs in the magazine publishing industry, where editors (and the publishers they work for) typically share with freelance writers the risk that the article won't come out as planned. If the magazine agrees to pay the full fee just for completing the article, the writer won't necessarily have an incentive to turn in high-quality work or be available to promptly answer editors' follow-up questions. At the other extreme, if the writer agrees to write "on spec"—getting paid only if the editor likes the piece enough to publish it—the writer not only assumes all the risk but also gives the editor no incentive to actually read the submitted piece or work with the writer to make the piece publishable. Instead, the industry uses so-called kill fees, some fraction of the full fee paid to the writer if the editor finds the piece unacceptable. Kill fees vary, but they tend to favor the magazine, usually ranging from 10 to 33 percent. For example, two of the largest American magazine publishers, Condé Nast and Hearst, routinely offer kill fees of 25 percent.

Not surprisingly, writers don't like kill fees, one describing them as "profit-sucking vampires that deserve a good stake through their hearts."[40] Writers think it's as outrageous to pay a writer a mere 25 percent for an article that didn't come in as the editor envisioned it as it would be to pay a house painter 25 percent if the color doesn't come out as expected. It can also be argued that a magazine is in a better position than a writer to handle a risk and that the risk burden should be mainly on the magazine. But these are moral arguments, not economic ones. Indeed, some writers do manage to strike kill-fee clauses, increase the percentage owed them, or clearly define and limit the conditions under which the magazine can pay a kill fee rather than the full fee. For example, well-known writers, who have both bargaining power and a stronger reputation, can get higher kill fees.[41] But the fact is that in the highly competitive magazine industry, magazines usually have more clout than writers, and many writers agree to kill fees; they either don't question them or, if told the contract is nonnegotiable, accept them as better than the alternative. As this example shows, risk isn't the only force affecting behavior—even when risk considerations are very important, incentives and environments (such as the parties' relative market power) also affect how people behave.

You also need to be careful about adverse selection. Whereas moral hazard has to do with how the people in your risk pool behave, adverse selection is about who becomes part of your risk pool to begin with. If you assume too much risk, you'll end up attracting too many risky customers. Again, let's take an example from the insurance industry. If a company sells trip-cancellation insurance at the same price to everyone, then the people who know they're especially likely to cancel their trip (because, say, they have an ill family member) will be especially likely to buy the insurance, whereas those who think it's unlikely their travel plans will change will consider the same price too high and opt out of the coverage. The result is a policyholder pool that's not at all random, but rather the antithesis of the diversification insurers want. Insurance companies have several strategies to guard against adverse selection. The travel insurer, for example, might restrict the reasons for which you can file a claim. They might exclude "preexisting conditions," or they might charge a higher price for policyholders with such conditions.

Adverse selection can affect other industries. An overly liberal returns policy can systematically attract customers who abuse the policy, including outright fraudsters. So retailers often limit returns to a short period (such as thirty days after purchase), require a receipt, charge a restocking fee (or nonrefundable "shipping and handling charge"), or keep track of the names of customers who make returns. The restocking fee is an interesting strategy because it simultaneously guards against adverse selection and moral hazard. On the other hand, the restocking fee may backfire, either deterring risk-averse customers from buying from you in the first place or appearing to penalize customers unfairly, leading them to argue with the company's reps and badmouth the company to others.[42] But even so, restocking fees may be good, depending on your business. For Best Buy, the fees do lead to some disgruntled customers, but they also weed out people who would abuse the policy. The right policy depends on the business environment. For example, in the late 1990s, Kay-Yut worked with the computer products division to test and compare two possible return policies between a manufacturer and a retailer. If you're the manufacturer (like HP), is it better for your business to have a generous return policy with your retailers (unlimited returns with a full refund) or a more restrictive one (such as placing a cap on the number of returns, or charging a restocking fee with unlimited returns)? It's clear that charging a restocking fee forces the retailer to share some of the risks of unsold goods: although the retailer can return the goods, there'll be a price to pay for each item returned. On the other hand, given a more restrictive return policy, the retailer will in theory stock at least a little less to limit his exposure—and that's not good for the manufacturer, who wants to maximize sales. On balance, then, is a restrictive return policy better or worse for the wholesaler?

To get a realistic answer, the experiment mimicked an actual business environment. Participants played the roles of retailers, and they competed with one another for the same group of end consumers. Like real retailers, they needed to price and stock several different products, decide on an advertising budget, and so on. At the end of the experiments, they were paid real money according to how well their retail operation actually did.

The experiments tested two different return policies: an unlimited, full refund policy, and one with no limit on the number of returns, but a 21 percent restocking fee. Not surprisingly, the restocking fee greatly curbed the rate of returns—there were 28 percent fewer returns under the policy with the restocking fee than with the full refund. This means that if you're the manufacturer, having a more restrictive return policy means lower costs. But what about the effect on revenue? The surprising result is that participants did not stock significantly less, nor did they shift away from selling products with a more stringent return policy. In other words, the manufacturer got away with absorbing less risk from the retailers with few negative consequences.

Does this mean a restrictive return policy is always a good idea, or that 21 percent is the optimal restocking fee? Not at all. As we saw in the consumer mail-order study, people value the option to return products. In the HP experiment, however, the restrictive policy seems to have worked well because the manufacturer had market power, which enabled it to use competition among the retailers to drive down the amount of "insurance" the manufacturer needed to give. It's easy to imagine a different business environment in which different manufacturers (say, HP, Dell, and Sony) compete for a single retailer (such as Walmart) that's powerful enough to call the shots; in this environment, the retailer can shift business away from manufacturers with restrictive return policies. Ultimately, a retailer's market power can force all manufacturers to offer more generous return policies.

Beyond Risk Aversion

Being risk-averse rather than risk-neutral is only one of the many ways people tend to behave in uncertain situations. There are many, many others. Unlike scientists, most of us make large inferences from tiny (and often nonrandom) samples, such as personal experiences or dramatic stories we've heard from friends or on the news. People are terrible at figuring out odds—and, even knowing the odds, making good decisions based upon them. (If we were good at making these kinds of decisions, we'd never play the lottery.) And we're notoriously prone to seeing nonexistent patterns in randomness—for example, at times we believe in either the Hot-Hand Fallacy ("I'm on a roll!") or its opposite, the Gambler's Fallacy ("After all these losses, I'm bound to win now!").[43]

Those in the business of buying and selling risk—especially casinos and insurance companies—don't make these mistakes, because accurately assessing risks is their bread and butter. They hire actuaries and statisticians to make sure they'll always come out ahead. If managing uncertainty is a significant part of your business, too, you might consider enlisting professional help.

In this chapter, you saw how much most people hate uncertainty and some of the lengths they'll go to reduce it. Keeping in mind people's attitudes toward risk suggests ways to take these preferences into account with the people you face in your work. That's just as true of social preferences, particularly fairness and reciprocity, which we explore in the next two chapters.

2

. . . .

Fair's Fair

In April 2005, the Washington Ballet canceled an Italian tour months in the making. The esteemed dance troupe had planned to perform at three Italian dance festivals that summer, serving as a cultural ambassador of the United States while deepening donors' involvement. At the Florence festival, the troupe was to be the centerpiece, so its last-minute cancellation left festival organizers in the lurch. But there was no way around it—negotiations had broken down between the dancers and the company's management. The point of disagreement: the dancers' per diem allowance.

The dancers wanted $150 per day to cover meals and other travel expenses; the number seemed reasonable based on the State Department's per diem rates in the festival cities. But the owners, who argued that they were already losing $90,000 on the tour, offered a per diem of only $55. When the dancers balked, the owners offered $150—but with a salary cut to match. This was a clever move, since lower salaries meant lower taxes, but it wasn't enough to salvage the deal.

The collapse of negotiations sent ripples well beyond the ballet company. Italian festival organizers were furious at the last-minute pullout, deeming it arrogant and unprofessional. Even American consulates throughout Italy expressed disappointment.[1]

That all this happened over something as minor as per diem

allowances seems to make no sense. Experienced negotiators know that if a proposed agreement is better than your fallback option, you should accept it—and reject a deal only if it's worse than your alternative. Surely the negotiators on both sides of the ballet company knew these rules, too. So how could they have thought that canceling the tour would be better than giving in on the per diem amount?

The situation was complicated. Some dancers thought that the ballet company's management didn't really want a deal and were seeking an out. In light of the tour's mounting expenses, the managers may have purposely offered a deal the dancers' union would refuse. That way the dancers, not the management, would take the heat for the cancellation. In fact, the dancers' union went on to claim that management had bargained in bad faith. But emotions played a big role in the collapse of negotiations. The dancers were already unhappy with working conditions, and a few months earlier they had organized into a union. More recently, two dancers active in union organizing had been let go, supposedly for artistic reasons—something the other dancers refused to believe. So there was already bad blood going into negotiations. Things only escalated when both sides brought in abrasive lawyers. At one point, the board's lawyer used a loudspeaker to dismiss the dancers' request for bottled water: "Well, if there's no water, there's no water," the lawyer said, further fanning the flames. As emotions ran high, considerations beyond logic factored into the decision making. It's reasonable to conclude, as one observer put it, that the dancers might have been "more open to concessions if they'd perceived their initial requests as being met with concern for their welfare rather than contempt." We can't know if a deal was even possible, but mounting anger spelled certain doom.

It's not an isolated case: time and again people act as if they prefer getting nothing at all to getting what feels like an unfair deal.

So what was unfair about the company's offer? Mainly that, for whatever reason, the dancers found it so. Think of the problem from both sides' perspectives. The dancers had a good case for a higher per diem than they were offered: they only wanted what other official travelers were getting. Management had a point, too: the company was already losing money on the tour. But what matters in the end isn't who's "right," it's what both sides will accept. Right or wrong, to strike a deal the company's owners needed to offer what the dancers would accept—what the dancers thought was fair.

Paying for Fairness

Fairness is so important to us that, in effect, we're willing to pay a price to get it. In some situations, we purchase fairness even when we get nothing else in the process. The simplest illustration of this phenomenon comes from a classic bargaining experiment called the Ultimatum Game.

The Ultimatum Game is one of the most elegant social experiments ever designed. In the years since 1982, when German economist Werner Güth invented this deceptively simple game, versions of it have been used in hundreds of studies around the world.

Here's how it works. When you show up for the experiment, the researcher gives you a sum of money—say, $10—and tells you to offer whatever part of it you want to another player. You can give the other player all the money, none of it, or anything in between, keeping the rest for yourself. But there's a catch: the other player, whom you don't know, can reject your offer. If she does, neither of you gets anything. If, on the other hand, she accepts your offer, you both keep your portions. There is no back-and-forth: your offer is an ultimatum, a take-it-or-leave-it deal.

Of course, it's just as likely that when you play the Ultimatum Game, the researcher will put you in the role of the Responder, the player who gets to veto the offer. But for now, assume you're the Proposer. Knowing the rules of the game, how much should you offer?

Before we tell you what most Proposers do, let's see why economists are so fond of the Ultimatum Game. The game distills the essence of bargaining: in any bargaining process, whether it's negotiating a salary, haggling over the price of a car, or agreeing on a per diem for a tour to Italy, the two parties are trying to split a pie.[2] The more one side gets, the less the other side keeps. And if the sides can't agree on a split, there's no deal. But to study real-world negotiations is messy and logistically complicated: how do you get people to negotiate a salary in a lab? To run a clean, controlled experiment, economists prefer to boil a problem down to its essence, and the Ultimatum Game does just that.

So what's the best strategy for the Ultimatum Game? If you've been schooled only in traditional economics, and ignore everything you know about human nature, you would say the best strategy for Proposers is to offer the smallest possible amount. If the researcher gives you $100, you offer the Responder $1; if the researcher gives you $10 in pennies, you offer 1 cent. The reasoning behind this low offer makes sense in the unrealistic world of perfectly rational and selfish players. After all, any amount is better than nothing, so no players will reject a low offer. Therefore, you should offer a really low number.

But, of course, that's not what most people do—and for good reason. No one will accept so small a share, so no one offers so little.

How people play the Ultimatum Game depends on who they are and how the game is set up, something we'll say more about later. But Werner Güth's classic study shows results that are typical for most players.[3] The Proposers' average offer was a little more than 30 percent. Responders rejected about a fifth of all offers.

What does this mean? This result is the outcome of a clash between two forces: pure self-interest and something else. That something else is an interest in fairness.

Put yourself in the Responder's shoes. If the Proposer offers you $2 (out of $10), do you take the $2, knowing the Proposer will get $8? Chances are you won't. Most people reject what they deem unfair splits in an impetuous huff: across many studies, when offers fall below 30 percent, they're almost always rejected.

If you decide you'd rather have nothing than let the brazen Proposer get more than he deserves, you're making a poor choice only if your main goal is material gain. But if, like most people, you enjoy righting a wrong, then by rejecting an unfair offer what you're doing is, in effect, paying a small price for the pleasure of getting back at the other player. It's not about being rational; it's about emotions—the anger at a low-ball offer and the satisfaction of retaliating against it.[4] Brain scans of people playing the Ultimatum Game have confirmed this: evaluating Ultimatum offers creates activity in both cognitive and emotional regions of the brain—the former advocating rational economic self-interest and the other pushing for spiteful rejections—and unfair offers generate more activity in emotional areas, causing emotion to triumph over reason.[5]

Rejections of unfair offers are interesting for another reason: that they happen at all tells us that people don't agree on what's fair. Let's say you think a fair offer is anything over 20 percent. Therefore, you offer $3 and keep $7, congratulating yourself on your generosity. But your Responder balks! She thinks it would be unfair for you to keep any more than 60 percent. Not only do we disagree on what's fair, but we aren't very good at guessing what other people consider fair. Think of it this way: if we were good at guessing what others thought was fair, our offers would never get rejected.

Think about the implications of this research. Even in a simple game like this one, different people have different notions of what's fair. So don't assume that what you think is fair will seem fair to the people you're dealing with, and don't be surprised when a seemingly fair offer gets rejected. For yourself, avoid using the vague notion of fairness as a criterion for a good deal. Instead, consider whether the deal is beneficial to both parties, whether both parties are better off compared to before, and whether either party can get a better deal somewhere else. Finally, knowing that emotions can be a powerful force for decision making, avoid situations where your emotions will reign. For example, give yourself time to deliberate on a deal; you'll be less likely to decide based on anger and spite—and more likely to make a good decision.

The Acid Test of Fairness: The Dictator Game

Let's make one point perfectly clear: the Ultimatum Game does not show that fairness trumps greed or even that people want to be fair because it's the right thing to do. While some people made even splits out of pure generosity, many shared generously only because they knew that unfair splits would be rejected.

We know this because of the difference in results between the Ultimatum Game and another simple experiment, a pared-down version of the Ultimatum Game called the Dictator Game. In the Dictator Game, the second player has no veto power.[6] In fact, there doesn't need to be a second player at all except in the first player's imagination: the participant in the experiment decides unilaterally how much money to keep, and the game ends.

With this crucial change in the rules, the results change drastically. Most of the Dictators in the original experiment offered very little—much less than in the Ultimatum Game. In fact, the most common offer in the Dictator Game was $0. This difference between the two games tells us that a 50-50 split is more likely to come from the fear of failed deals than from the desire to be fair. Knowing that a rejected split would leave the Proposer with nothing, the Proposer offered a fairer split. Put another way, many of the fair splits in the Ultimatum Game were not the result of high-minded aspiration for fairness, but selfish, calculated moves.

But there's a wrinkle to the Dictator Game. While most people give very little, some people do split the money evenly. And these weren't just a couple of easy-to-dismiss outliers. In the first study of the game, five out of twenty-four of the players made 50-50 splits—just as many as those who offered $0. (The most common offer, made by seven players, was $3 out of $10.) This spread reveals an important insight into human nature: people vary, in this case in their desire to be fair. As a result, one-size-fits-all strategies are bound to fail much of the time.

Nonetheless, the overwhelming trend in the Dictator Game is splits that are far less generous than in the Ultimatum Game. Across many studies of the Dictator Game, about 60 percent of players give something, and players share an average of about 20 percent of the pie.[7]

The level of giving is even lower when the experiment reframes the situation. In the standard Dictator Game, the situation invites at least some generosity, since participants have ten ways to give (anywhere from $1 to $10) and only one way *not* to give ($0). But what happens if the options aren't skewed this way? John List explored this question in a clever twist on the Dictator Game in which he changed the range of options from the original $0–$10 to a new range: –$5 to $5.[8] Now, participants have the option to give the other player up to $5 or *take* up to five additional dollars back. Even though the number of choices hadn't changed, their mere shift produced dramatic results: now only five out of fifty participants—just 10 percent—gave *any money at all,* compared to 71 percent in the control group, which saw the typical Dictator choice of $0–$10.[9] And whereas the average offer in the control group was $1.33, the average offer in the experimental condition (that is, among participants who could give up to $5 and take up to $5) was –$2.48—almost half of what it was possible to take.

This finding introduces a theme that runs throughout this book: the situations people find themselves in can affect their economic choices just as surely as differences between people can. Some people are inherently more generous than others, or more trusting, or more hardworking—but in the right (or wrong) situation, they'll be less generous, more suspicious, and work less hard. It's an important point to keep in mind as you judge the actions of the people around you—and as you shape environments to bring out people's best behavior.

There's another interesting way in which the standard Dictator Game experiment overestimates people's generosity. In that experiment, as in most lab studies, participants are a representative sample of the larger population—but out in the real world, people often choose their environments. A writer, for example, might gravitate toward the arts scene and avoid the world of business—but in a lab experiment that samples the general population, English majors will be just as likely to participate as students of any other equally popular major. Similarly, a standard Dictator Game attracts generous people and stingy people alike—but aren't stingy people likelier to avoid the Dictator Game entirely if given the choice?

To answer this question, a team of researchers led by Edward Lazear gave participants an opportunity to choose whether or not to play the Dictator Game. The investigators explained to all would-be Dictators who showed up for the experiment in Berkeley and Barcelona how the game works—and then gave them a chance to opt out and keep their $10 or 10 euros. Opting out, therefore, was tantamount to not sharing. The opt-out rate was 72 percent in Barcelona and 50 percent in Berkeley. So when given the opportunity to avoid the sharing environment altogether, at least half did so. Many of those who do share in the standard Dictator Game, the researchers conclude, do so reluctantly.[10] The level of sharing in one-shot interactions with strangers in the real world, therefore, is even lower than the disappointing levels the standard Dictator experiment shows.

Fairness in Pricing

The Dictator Game shows that people in general aren't particularly generous to others, whereas the Ultimatum Game shows that people do want fairness and generosity toward themselves. These findings have important and underappreciated implications for many aspects of business, particularly wages and prices. In this section, we focus on prices.

To start, consider the following question posed in a seminal study by Daniel Kahneman, Jack Knetsch, and Richard Thaler:[11]

> A hardware store has been selling snow shovels for $15. The morning after a large snowstorm, the store raises the price to $20. Please rate this action as: Completely Fair, Acceptable, Unfair, or Very Unfair.

Eighty-two percent of respondents to the questionnaire rated the store's action as unfair. In a way, that's unfortunate: if a store concerned with customers' perceptions of fairness refuses to raise prices to meet a spike in demand, it's guaranteeing a shortage. Here's why. Prices solve the scarcity problem: when something (like shovels) is scarce, people bid up its price. That way, the people who are the most willing to pay for a shovel will be the ones who'll get the shovel. Of course, some people see this system as inherently unfair, questioning why someone who happens to have plenty of money should get the shovel over someone who needs the shovel just as much but must choose between buying the shovel and, say, feeding the family that evening. But the results of this survey question suggest that many *more* people—the 82 percent can't all be collectivists—think that under certain conditions (in this case a snowstorm) it's unfair to raise prices. If a business ignores these considerations of fairness, it risks alienating customers. Yet by being sensitive to customers' sense of fairness in pricing, the store won't raise prices enough to bring down the demand—ensuring that demand outstrips supply.

Still, it's a good idea to keep fairness in mind in making pricing decisions. For example, a group of economists conducted a field test to investigate what happened to a company's revenues when it charged more for large-sized women's clothing. Customers who would otherwise buy these clothes found the prices unfair and didn't buy as much.[12] You might think this isn't surprising; after all, whenever you raise prices, you can expect demand to fall. But the researchers tested several different versions of the catalog to separate the typical effect of a price increase from what they call the "fairness effect." For example, in one catalog, they raised the prices of both large and small sizes, making them equally high. As they expected, they found that customers balked not so much at higher prices as at perceived price unfairness, or the difference in price between different sizes of the same item. As a result, gross profits in the "unfair price" condition were about 6 to 8 percent lower than they had been.

Customers also sometimes see a financial penalty as unfair. A business manager may think that penalties, such as late fees, are an obvious way to keep customers doing the right thing, but customers may have a different idea, seeing late fees for video rentals as unfair and exploitative (because why should you pay more for returning a DVD a few days late than it would cost the store to replace the DVD entirely?). A study of independent video rental stores by economists Peter Fishman and Devin Pope found that customers charged a late fee were 27 percent more likely not to return to the store.[13]

The long-term consequences can be even more far-reaching. Netflix president Reed Hastings has said he founded his company after incurring $40 in late fees himself.[14] Today Netflix uses the promise of "No late fees" in its advertisements, clearly differentiating itself from Blockbuster, its chief competitor.[15] Of course, how long you keep your DVDs out is built into the current Netflix pricing model, too—you don't get more movies from your queue until you've returned the ones you already have. But the way the model is set up—paying a monthly subscription fee based on how many movies you're allowed to have out at a time—feels more fair. If customers perceive your competition as acting unfairly, you have an opportunity to attract customers with fairer treatment.

There's another takeaway here. The same numbers can sometimes be presented in two different ways, one of which is easier for people to swallow. For example, if your goal is to get clients to pay within two weeks of receiving an invoice, you can either charge a penalty for paying late or offer a discount for paying early. To many clients, the penalty will seem harsh and perhaps unfair, whereas the discount will seem more palatable—even though the price for late payment amounts to the same thing in both cases.

When a Good Offer Feels Unfair

Sometimes even an objectively good deal can seem unfair. Think back to when you were a child. Unless you grew up without siblings, this scene should sound familiar: your mom gives you a lollipop, a nice round one with a chewy center. It happens to be your favorite candy, and you weren't expecting the treat, so you're delighted. Then your sister skips into the room, sucking a lollipop—and clutching a second lollipop in her other hand! Suddenly you're no longer thrilled. You might even wail, "That's not fair! She got *two* lollipops and I only got *one*."[16]

Chances are your mom didn't respond with a lesson about how life's not fair. She tried to persuade you with a good explanation for the apparent injustice—your sister is older, or you got an extra piece yesterday, or you'll get your second one after dinner. And her words might make the situation seem less unfair. But the point is that you thought you were getting a good deal until you found out somebody else got a better one. You're not just watching for how somebody splits a pie with you, but also for how they split the pie with somebody else.

This is true for more than just siblings. One of several experiments along these lines is the Envy Game, in which children can choose between two options—A, one piece of candy for themselves and one for another child, or B, one piece of candy for themselves and two for the other child. By the time children are five or six years old, most of them (more than 80 percent) opt for A, even though Option B doesn't cost them anything.[17] (Younger children were actually less prone to envy, only about 40 percent of three- and four-year-olds choosing Option A.) In a variation of the Ultimatum Game where players are told how much a Proposer has offered another player, Responders were more likely to reject offers that they knew were lower than another player had gotten.[18] This concern with getting a fair share relative to others seems to have deep evolutionary roots: even capuchin monkeys have been shown to compare their rewards with those of others and to refuse "unfair" rewards.[19]

We see this pattern in everyday life. At work, you're not sure how you feel about your bonus until you find out what kind of bonus your coworkers got. Likewise, you might be happy with the raise you're getting at your new job—until you find out that others in your position are getting $5,000 a year more.

In discussing this quirk of human nature, it's common to quote the writer and critic H. L. Mencken, who said, "A wealthy man is one who earns $100 a year more than his wife's sister's husband." Of course, these days it might take more than $100, but there's a lasting truth in Mencken's comment: we compare ourselves with people close to us in some way. Warren Buffett's wealth, for example, doesn't make you feel poor unless you're a lower-ranked billionaire, or his neighbor, or perhaps a professional investor. We don't compare ourselves to Buffett but to people in our own company, profession, or neighborhood.

Whom we compare ourselves to has practical implications. For example, in a study of charitable giving, economists Rachel Croson and Jen Shang looked at the effect on donations to an actual radio station after revealing how much other listeners had already given. As you might expect, people who were told that somebody else had given $300 made larger donations than people who hadn't been told anything. This is consistent with a psychological theory of influence that says people look to the behavior of others in ambiguous situations, situations where it's not clear what the right thing to do is.

But ambiguity alone is not enough for other people's past actions to influence you: they must seem relevant to you. In another experiment at the radio station, Croson and Shang told one group of callers that others had given $600 and another group that others had given $1,000. While information about the $600 gift increased donations, information about a $1,000 gift didn't—in fact, the resulting donations were lower than for the first group. That is, when listeners were told that someone had given vastly more than they themselves could give, donation levels *declined*. The comparison backfired.[20]

Now try this thought experiment. Suppose you have two options. Option 1: you can earn $50,000 a year while other people earn $25,000. Option 2: you can earn $100,000 a year while other people get $250,000. Which option would you choose? It turns out that researchers conducted a real experiment on this very question, using participants from the Harvard School of Public Health.[21] Under those conditions, half the participants said they'd rather get $50,000 than $100,000. And it's not because of concerns that other people's higher salaries would reduce the participants' own buying power. The researchers had made clear that, with both options, prices would stay the same. Our consideration of relative income sometimes defies logic: in effect, we're willing to give up a lot of money to make sure our neighbors aren't much better off than we are. Yet it seems to be human nature to want to keep up with our peers.

Unfortunately, our fairness radar activates in many situations where we compare ourselves with another group or reference point and find ourselves short. Consider this incident in Kay-Yut's lab. He and his colleagues have run hundreds of experiments over the years, and most of the time things go smoothly: participants show up, play for a few hours, and get paid for their efforts. But sometimes things don't go as planned. One day, a local student was one of several people who came in to participate in an experiment. The researchers made clear to all the participants that they'd get $25 for showing up, but that how much they took home depended on how well they played the game. As a result, some people would end up with more, others with less. And no matter how badly they played, they wouldn't have to pay the lab out of their own pockets. Their losses would come out of the $25 they started with. Sounds fair, right? But this particular student did so badly that at the end of three hours of play she came away with only $1.35. To her, that didn't seem fair. Even though she didn't gamble away her own money, she felt that her time was worth more than $1.35. She was upset enough to complain to Kay-Yut and, eventually, to his boss. The two stood by the rules. Doing otherwise wouldn't be fair and would change the dynamics of future games. But the researchers learned a lesson: people compare against a benchmark (whether it is the minimum wage, the $25 baseline, or what most players were earning in the same game). So when people ask how much others earn in the same game, the researchers now give a stock answer that doesn't reveal much except an unwillingness to invite comparisons.

The Washington Ballet incident can be understood in the same way: the dancers felt shortchanged because their per diem was less than the going rate. Would their reaction be different if they'd learned that other touring groups were getting a $50 per diem? We can't know for sure, but we have good reason to believe they'd be happier. Here's why. It's hard to know how much it will cost to eat in Rome or what quality of meals to expect an employer to subsidize; it's much easier to look over your shoulder and see what somebody else is getting. When we get more than that, we feel we're getting a decent deal; when we get less, we feel cheated.

But there's another issue that makes it hard to reach agreement: when people in a negotiation can choose which group to compare themselves with, they'll make a self-serving choice—and, of course, that choice is likely to be different for the two parties in a negotiation. For example, Carnegie Mellon economists Linda Babcock and George Loewenstein surveyed presidents of school boards and teachers' unions all over Pennsylvania to see which districts the two groups considered comparable to their own for purposes of salary negotiation. This is the kind of information both sides use to set their targets for a fair negotiation outcome, much as the Washington Ballet dancers used data from the State Department. The teachers tended to list districts whose teachers earned salaries higher than theirs, while the school boards listed districts with lower-paid teachers. The average salary difference between the two groups' numbers—$711 per year, or 2.4 percent of the average teaching salary—is huge when you consider that the average raise at the time was less than 5 percent per year. For example, suppose teachers in one district earn $35,000 on average. They compare themselves to teachers in a district where the average salary is $36,700—a number that would require nearly a 4.9 percent raise to reach. Instead, they ask for a "modest" 4 percent raise, which would bring their salaries up to $36,400—not quite as high as they'd like, but in their view a decent compromise. The school board, on the other hand, sees this as an unreasonable demand because the board's reference point is a school district with an average salary of $36,000 (or $700 less than the teachers' reference point). So the school board offers $36,200, which it sees as "more than generous." The result: although both sides made concessions, they still couldn't reach agreement—and each thought the other side was making unfair demands. Indeed, when the researchers analyzed the data, they found that these biased judgments of what's fair were leading to teachers' strikes. For example, strikes were more likely to occur in districts with more varied districts around them, where the gap between teachers' and school boards' perceptions of a fair comparison was wider.[22]

When Price Discrimination Is Unfair

Businesses that overlook the issue of relative fairness can strain relations with employees or customers. Amazon's ill-fated experiment with price discrimination is a case in point.

The word "discrimination" sounds bad, even bigoted, evoking images of women getting paid less for the same work as men, or minorities being denied jobs and housing. But price discrimination is a different story, a time-honored and well-accepted marketing practice. Price discrimination happens whenever two people pay a different price for more or less the same good or service: when you use a dollar-off coupon to buy laundry detergent. Or wait until a book you want to read comes out in paperback. Or see a movie for a few dollars less during a matinee. Price discrimination also happens in less obvious ways, like when you pay more for an airline ticket because you're not spending a Saturday at your destination (thus telling the airline that you're probably traveling for business, not pleasure). Hardly anybody balks at these price differences.

By letting a seller sort its market into different price categories, price discrimination is clearly great for the seller, who doesn't have to leave money on the table. But it's also good for buyers: if we don't care about the price, we just don't mind paying more, and if we're price-sensitive (and don't mind clipping coupons or seeing a movie during the day), we enjoy a lower price. So how did Amazon go wrong?

Before we get to that, let's look at two crucial elements of price discrimination done right. First, the product or service offered at different prices has to be different in at least a subtle way. For example, you may be seeing the same movie or reading the same story, but the experience is different if you're seeing the movie at 11 a.m. or reading the book months after it hits the bestseller list. Think of all the kids who lined up before midnight to buy the latest Harry Potter installment the moment stores could sell it; those who waited to buy it in paperback got the same content for less, but they had missed out on a lot of the fun.

These small differences in quality can justify large differences in price, but customers are fine with that. Sure, some may decide it's not worth paying twice as much to read a book when it first comes out, but others won't have a problem with the higher price. It's up to you and every other customer, and that's the second key to price discrimination done right. You can get a lower fare if you choose to spend Saturday in Minneapolis. You can spend a few minutes looking for coupons, or pay a higher price by skipping this step.

You wouldn't feel nearly as good if you found out somebody else was getting a better price than you, just because.

In September 2000, Amazon took advantage of its remarkable store of customer data to test different prices with actual users. A DVD aficionado discovered that Amazon's price for a DVD changed depending on whether he was logged in as himself ($26.24) or as a new user (making the price fall to $22.74). Although customers might expect better treatment for being loyal, it appeared that Amazon was taking advantage of an insight into customer loyalty: a customer's loyalty might mean the customer is already sold, won't bother comparing prices at the competition, and will be willing to pay more than a new customer. The DVD buyer mentioned his experience on a DVD fan site and before long Amazon had a PR disaster on its hands.[23] "Few things stir up a consumer revolt quicker than the notion that someone else is getting a better deal," said David Streitfeld in a *Washington Post* story about the incident. Amazon denied that it was engaging in "dynamic pricing," insisting that it was merely running a test to see if it could make as much money selling DVDs for less. But the test was a failure.

Amazon probably got more flak because its tactic wasn't just unfair—it also seemed underhanded, since Amazon didn't advertise the new pricing scheme. But being open about low introductory rates can alienate customers, too. Magazine subscribers sometimes have to pay more to renew than to get a new subscription,[24] and cable and Internet customers often get a better deal by switching providers than by staying loyal to their existing one. Whenever different customers get different prices and have no say in the matter, price discrimination risks angering them.

A classic example comes from Coca-Cola. For a time, the company was touting plans to use gee-whiz vending machines that, sensing the temperature outside, would adjust the price of a drink. Hotter days, higher prices. It's a scheme most economists would approve of: raising a price of a scarce, in-demand item ensures that people who really need it (and thus are willing to pay for it) will get it. But most people don't see it that way, and we have a name for charging $3 for a can of coke: gouging. After all, if it costs no more to run a vending machine on a hot day than a cold one, why should the vendor get a higher price? When word got out, the public recoiled, and though the machines are technically feasible, Coca-Cola never implemented them. The company backpedaled, saying the CEO had been speaking hypothetically.[25]

Maybe there's something about cold drinks. In a famous study often called "Beer on the Beach," the pioneering behavioral economist Richard Thaler asked participants how much they'd be willing to pay for a beer.[26] Both groups of participants would be sending a friend to buy them a beer, with instructions for the most they'd be willing to pay. But one group would be buying the beer at a resort hotel, while the other group would be getting the beer at a beach stand. Same beer, different merchant. Participants who were asked about the resort were willing to pay an average of $2.65 (in eighties dollars), but at the humble stand they'd only pay an average of $1.50.[27]

Why is it okay (in the eyes of the participants) for a resort to charge almost twice as much for the same product? Because customers aren't just looking at the absolute price—they're also considering how much money the business is making, and they have some sense of what is a fair markup or profit. In other words, in determining what would be a fair price, they first account for the cost of doing business. Hence the higher price at the resort, even assuming the same markup. Customers feel it wouldn't be fair for a merchant with much lower overhead to charge as much and thus get an exorbitant profit. Profits are okay, but profiteering is not.

The size of the markup—that is, the perceived cost of the good relative to the price paid for it—is just one factor determining what people will generally accept as a fair price. Others include what's customary in a particular place or industry (which is why price discrimination for identical items on Amazon seems less acceptable than price discrimination for the same airline seats), getting what you pay for (that is, getting your money's worth), and other factors that businesses ignore at their peril.[28]

Sometimes Fair, Sometimes Foul

Something strange is at work. On the one hand, interest in fairness seems to be a universal human trait. On the other hand, we've seen that not everybody agrees on what's fair—let alone can predict what the other side will consider fair. What accounts for the differences?

It turns out there are several answers to this question, and we'll focus on three of the most important.

Around the World

To explore the role of culture in bargaining, a team of economists led by Al Roth ran the Ultimatum Game in four very different places— Pittsburgh, Tokyo, Jerusalem and Ljubljana, Slovenia.[29] The differences between countries were striking. The general pattern was the same— some Responders rejected offers and some Proposers offered substantially more than the "rational" minimum—but how much people offered and the rejection rate for each type of offer differed from place to place.

Participants in the United States and Slovenia offered more money than those in Israel and Japan. The most common offer in the United States and Slovenia was 50 percent; in Japan, the most common offers were 45 percent and 40 percent; and in Israel it was 40 percent. So perceptions of fairness are different in different cultures. But there's a more interesting phenomenon at work: whereas Israeli and Japanese Proposers offered less than Proposers in the United States and Slovenia, rejection rates in Israel and Japan were *lower*. So it's not as though Israelis and Japanese are tougher negotiators; if they were, rejection rates in those countries would be higher. Instead, these cultures have more agreement about what's fair. As the spread in offered prices shrinks—as it did in Israel and Japan compared to the United States and Slovenia—the rejection rate falls.

We can only speculate about the reasons for differences between countries, though research on other countries provides some clues. There appear to be two factors that determine how high the offers will be in a particular society: payoff for cooperation and market integration. The highly interdependent Lamalera whale hunters of Indonesia make higher offers than the relatively independent Machiguenga people of the Peruvian jungles because the payoff for cooperation is much higher for the Lamalera. Likewise, societies where people have frequent market interactions make more generous offers than groups with less market interaction.[30] But whatever the reason, culture matters. It's one of the major factors affecting differences in what people consider fair. And because an offer considered fair in Japan may not be considered fair in the United States (for example), you need to be sensitive to the cultural backgrounds of the people you negotiate with.

Small Talk, Big Difference

So far, we've talked about how culture affects people's sense of what's fair. But we can't do anything about someone's culture, other than work with it in mind. There are, however, some fairness factors we can control.

The big one, as shown in a study by Al Roth, is face-to-face communication.[31] In one experiment, Roth used the standard Ultimatum Game as a benchmark and compared those results with two variations. In the first, participants could talk face-to-face about anything, including how to divide the pie. In the second, they were allowed to talk face-to-face, but not about anything related to the experiment. The communication was purely social.

What happened? Remember that in the basic Ultimatum experiment, half of all splits were fair—within 10 percent of 50-50. Adding face-to-face communication increased the number of such splits to a whopping 83 percent. The rate of rejections went down from 33 percent to 5 percent.

What's most interesting is that the results didn't depend at all on the type of communication. Whether participants talked about the negotiation or just made small talk, the resulting offers were fairer and much less likely to be rejected. It's the face-to-face interactions that made all the difference. We now know from another series of experiments, which entailed haggling over the price of a car, that people who are given an opportunity to make small talk before a negotiation are more likely to reach an agreement. These were more complicated negotiations than the Ultimatum Game, yet participants in the schmooze condition were able to reach an agreement, apparently because it's easier to build rapport in person than through e-mail.[32]

There's a lesson here, of course. It's an understatement that we live in a culture that values efficiency. We work with far-flung colleagues and conduct important business entirely through e-mail, saving ourselves the trouble of making our way over to the next cubicle, let alone another city. To Americans, cultures like China and Japan, where it's customary to spend hours getting to know one another before getting down to business, seem wasteful. Even the American three-martini lunch seems like an indulgent throwback to a less enlightened era. But Roth's experiment, along with others like it, shows that we lose something when we shed these "wasteful," seemingly irrational practices. Small talk, especially done face-to-face, can make a big impact.

One reason for this effect is that face-to-face contact forces you to see someone as a flesh-and-blood human being. You're more likely to feel empathy for someone you've broken bread with than for a disembodied voice, and more motivated to see things from the other's point of view—especially in moments of conflict. The head of Japan's largest mobile phone operator, Ryuji Yamada of NTT DoCoMo, recently put it this way when asked for advice he gives his younger employees:

> These days, many Japanese grow up as an only child or with one sibling, spending a lot of time in front of their computers, and they become poor face-to-face communicators. In offices, they exchange emails even though they might be sitting right next to each other. That's fine when things are going well, but not when there is a problem to be solved. At those times, they have to look one another in the eye in order to respect their position and understand their vantage point.[33]

How Children Play

Kay-Yut's younger son, a sixth grader, recently followed in his father's footsteps, opting to do a science project around the Ultimatum Game. He observed how his classmates played the game, and found behavior that's similar to how adults play. For example, about 43 percent of the offers were for a 50-50 split. The one sixth grader who offered nothing had all his offers rejected. But excluding this outlier, the average offer was 39 cents (out of $1), and sixth graders rejected 29 percent of offers below 50 cents.

Coincidentally, a pair of scientists had recently published a study that also looked at sixth graders playing the Ultimatum Game, comparing this age group to younger children and adults. (Kay-Yut's son had not done a thorough "literature review" before conducting his own experiment.) Looking at how children play the Ultimatum Game offers clues to how ideas of fairness and retaliation develop, so Shelly Fisk and Yoella Bereby-Meyer had children of three different ages play the game: kindergartners (aged five), second graders (aged eight), and sixth graders (aged twelve). The procedure was similar to the usual Ultimatum Game, except that instead of money the researchers used tokens that the children could later exchange for school supplies. Also, to keep things simple, the researchers limited the types of offer to either a fair split (5-5) or an unfair split (8-2).

Most of the older children, second graders and sixth graders alike, played the game just as adults do, all of them making fair offers and usually rejecting unfair offers. But the kindergartners played very differently: 60 percent of them proposed unfair offers and, when put in the role of Responder, only 20 percent of them rejected an unfair offer. In other words, most of them acted just as rational and self-interested economic agents would— prompting the researchers to call their paper "Is Homo Economicus a Five-Year-Old?"[34] Fairness, it seems, isn't inborn but becomes an important social consideration once children reach a certain age.

The researchers created another interesting variation: having some of the offers come not from another child, but from a bingo machine that randomly spat out balls corresponding to either a fair or an unfair offer. We know from other studies that adults are more likely to mete out costly punishment to another person than to a computer—a finding that suggests people reject offers to punish the other player.[35] But would children of different ages make this distinction? Here again, the older children acted like most adults, rejecting unfair offers from another child much more often than the randomly generated offers. For example, 60 percent of the twelve-year-olds rejected unfair offers from other children, but only 10 percent rejected offers from the bingo machine. The five-year-olds, on the other hand, rejected both types of unfair offers at a rate of only 20 percent.

There's another way we can tell that young children aren't thinking of the other person: by comparing their behavior in the Ultimatum Game with that of the Dictator Game. Younger children make greedy offers in both games, oblivious to the possibility that in one of the games the other player can reject an unfair offer. By the time children are eight years old, most of them don't make this mistake.

But notice that this growing social sophistication pays off only for the Proposers. In other words, thinking of the other player's intentions and actions helps you only when you're choosing what offer to make; when it comes to deciding about rejecting an unfair offer, you're better off acting like a five-year-old.

Fairness Isn't Everything

You might be wondering why we're devoting so many words to fairness. Is it really that important? Absolutely. Fairness is a major consideration for people all over and—as we've seen with negotiation and price discrimination—it drives many business outcomes. But the issue is underappreciated. People are quick to feel they're being treated unfairly, but they aren't quite as attuned to others' sense of fairness. We can't know whether the Washington Ballet could have averted its negotiation failure, but it seems clear that success would have been more likely had the owners not done something so blatantly unfair as offering a per diem that's nearly two-thirds lower than what others were getting.

So fairness is crucial, but making sure we get our fair share (and, to a lesser extent, making sure others do, too) is only one of several social considerations that affect our decisions in ways traditional economics wouldn't predict.

These considerations, which economists call "social preferences," also include status—our social standing compared to others. Having high status means you and others in your group know you're near the top of the pecking order, and it comes with privileges: status brings power, respect, influence, and usually more money. Now, it's perfectly reasonable to seek status as a way to gain power or money; for example, an impressive job title from your current employer tells future employers that you held a high-powered job and makes it more likely that they will offer you a higher salary. But in one experiment conducted in five countries, researchers showed that we also seek status for its own sake, not just as a means to an end. American participants, for example, invested 10 percent more for the chance of a financial reward if their success was publicly applauded—that is, they were willing to pay a 10 percent premium to gain status.[36]

We value status, but we have other social preferences (see table). Some of our preferences—particularly status seeking and resource striving—put us at odds with the people around us. These preferences are essentially selfish and competitive. But there's another set of social preferences that pull us in the opposite direction—altruistic, cooperative preferences that include our desire for fairness, the desire to belong to a group, and (the topic of our next chapter) our tendency to reward like with like.

Competitive Forces[37]	Cooperative Forces
Resource Striving: the craving for money and material goods	**Fairness and Reciprocity:** the demand for fairness from others and the willingness to punish unfairness, as well as a tendency to repay kindness with kindness
Status Seeking: the craving for status as an end in itself	**Group Identity Seeking:** the desire to belong to a group, as well as the tendency to favor members of your own group

Traditional thinking in business and economics has stressed competition, especially in resource striving, and has given short shrift to our cooperative tendencies. But all of these preferences affect business outcomes, and ignoring their pull can mean errors in predicting how people will behave.

Consider contracts. Conventional wisdom says a contract should be ironclad, covering every possibility and closing every loophole. But that idea assumes that people only want to win, and, given any opportunity, will take advantage of a situation. There's certainly some truth to that: a selfish part of us does want to best the other side, even by cheating. But that part of us must struggle with our other half: while we want to win in the short term, we also want to cooperate, preserve our relationships, and be seen by others as worthy of their trust.[38] A contract that doesn't take that into account may work less well than one that rests on a solid basis of trust and doesn't try to cover everything.[39] An overly legalistic contract may drive out the motivation to behave out of a sense of cooperation, out of respect for social norms.

Some people think the forces of competition are much more powerful than the forces of cooperation. They believe that we are by nature selfish, and only the rules of culture keep us from acting that way. But most social scientists—including psychologists, anthropologists, and even economists—no longer accept this story. That's because the pre-ponderance of evidence points in a different direction: that we're born with a dual nature, with great potential for selfishness and altruism, greed and generosity, status-seeking and fairness-seeking.[40] We can't run experiments on the origins of human nature, but indirect evidence sug-gests that millions of years of evolution have built us this way.

Playing the Ultimatum Game makes us very conscious that generos-ity works out better in the long run. Most of our responses to the world, whether in the form of cooperation or competition, are of the knee-jerk variety—working at an emotional, subconscious level. Poor resources and low status make us envious. Taking advantage of another person makes us feel guilty. Unfairness makes us angry. And all these uncomfortable feelings, these negative emotions, drive us to do what it takes to make things right.

Positive emotions drive our actions, too. Acting kind and belonging to a group make us happy. Receiving kindness from others makes us grateful—which in turn makes it more likely we'll reciprocate in kind. With no conscious reasoning on our part, our emotions affect our thoughts and actions. This is an efficient, if imperfect, way of making decisions. We don't have time to calculate and weigh the costs and benefits of dif-ferent courses of action for every decision; emotions are a shortcut.

But just as we don't want to consciously calculate the trade-off in every decision, we also don't want to become slaves to our emotions. When we have time to be rational, it's smart to keep our emotions in check.

If it's a good idea to keep your own emotions in check, do you want other people, such as your rivals, to succumb to their emotions and make worse decisions because of it? Sometimes. Advertisers do this all the time, using emotional appeals to get you to buy products you may not need or pay more for them than you really should. This strategy isn't just morally dubious—it also risks backfiring if your counterpart is on to you. And even if you win the battle, you may lose the war if the other person retaliates down the road. In the long run, you'll often do better by treat-ing others as you would have them treat you. In fact, this principle of reciprocity is the subject of the next chapter.

3

....

What Goes Around: Reciprocity

As Jim Goodnight was starting his company in 1976, he didn't want to re-create the work environment of his previous jobs.[1] When the statistician had worked at GE, for example, employees had to pass a security guard and sign in to get to their desks; when they wanted a cup of coffee, they had to buy it from a vending machine. "A lot of these things I found somewhat offensive," recalls Goodnight, whose business, the analytics giant SAS, has grown into the largest privately owned software company in the world.

Today, the North Carolina–based company (whose name rhymes with "class") offers its workers much more than free coffee. Among the many subsidized on-site perks: an upscale cafeteria, a state-of-the-art fitness and recreation center, convenient child care, and a health clinic where employees can get everything from an allergy shot to a psychotherapy session. The point of all this largesse isn't to keep employees at the office longer; in fact, the company encourages thirty-five-hour workweeks. But neither is the generosity entirely selfless, something company executives readily admit. "We're not altruistic[2] by any stretch of the imagination," the HR director has said. "This is a for-profit business and we do all these things because it makes good business sense." For example, in an industry where 20 percent of a company's workers leave each year, the turnover rate at SAS hovers at about 4 percent. This past year only

2 percent of SAS employees left, and SAS was ranked No. 1 on *Fortune* magazine's list of 100 Best Companies to Work For.

In interview after interview, SAS managers and employees repeat some version of an unofficial but well-understood company covenant: "We're willing to take care of you if you're willing to take care of us."

Testing for Reciprocity: In the Lab

This is a simple statement of the principle of reciprocity. The principle is extremely well established in the social sciences and in folk psychology alike, captured in common phrases like "an eye for an eye," "give and take," and "you scratch my back and I'll scratch yours." But reciprocity is a departure from traditional economic thinking, which predicts that people will give only as much as they have to and only if giving will produce a future benefit. According to this logic, if you've finished a meal in a restaurant you never plan to visit again (because you're on vacation), you won't leave a tip no matter how wonderful the service. Or, if someone pays you to do a job, and this employer can't tell how hard you're working, you'll do the bare minimum. But most people do tip for good service, and they work even when the boss isn't around, and many subscribe to some version of the Golden Rule, treating others as they would like to be treated themselves.

But is treating employees better than they expect indeed good business, as the SAS HR director suggested? You certainly can't conclude from the SAS story that treating employees well is responsible for their loyalty or hard work. After all, perhaps it's the other way around: that good workers like to work for successful companies, and that it's these successful companies, like SAS, that can best afford to treat employees well. So how can we be sure that treating employees well can change how hard they work?

As usual, through experiments. These experiments tested a notion developed by Berkeley economist George Akerlof (whose most famous idea we'll have much more to say about in chapter 5). Akerlof envisioned the relationship between a worker and an employer as a "partial gift exchange."[3] To be sure, there's real money changing hands just like in any market transaction—but part of the transaction, Akerlof argued, is often governed by an unwritten but compelling rule: the norm of reciprocity. In such a system, the employer voluntarily pays more than is necessary (that is, more than the worker could earn at a different company) and, to reciprocate the kindness, the worker puts in extra effort (more than the minimum that the job calls for). The system seemed to be working: one employer he looked at chose this system over a simple incentive system even when the employer could easily see and measure each worker's productivity. In other settings, the hope of a promotion might motivate employees, but in this case workers sometimes turned down promotions, which came with more responsibility but no raise. It was reciprocity, not the hope of a future reward, Akerlof reasoned, that explained both high wages and high productivity in this setting.

To test this idea, many economists have used an experiment called the Gift Exchange Game. A typical setup, designed by a team of Austrian economists led by Ernst Fehr, has some participants playing the roles of employers and another group playing the workers, with more workers than available job openings—and a minimum wage that the employers cannot go below.[4] The game has two stages. In the first stage, the employers post wages publicly, and any worker can accept any offer. Once an offer is accepted, it becomes a binding contract. In the game's second stage, each worker with a contract chooses the "quality" of work to perform. This quality or effort level is a number between 0 and 1, but quality isn't free—the higher the number, the higher the cost to the worker. The idea is that, as in the real world, the worker needs to work harder to produce higher-quality work, and the more effort he puts in, the more it costs him.

The payoffs in the experiment work as you might expect: each worker receives his or her wage minus the cost of whatever quality level the worker has chosen. Employers, meanwhile, earn profits based on the quality of the work minus the workers' wages.

How should selfish, rational people play this game? If the worker is selfish and rational, he should always choose a quality of 0 because the wage has already been set by the time he is making that decision.

Similarly, the selfish and rational employer should always offer the minimum wage because of the surplus of labor: more workers than jobs should make workers take any wage, even the minimum wage. In this setup, it's not possible for employers to entice workers to work harder for higher wages because the quality decision is made *after* the employer and worker strike a deal.

And that's exactly why the results of the experiment aren't what you would expect of selfish, rational players. Employers *did* want to entice workers to produce higher-quality work, so they paid more, on average, than the minimum wage. They seemed to anticipate that if they didn't pay high wages, workers would lower quality. As for the workers, they chose quality levels whose median was higher than 0, an effect that's best explained through reciprocity. Indeed, more than half of the workers chose a higher level of quality when they received higher wages. And as wages increased, so did the median quality level. For example, when the wage rose from 30–44 to 90–110, the median quality rose fivefold, from 0.1 to 0.5.

The experiment went further: in a second condition, the researchers took away the opportunity for workers to reciprocate. That is, rather than letting the worker choose a level of quality, the researchers set this level at 1. What happened? Wages plummeted, falling far below their level in the first condition, when workers had an opportunity to reciprocate high wages with high effort. That suggests not only that workers will reciprocate when they can, but also that employers anticipate this reciprocating behavior and set wages accordingly.

All this has far-reaching consequences, going a long way toward explaining why some people can't find jobs no matter how much they're willing to sacrifice wages. After all, if the price is right, supply and demand should (in theory) perfectly match, with exactly the same number of jobs as there are people willing to take them. In a deep recession, for example, wages should fall as workers compete fiercely for fewer jobs—to the point where everybody who wants to work for these low wages can find a low-paying job.[5] So why should there ever be involuntary unemployment? One answer, put forth by Akerlof and Janet Yellen, is that employers don't lower wages *even when they can;* lower wages would lead to disgruntled workers who don't put in enough effort. And if wages stay above the "market-clearing" price, there will be a labor surplus.[6] And that's exactly what we saw happening in the lab experiments by Fehr and his colleagues.[7]

Testing for Reciprocity: In the Field

There's a real problem, though: when other researchers ran a field experiment to test the effects of employer generosity, they got decidedly mixed results. Uri Gneezy and John List, economists with a knack for constructing fascinating experiments, wanted to see how well the lab findings on gift exchange carried over into the real world. This is a crucial question with all lab research because all tightly controlled lab experiments are artificial by design: to tease out the effect of each variable, lab tests purposely strip away many of the messy details of the real world. But what if you strip away too much—what if what appears irrelevant to the lab scientist actually influences behavior outside the lab?

For example, many lab studies have participants communicate through computers, in part to reduce the contaminating effects of extraneous factors like physical attractiveness, race, rapport, and the like; yet some "extraneous" factors aren't extraneous at all—they can affect outcomes in crucial ways, as you saw in experiments on the Ultimatum Game, where face-to-face interactions resulted in fairer splits than computer-mediated game play. Similarly, time can play an important role in how people play. In Fehr's Gift Exchange experiments, as in most lab studies, participants play for only a couple of hours; the experiments condense interactions that, in the real world, would span days, weeks, even years. A lot happens when time stretches out: people can afford to deliberate, for example, thinking through decisions more carefully than they might in a rapid-fire lab session. On the other hand, they may be more likely to get more bored and tired over the course of a day's work than during one or two hours in the lab. And sometimes just knowing you're a participant in an experiment—a player in a game rather than your true self—might affect how you think and act. For all these reasons and others, economists like to supplement lab tests with field experiments.[8]

That's what Gneezy and List did with gift exchange in the workplace. They hired college students for two real jobs without telling them they'd be participating in an experiment. In one, the students had to catalog library books, entering data about each book into a computer. The other job was door-to-door fund-raising for an on-campus research center. Both jobs would take about six hours, far longer than the lab studies took. What's more, by seeing the student workers' efforts at a real job, the researchers could track the workers' actual productivity, as opposed to a quality number entered in a lab terminal.

Would an above-market wage improve productivity? To answer this question, Gneezy and List recruited all their workers by advertising a market wage: the library job would pay $12 an hour, and the fund-raising job (in another part of the country) would pay $10 an hour. Students who applied for these jobs, we can assume, were willing to work for these wages. But would these same students work harder if the wages were higher? This is where the researchers threw in a gift—when the students showed up for work, half of them got a surprise boost in pay. That is, unbeknownst to the control groups for both jobs, half the library workers and half the door-to-door solicitors would get $20 an hour.

The effect of this unexpected gift was dramatic—but only at first. In the first ninety minutes on the job, each library worker in the control group, working for $12 an hour, logged on average about forty-one books; the workers who'd gotten $20 an hour, on the other hand, logged about fifty-two books on average. This is a startling difference, especially given that the workers were the same type of person, randomly assigned to get the gift or not. It's not as if the higher wage had attracted a more productive worker.

We should add that the researchers made sure the workers knew these were onetime jobs; in other words, the workers didn't have to worry about getting fired for not living up to the employer's expectations. If the students worked hard to make a good impression, this effort had nothing to do with the desire for more of such high-paying work in the future. In other words, the researchers were looking for evidence of strong reciprocity—and, for the first hour and a half on the job, that's what they found.

But for some reason, the workers slacked off after that. Whether they were doing data-entry work or door-to-door fund-raising, the students who'd been paid more than promised didn't produce any more than the control group. They had stopped reciprocating the gift of a higher wage.

This is a troubling finding. It calls into question the results of lab studies on the Gift Exchange Game and suggests that simply paying a higher wage isn't enough to sustain high levels of morale and productivity. But anybody who's gotten a raise or changed jobs knows this already, at least on some level: you're happy and extra motivated at first, but the effect wears off. How fast it wears off depends on a lot of factors—the type of work, the size of the pay boost, and considerations of how much your coworkers are making, to name a few—but sooner or later, you're bound to want even more. And not necessarily money, either; it might be a promotion, or a special perk, or recognition in front of your peers—or maybe just the inherent stimulation of a new and interesting assignment. But whatever it is, most of us understand that we need to keep things fresh to stay at our most productive. If you're managing people, you undoubtedly know this about motivating people. Even so, perhaps you're not doing this as effectively as you could. Here's why.

Annual salary reviews and the small raises that accompany them may not be enough. In fact, by the time performance reviews roll around, your employees may have all but forgotten the last raise and the last set of goals—perhaps being so disenchanted with the job that their performance has suffered, leading you to believe a raise isn't called for! Not only that, but raises that come like clockwork become expected—not so much a gift as a "given."

Fortunately, unless you're constrained by an unyielding bureaucracy, you probably have other tools at your disposal besides annual raises and bonuses. HP, for example, gives managers the discretion to reward outstanding work with unexpected, ad hoc tokens of appreciation, typically a choice between a restaurant dinner and its value in cash. Many companies do similar things. FedEx has long given "Golden Falcon" and "Bravo Zulu" awards, which combine financial rewards (such as grants of company stock) with public recognition (which appeals to many people's desire for status). If your company doesn't do anything of the sort, perhaps you can help change that. And if you need proof that small gifts can work, consider the following experiment.

A group of Swiss researchers led by Sebastian Kube wondered if the field test by Gneezy and List didn't make the employers' intentions clear enough.[9] If the student workers weren't sure why they were getting a higher wage than promised, they might not have interpreted this windfall as a gift. If so, perhaps their extra effort at the beginning of the experiment wasn't due so much to reciprocity as to the extra oomph that any pleasant surprise gives us. Would making the gift nature of the gift more obvious affect worker productivity?

To answer this question, the researchers used a library task similar to the one used by Gneezy and List—but they used three different treatments. In one, they paid students 12 euros per hour for the three-hour job, just as advertised. A second group received an extra, unexpected 7 euros—not per hour, but as a onetime gift—which the researchers presented to them at the beginning of the study by saying, "We have a further small gift to thank you: you receive 7 euros in addition." The third group got a gift worth 7 euros—a small, gift-wrapped thermos—which the researchers presented by saying, "We have a further small gift to thank you: this thermos bottle in addition."

Which condition would you expect to produce the best results for the employer? It turns out that the cash gift of 7 euros had no effect on productivity. In fact, since the employer spent almost 20 percent extra (7 euros out of the 36 euros advertised) to get no productivity gain, the gift was counterproductive. But look what happened to the students who'd gotten the thermos: their productivity rose by 30 percent! And it stayed high throughout the three-hour experiment. The noncash gift was clearly a better use of the employer's money. As much as workers say they'd prefer cold, hard cash, under the right circumstances a noncash gift can achieve more.

As you think about what all these Gift Exchange experiments might mean for you, you need to keep a few points in mind. Remember that although Gneezy and List did their experiments in the real world using real work, the jobs were (by design) onetime gigs. The same was true for the Swiss study. All these researchers wanted to make sure that workers' concerns about the future wouldn't affect the data or confuse their interpretation of the results. But many real-world employment situations entail an ongoing relationship. In other words, workers aren't thinking about being nice to the employer only because the employer was nice to them (strong reciprocity), but also because they know that doing a good job will make it likelier that their employer will pay them more later, or promote them, or at least not fire them (weak reciprocity). Suppliers, too, usually care about the prospect of future work. When both strong and weak reciprocity enter the picture, we can expect the relationship between an employer's gifts and an employee's effort to be even more solid than in the one-shot experiments. This combination of forces is part of what makes companies like SAS so successful.

There are other insights from the Gift Exchange Game. If you've ever been told that you're overqualified for a job that you'd have been happy to take anyway, you now have a clue about why your prospective employer was reluctant to offer you the job. True, there's a chance that "overqualified" is a polite way to package age discrimination. But there's a legitimate reason to think someone's overqualified: the hiring manager might have feared you'd quickly grow bored and resentful, jumping ship at the first chance of a better job—or simply thought she'd find someone more likely to give the job their all. Hiring a skilled senior worker for a junior-level job and a junior-level salary is often no bargain in the end. And that's a lesson to those on the hiring end, even if you're merely choosing a supplier or a temporary contractor. You might feel pleased at getting someone to agree to do work for less, but if the person feels put upon, you risk getting exactly what you paid for.

Also, keep in mind that the right wages depend on a host of factors, including the type of work and the competitive environment. For example, you can pay cashiers at your fast-food franchise twice the minimum wage, but even if that does improve how well they work, the difference isn't likely to matter enough to be worth it in a business customers turn to for fast and cheap food, rather than superior customer service. So high wages and generous gifts aren't the answer for every situation.

Finally, if you want to create a culture of give-and-take, you need to repeatedly give as good as you get. Again, it's not just about money. For example, if a company expects professionals to work as long as it takes to get the job done, never paying overtime for occasional nights and weekends, many employees will take offense if the company changes its tune in terms of time off, becoming clock-watching bookkeepers over every half-day of vacation taken. This double standard will violate reciprocity norms, which demand that either you account on both ends, as you would for an hourly worker—or you don't keep tabs, maintaining a relationship of mutual obligation, as in a family or a friendship.

The Thought That Counts

As the Swiss experiment suggested, the nature of the gift matters. One reason the thermos may have worked better than the cash gift is that it may have suggested better intentions on the part of the employer. For example, although the thermos may be worth no more than 7 euros, the workers may have sensed that the noncash gift took some thought and effort to buy. Also, whereas people are used to getting paid in cash for work, noncash gifts are special. Technically, unexpected cash and an unexpected thermos are both gifts, but the gift-wrapped thermos *looks* more like a gift than a cash payment does. It tells the recipient loud and clear that the employer is purposely being nice. And that's important because we know from other experiments that employees care why their employer is compensating them well. For example, UC Santa Barbara economist Gary Charness found that workers put in more effort when they sensed that their employer was keeping their wages high on purpose.[10] In other words, given the same high wage, two workers will respond differently depending on whether they see their manager giving the raise freely or, say, because of union pressure. Intentions matter.

But what happens in more complex situations, where intentions are hard to interpret? Often you don't know why someone's being nice to you. In those cases, is reciprocity still a strong driver of behavior? That's one of the questions probed in an experiment by INSEAD professor Christoph Loch, a pioneer in social preferences research, and his colleague Yaozhong Wu.

Imagine the following supply-chain scenario. You're a wholesaler selling widgets through a retailer to consumers. You decide on a wholesale price to charge your retailer, and the retailer decides on a street price to charge the end customers. Given the same wholesale price, you as the wholesaler make more money if the retailer charges a low street price because lower prices generate more sales. The retailer, on the other hand, may not want to set a low street price because low prices mean lower margins on all those sales. Still, the lower the street price, the more customers will show up. This is the classical trade-off where a higher price allows retailers to make more money per unit, but a lower price generates more sales, and it's one participants playing retailers in this experiment understood.

As a wholesaler, you might reason like this: if you set a low wholesale price, the retailer can make more money—either by being able to sell more widgets or by having more room to raise the street price before he runs out of customers. Either way, giving him a low wholesale price can be construed as being "nice," the kind of behavior that engenders niceness in kind.

The experiment strips away some of the details (such as demand uncertainty) to zero in on the core question: if you set attractively low wholesale prices for your retailer, will the retailer reciprocate your niceness by passing on the lower price to his end customers?

There's a challenge to answering this question, though: it's not at all clear what constitutes a low price in this situation, in which retailers have only one source of widgets. It's not like the Gift Exchange Game studies, where participants saw the normal wage and then compared their new wage with it. The same can be true in the real world. Not only that, but even if the retailer does consider your price to be low, he may chalk this up to an error on your part. In other words, it's really difficult for the retailer to figure out whether you're being nice to him and, if so, whether that's your real intent. Given this ambiguity, will the retailer reciprocate?

Although these challenges made it impossible to measure absolute reciprocity, by manipulating social conditions the researchers found a way to measure *relative* reciprocity, compared to the behavior of a control group. The idea is that if reciprocity comes from feelings and relationships, then reducing the social distance between participants should increase reciprocity's effect relative to the control group, in which anonymous pairs of participants played the wholesaler-retailer game for fifteen rounds, interacting only through computers. Because the players don't know each other and remain anonymous throughout the game, their social distance is large. Note, however, that there is a selfish reason for both players to reciprocate, regardless of anyone's intentions for being nice: in the long run, lower prices can potentially help both players earn more money. Of course, reciprocity doesn't always make money. To use an extreme example, if the wholesaler sets the price at 0 above cost, and the retailer sets the price at 0 above that, then neither makes any money.

In the experimental condition, the researchers established a social relationship between each pair of players. Before the game, the two players briefly met face-to-face and introduced themselves. To reinforce this social relationship, the researchers showed the participants the following short paragraph before the start of the game:

> You have already met the person with whom you will play the game. Now the person is no longer a stranger to you. You can imagine that the other player is a good friend. You have a good relationship and like each other.

This way the researchers shortened the social distance between participants (compared to the control condition) without changing any of the financial incentives or offering any additional information about the players or the game.

So what happened? Reciprocity prevailed: participants with social relationships were indeed nicer to each other than those in the anonymous condition. We know this because wholesalers who were "friends" with the retailers set their prices lower than did anonymous wholesalers ($5.18 compared to $6.30), and the friendly retailers set street prices that were lower than those set by anonymous retailers ($10.10 compared to $11.63).

What's more, both the retailer and the wholesaler in the social relationship made more money than anonymous pairs: when you add the average wholesaler's profit to the average retailer's profit, that sum was higher in the social relationship condition. We saw earlier that mutual niceness leads to higher profits even when both players are being calculating—that is, even if players are only thinking about the future of the relationship, rather than simply feeling good about where it stands. But the face-to-face experiment shows that the reciprocity effect is even stronger when the players have an existing relationship. The relationship engenders even more reciprocity and even higher profits, all without changing the rules of the game.

Amazingly, this can occur even when the relationship is merely imaginary. In another version of this experiment, the researchers kept the participants anonymous, but induced the feeling that they had a relationship by showing them the following paragraph:

> From the instructions, you already know that you are going to play with another person. You can imagine that the other person in the game is a good friend of yours. You have a good relationship and like each other.

In this condition, which is something of a cross between the purely anonymous control condition and the face-to-face meeting condition, participants treated each other more nicely than in the control condition, lower prices leading to higher profits for everyone.

As we saw in some of the Ultimatum Game experiments, social considerations can have a powerful effect on behavior and the bottom line, even when these considerations seem irrelevant to the task at hand. And even when it's not clear that someone is being nice, that niceness can pay off in the long run.

First the Carrot

The force of reciprocity can work especially well in situations that, unlike employee-employer relationships, call for selfless acts of giving. Charitable giving is a case in point.

The German economist Armin Falk, an expert on reciprocity, conducted a simple field experiment: working with a major international charity, he crafted three different types of fund-raising appeals.[11] All three contained letters asking people in the Zurich region of Switzerland for money to fund schools for street children in Bangladesh. Of the nearly ten thousand solicitations they sent out, two-thirds contained a gift that the fund-raisers said was from the children. The remaining third contained no such gift. And although all the gifts were similar (postcards drawn by the children), they differed in one important way: some letters contained just one postcard and one envelope, while others contained four postcards and four envelopes.

The question Falk hoped to answer was what effect the gifts would have on donation rates. We know that some people give just because it feels good—these are the people who would donate money simply because the solicitation letter, with its description of needy children, pulled at their heartstrings. But what effect would the gifts have over and above the effect of altruism—and would the size of the gift matter?

Sure enough, some people (about 12 percent) gave money even without receiving a gift. But more people gave money after receiving a gift. When the gift was small, about 14 percent gave money. That may not seem like a large difference, but it actually amounts to an increase of 17 percent—to be exact, 465 people out of 3,237 gave money after receiving the one postcard and one envelope, whereas only 397 out of 3,262 did when there was no gift enclosed. So the inclusion of a very small gift had a significant effect on donation rates.

But the really striking effect came from including what Falk writes about as a large gift—the four postcards and four envelopes. Incredibly, the donation rate rose by 75 percent. Whereas 397 out of 3,262 people in the no-gift group donated money to the street children, 691 of the 3,347 people who'd gotten the large gift did.

Now, including a small gift with a solicitation is something that many charities already do; enclosing a greeting card, personalized address labels, a pen, or the like is a time-honored technique that goes back at least to the psychologist Robert Cialdini's book *Influence,* in which he specifically chalks up the success of this technique to reciprocity. But it's very different from what many fund drives do, which is to dangle in front of you a gift you can receive *in exchange* for a donation. Instead of telling would-be donors that they would get, say, a T-shirt as a thank-you gift for a certain level of donation, or a hardcover book for a higher level of donation (as public-television stations in the United States often do), the charity in Falk's study is going out on a limb a little, giving away an unconditional gift before the donor gives anything at all. But because of the power of reciprocity, all gifts have strings attached, so gift givers can count on at least some portion of their recipients to reciprocate.

In Falk's experiment, even though many recipients kept the gifts without donating anything at all (or perhaps simply tossed the postcards or solicitation requests unopened), sending out the gifts proved hugely profitable. Not only did the participation rate rise with the inclusion and size of the enclosed gift, but the size of the donation per donor remained fairly constant across the three conditions. In other words, it's not as if people given the gift were simply "paying back," giving only enough to cover expenses or giving in proportion to the cost of the gifts. The cost of the postcards to the charity was about 2,000 Swiss francs, and total revenue from all donors was 92,656 Swiss francs—about 22 percent more than had the organization not used gifts at all to evoke reciprocal donations. Had the charity spent 4,800 Swiss francs to send the larger gift to all the would-be donors, Falk infers that revenues would have risen by 40,976 Swiss francs—a total that's 55 percent higher than if the charity had not used gifts at all. Spending 4,800 Swiss francs to earn an additional 40,976 Swiss francs—that's an impressive return on investment.

We have to be careful not to make too much of this one experiment, however. If one postcard increases the donation rate, and four postcards increase it even more, will ten postcards—or a more expensive gift—go even further? Not necessarily: it could be that four postcards hit at the sweet spot and that costlier gifts would backfire. Without further testing, we can't be sure. And there are other factors at play here. The gifts came from the children themselves—the direct beneficiaries of the donors' gifts (as opposed to, say, postcards ordered by the charity). What's more, they're the children's own handiwork, the images on the cards calling to mind the poor children's plight. (One boy's colorful drawing, signed by the eight-year-old artist himself, depicts a scene whose cheer and optimism contrasts poignantly with the boy's current situation—the image itself evoking a desire to give.) Finally, the gifts were unexpected, and had the donors been receiving the same postcards year after year, from this or other organizations, the effect would likely not be as strong, much as for a routine raise at work; under some circumstances, the effect might disappear entirely.

Here's what we can say with some confidence. Reciprocity is a powerful force that can be harnessed for a good cause. When you want people to give money, give of their time, give blood, or give whatever it is you're asking for, you might feel tempted to dangle a carrot in front of the would-be donor; instead, all the reciprocity experiments suggest you might consider giving a carrot *first*. Finally, and at the risk of overextending the metaphor, think about the size of the carrot, the type of carrot, and from whom the carrot is coming.

But what about a gift after the fact, given to thank the generous donors—doesn't this work, too? Not necessarily. In fact, if the thank-you gift is too small, it can actually *reduce* donations. This is the famous crowding-out effect, in which positive or negative extrinsic incentives (especially money) push out intrinsic motives (like the feeling of being the kind of person who does good things).[12] Uri Gneezy famously found crowding-out in an Israeli child care center, where parents under threat of a 10-shekel fine for picking up their children late began to arrive late *more* often.[13] Gneezy explains this effect by saying that market incentives "kill the social norm."[14] The same thing can happen with donations to public-televisions stations. Instead of giving money to the station because it's the right thing to do, viewers switch from communal relations to the thinking of market exchange, wondering whether the enticement (say, a book valued at $25) is really worth a $100 donation. If the gift isn't large enough, the TV station is better off with no gift—an effect found across many studies. That's why Gneezy says you should "pay enough or don't pay at all."[15]

Reciprocity on Behalf of Others

We've already seen how people are willing to retaliate against cheaters. The Ultimatum Game showed this in the many players who would rather take nothing (and punish the other player) than accept an unfair offer.

It's remarkable that this kind of punishment even at a cost to yourself happens in situations involving multiple players as well—what social scientists call "social dilemmas" or "public-goods games." Games like this are really a multiplayer version of the Prisoner's Dilemma, the very common situation in which the best choice for both players is different from the best choice for either player. To see what a multiplayer Prisoner's Dilemma looks like, consider the Unscrupulous Diner's Dilemma.[16] The dilemma is that when a group of people are eating out and splitting the check, it's in each person's self-interest to order more lavishly than she would if paying her own way—but if everybody orders this way then each person in the group is stuck with a higher tab. This temptation to free-ride sometimes leads to total depletion of group resources, a dismal fate famously called the "tragedy of the commons."[17] In the Unscrupulous Diner's Dilemma, the tragedy of too many unscrupulous diners might be a restaurant tab so large that the diners never want to eat out with the others again. In practice, things rarely go that far, as people look to see what others are ordering, know that it's customary to pay more for ordering extras, and care about how others see them. Nonetheless, we know that bills split evenly tend to be higher than when diners agree in advance to use separate tabs.[18]

The Diner's Dilemma is just a colorful demonstration of a far more general problem: the more participants you have (whether it be members of a community or of a work group), the harder it is to sustain cooperation by all parties because the temptation to cheat (by free riding on the cooperative efforts of others) increases.

One type of social dilemma involves providing public goods. In a typical public-goods game, everyone in the group has the option of chipping in toward a public resource. The collective contributions then benefit every-one in the group, even those who didn't contribute their share. Of course, for every freeloader, the whole group suffers. At some point, if there are too many cheaters, you'd be a chump to keep chipping in, so even cooperators will begin to cheat—a downward spiral that leads, again, to the tragedy of the commons. Nobody wants that—not even the cheaters, who'd prefer to have resources to exploit. That's why most people resent the cheaters in their midst. For example, in one experiment, Ernst Fehr and Simon Gächter posed the following scenario to their participants:

> You decide to invest 16 francs to the project. The second group member invests 14 and the third 18 francs. Suppose the fourth member invests 2 francs to the project. You now accidentally meet this member.

They then asked participants to rate, on a scale from 1 to 7, how angry and annoyed they are with this person, with 7 indicating the most intense anger. The result: 47 percent of participants answered 6 or 7. Another 37 percent gave it a 5.[19]

It's this anger, then, that prompts people to punish cheaters. The pun-ishment is not always rational from an individual's economic perspec-tive: many times, not only do individuals not gain any material reward for punishing freeloaders—they actually lose money in the process.[20] But economic rationality has nothing to do with it: altruistic punishment is an emotional response.

In everyday life people show similar feelings toward freeloaders of all sorts, referring to them as moochers, leeches, or more specific epithets for particular public-goods situations: from scabs and slackers to lurkers and litterbugs. Years ago, Marina worked with an engineer who called parents "breeders," as if bringing even one child onto our crowded planet amounts to selfishly taking more than your fair share—an extreme version of an attitude common among ordinary people toward those with many kids.[21]

Though such derision makes clear to a group what behaviors you don't approve of, name-calling and gossip go only so far in keeping people in line, especially in modern societies, where people typically aren't stuck in any one group. To keep the level of cooperation high, groups that thrive go beyond name-calling. They ostracize, they impose fines, and they put people in jail; they also make credible threats to do all these things. On the flip side, they honor their most upstanding members with gratitude and status. In short, successful groups are very good at punishing freeloaders and rewarding do-gooders.

But punishing free riders is costly, and benefits you whether you punish or not. Therefore, punishment of free riders is itself a public good.[22] Despite the costs, people punish free riders all the time.

For example, look at Kay-Yut's buyer-seller experiments. These are the studies we mentioned in the Introduction, when Marina first learned of Kay-Yut's work, and which you'll learn more about in chapter 5 about reputation.[23] In these experiments, participants played the roles of buyer and seller in a mock online marketplace. Buyers ordered products from sellers; the buyers then had to pay for the products and the sellers had to ship them. However, each side had an opportunity and a short-term incentive to cheat: sellers could hope to pocket the order fee without actually fulfilling the order, and buyers could hope to receive the goods without paying for them. (Even in the short term, cheating paid off only if the other side was honest; if both buyer and seller cheated, neither side would profit. This aspect of the experiment was similar to the Prisoner's Dilemma.) After each side had made its choices, buyers and sellers saw the result on their computer monitors. Although there was a short-term incentive to cheat, in the long run traders' dishonesty caught up with them as buyers learned which sellers failed to fulfill orders and sellers learned which buyers didn't pay. This version of the Prisoner's Dilemma is called the Repeated (or Iterated) Prisoner's Dilemma.

It's pretty obvious that you'd avoid doing business with someone who's cheated you or even with players who'd cheated others. But something else happened in Kay-Yut's experiments: participants went out of their way to punish cheaters. They would strike a deal with a seller, for example, knowing full well the seller was a cheater—just so they could stiff the cheater. There was absolutely no direct economic gain from this activity; rationally, it's a waste of time to pursue dead-end deals when you could be focusing on profitable ones. But reciprocity, driven by the righteous anger Fehr and Gächter observed, drives people toward this kind of vindictiveness.

We've all seen similar behavior outside the lab. Consider the problem of employee theft. Such theft can include pilfering office supplies, embezzling company funds, and everything in between. Employees steal from all kinds of companies, but there's evidence that employees steal more when they feel shortchanged. For example, one manufacturing company made temporary 15 percent pay cuts to employees at two of its plants, while keeping pay the same at other plants, creating an opportunity for a natural experiment. Psychologist Jerald Greenberg, who studied the situation, found that rates of employee theft were much higher in the two plants that had cut employee pay than in a control-group plant that hadn't.[24] In addition to the natural experiment, Greenberg conducted a true experiment on the first two plants, randomly assigning the manager of one of the plants to give a thorough, regretful explanation for the pay cuts and the manager of the other to offer a more perfunctory, inadequate explanation. While both plants saw a spike in their theft rates during the pay cut, the theft rate was especially high in the plant whose workers had gotten an inadequate explanation for the pay cuts—a finding very much in line with what we've been saying about the importance of intentions and explanations, not just objective outcomes.

Employees also go far beyond just "getting theirs." They actively sabotage their employers even when their only reward is psychological. This corporate sabotage can take many forms, from destroying data and equipment to bad-mouthing companies on Internet gripe sites like Vault .com and GlassDoor.com. Disgruntled customers, who have less access to company resources, are even more likely than employees to malign the companies who've wronged them, taking the time to tell their horror stories on sites like PlanetFeedback.com and My3Cents.com, sites that wouldn't exist without the revenge instinct. Sometimes, of course, consumers have more direct ways of striking back at the businesses that have wronged them. One shopper, feeling that Best Buy was price gouging when it priced a DVD box set $60 higher than did Costco.com and refused to match the lower price, arranged for his own price match of sorts: "I bought the item at Best Buy and gave it to my buddy," he wrote on

PlanetFeedback.com. "Then I ordered the item from Costco and when it came I returned it to Best Buy." Other users of the site attacked him for this petty fraud, but he clearly felt he was only evening the score.[25]

From Bad to Worse: The Escalation of Conflict

A rosy picture might emerge from everything we've said about reciprocity so far. After all, it's wonderful that people repay kindness in kind, even if the effect is short-lived. And, as we've said, punishing wrongdoing keeps people in line and promotes cooperation.

But if things were so simple, our world wouldn't be so screwed up. Take wars, for example. They wouldn't exist if people only gave as good as they got: if one nation attacked another, and the target got even, that would be the end of that conflict. But we know that conflicts tend to escalate. And you don't need to look to the Middle East to see that. A couple once in love heads for divorce; a perceived slight in an e-mail spirals into an all-out flame war. How does reciprocity account for that?

The answer, according to an economic experiment, is that positive and negative reciprocity are not symmetrical: we retaliate against selfishness more than we reward generosity. What's more, this happens even when the slights are only illusory.

A team of University of Chicago researchers led by psychologist Boaz Keysar asked participants to play an interesting twist on the Dictator Game.[26] In this version, the participants started by playing the role of player 2 to the Dictator (who, unbeknownst to them, was a computer programmed to make even splits). After the split, the researchers reversed roles, with participants becoming the Dictators, who had to decide how to split a new $100 pie with the other player. The researchers wanted to see how the participants would reciprocate a 50-50 split depending on whether the splitting had been presented as an act of *giving* or an act of *taking*. So in one condition, participants started with no money and the (computer) Dictators gave participants $50 out of $100, whereas in the other condition the Dictators started with no money but *took* $50 from each participant's $100 stake.

Now, in one sense, the giving and taking conditions are equivalent: the Dictator and the other player both end up with $50. Yet after the role reversal, when the reciprocators became Dictators, those in the giving group were more generous to their partners than those in the taking group. For example, when told that the Dictator *gave* them $50, the participants proceeded to reciprocate with an average of $49.50—not as good as they got, but far more than participants who'd been told that the Dictator had *taken* $50 from them. These Dictators in the taking group made splits that averaged only $42. They were retaliating—but for what?

Apparently, for the mere act of taking money from them. Players didn't see taking $50 (when the other player had the option of taking $100) as equivalent to giving $50 (when the other player had the option of giving $0): in a separate experiment involving pairs of real people, when participants rated the Dictators' generosity, they judged the taking group inordinately more harshly than the giving group. For example, in this follow-up experiment some Dictators in the giving group split the money evenly, and some Dictators in the taking group took only $30, leaving the other player with $70, so the takers in this case were objectively more generous. Yet that's not how their counterparts saw them. "We found if I give you $50," Keysar says, "you think I'm more generous than if I take just $30 from you, which is mind-boggling."[27]

It is mind-boggling, but if you consider what we've said about the importance of intentions, this strange result begins to make sense. When people decide how to reciprocate an action, they don't just judge the action by its outcome; they also try to discern the other person's intentions. When you don't know or see the other person, it's hard to know their intentions, so you grasp at what little information you do have. In this case, the participants didn't even know that there were both giving and taking conditions—all they saw was the Dictator taking something of theirs, and they could only interpret this as a selfish act.

The fact that interpretations of intentions were driving the reciprocators' behavior also emerged from another result: takers did not realize how greedy they appeared to those on the receiving end. The takers understood their own intentions, and their partners assumed they understood the takers' intentions as well, but of course they were wrong; the takers, in turn, were wrong to assume their partners saw them as they saw themselves.

These mismatches led to increasing selfishness with each interaction: when, in a repeated version of the game, participants switched roles, the new Dictators responded to seemingly greedy splits with less generosity themselves, the pattern continuing with each subsequent role reversal.[28]

This is how conflicts can escalate. One side does something it sees as innocent, oblivious to the perceived effect on the other side. The "victim" sees the situation in a harsher light and retaliates out of proportion to the original slight. The first person sees this act of vengeance as undeserved, retaliates even more, and so it goes.

The research suggests that to stop this kind of escalation, it's not enough to give back what you took. To right a wrong you need to give more than you may even think is fair—whether it be by apologizing for hurting the other person (even when you think he or she is overreacting) or by making a more substantive concession.[29]

There are hints in these experiments about avoiding conflict in the first place. Try to see things from the other person's point of view, recognizing that what to you may seem like a kind or neutral gesture on your part may not seem as nice to another person. At times you may do well to be nicer than you are, to refrain from driving a hard bargain, and to assert your needs without stepping on anyone's toes.

Think, too, about how you interpret the behavior of other people. You may think your judgments are fair and objective, but there's a good chance you're as biased as the participants in Keysar's experiment, who thought worse of someone just for being in the role of taker rather than of giver. None of us may be perfectly objective, but if we're going to be biased it's usually better to err on the side of magnanimity. If you have doubts about someone's intentions, try suspending judgment until you can get more information; giving people the benefit of the doubt gives them a chance to prove your doubts wrong.

These first chapters have looked at what people want. But once you understand what people want, how do you know what they'll actually do? That's the question we tackle in chapters 4 through 7.

4

. . . .

Crossing the Bounds of Reason: Rationality

Today's trucking operations are a marvel of modern technology.[1] Thanks to route-optimization software and GPS, a large carrier like UPS, FedEx, Schneider, or Swift Transportation can quickly coordinate the moves of the thousands of rigs in its fleet: in the ideal case, each truck will pick up the most lucrative available jobs, take the fastest route to all its load and unload points, refuel at the lowest-cost gas stations, adjust course with changing road and traffic conditions, and manage to stay fully loaded for most of the way, all with almost no human intervention in making each of these decisions. To keep the busy trucker as happy as possible under this relentlessly efficient system, some of the optimization software can even take into account the driver's personal preferences, letting him pass through his favorite truck stops and arranging for him to swap trailers midway with another trucker, so that each driver can stay closer to home.

It wasn't always like this, of course. As recently as the 1980s, the logistics process was far more low-tech. After delivering one load of cargo, a trucker would radio a dispatcher, who'd use personal judgment to make the next assignment. Most dispatchers would make reasonable decisions, avoiding obvious mistakes like sending an empty rig across the country or forcing a trucker to drive fourteen hours straight. But no matter how smart or experienced, no dispatcher could make decisions that were truly optimal. There are simply too many variables for a human mind to consider.

Yossi Sheffi, the director of the MIT Center for Transportation and Logistics and a founder of several companies for automating transportation decisions, explains it this way: "Which truck goes where and how it is routed are very difficult questions because you have to simultaneously consider millions of possible movements. The number of decisions grows exponentially as you consider not only how the trucks go or how the freight is routed but all the possible combinations. And every time you change one variable, everything else has to change to achieve optimization."[2]

In other words, any decision about one truck ripples out in complicated, hard-to-imagine ways through the entire network, the way hitting a single billiard ball disrupts all the balls on the table. So even a decision that looks good for a given truck may well be suboptimal for the fleet as a whole, whereas a seemingly inefficient decision at the local level—like sending an empty truck out one hundred miles—can yield the most profitable set of freight loads in the grand scheme of things. Because people can't possibly compute all this, the tech-deprived carriers of a few decades ago were woefully inefficient by today's standards, unsystematically zigzagging across the land, logging too many empty miles, taking on not-very-profitable loads, and spending too much time making these suboptimal decisions.[3]

Eventually, the new technology became a requirement of doing business; companies that failed to adopt high-tech ways simply couldn't compete against their more efficient and thus more profitable rivals.

As you can imagine, similar changes have transformed other industries. Pharmaceutical companies' use of pharmacies' prescription data is an interesting case of this. Collectively, drugmakers spend billions of dollars each year on the free drug samples they give to doctors, with $18 billion worth handed out in 2005. The samples are a potent marketing tool, not only giving sales reps access to the busy docs but also helping to sway these physicians' prescribing decisions. With so much at stake, though, the companies want to make sure they're getting the best return on their investment. After all, giving too many samples to the "wrong" doctors eats away at sales, especially if the docs are giving large quantities away instead of writing expensive prescriptions. On the other hand, giving too few samples to a high-prescribing doctor leaves room for a competing drug to become the doctor's prescription choice. To find the right balance for maximum profits, drug companies are using software that analyzes prescribing patterns and allocates drug samples accordingly.[4]

Other businesses also use smart algorithms for quickly making sense of vast amounts of data. Think of the superb recommendations Netflix is able to offer its subscribers through its Cinematch movie-rating system, which analyzes recommendations by other users to predict what each user will like. Or, to use a more prosaic example, look at the rock-bottom prices Walmart can offer by squeezing efficiencies out of its complex supply chain. Its systems know who's buying what and where, and which truck or warehouse is holding each piece of inventory at any moment; feeding this data into complex inventory-balancing software helps Walmart balance supply and demand without spending more than necessary on carrying inventory and moving it from place to place.

Although companies like Walmart and Netflix are especially good at using technology to find useful patterns in their vast stores of data, these companies aren't the exception anymore: these days, no one would think of running any large enterprise without sophisticated decision-support tools. There's simply too much data for people to process on their own; even if they could, trying to do it without the aid of computers would take too long and cause too many costly errors.

Perhaps it's not surprising that human minds aren't up to the task of solving big, computationally intensive problems without software tools; what's more remarkable is just how little it takes to throw us, even those of us who should know better. In this chapter, we'll take a close look at several experiments that reveal patterns of suboptimal business decision-making. Though failures to optimize are only one by-product of the bounds of human rationality, we focus on these optimization errors because they can be enormously costly—while being largely preventable.[5]

Stocking *The Curious Gazette*

Imagine you're running a newsstand and are in charge of ordering newspapers to sell to your customers. Some orders are easy because you always sell the same number of copies each day. But one paper, which we'll call *The Curious Gazette,* is tricky because of its highly erratic demand. Some days you'll be able to sell 100 copies, other days you'll sell none, and the rest of the time it might be 12, 37, 89, or anything else between 1 and 100—all are equally likely. What's more, because you're selling newspapers, any unsold copies will be fish wrap tomorrow, so you'll lose what you paid for any copies you order and don't sell. On the other hand, if you sell out and customers want more, you can't order more—so when you underorder relative to actual demand, you sacrifice revenue.

Assuming you know your unit cost and profit margin, how many copies should you order? That's the newsvendor problem.

Before we answer this question, though, we should explain why the newsvendor problem is important. It's true that *The Curious Gazette* is unusual. But though the problem may sound academic and unrealistic, it appears time and again in various guises in all kinds of economic decisions, from deciding how many units of a new dress style to make in red (to sell before the fashion season ends) to how much money to put into your health care spending account (not knowing whether you'll use it all up by the end of the calendar year). Understocking is familiar to all of us: every holiday season, it seems, there's a "hot toy" that parents can't find enough of; as a result of the shortage, unexpectedly popular toys like Cabbage Patch dolls end up selling on the gray market, with the extra profits going to shady resellers rather than the toymakers or the retailers. But overstocking, though less visible to consumers, can also be enormously costly. A dramatic example of overstocking was IBM's ValuePoint line of computers, introduced in the early 1990s to compete with low-priced PC clones from the likes of Compaq, Dell, and HP. Despite the product's good reviews, sales fell short of the company's overly optimistic estimates. As a result, the company was stuck with $700 million in excess inventory one year.

Hindsight is always 20/20, of course, so order errors are glaring once you know what the actual demand was—whereas the decision makers we're talking about don't have a crystal ball. In fact, in retrospect every decision that turns out *not* to be dead-on is suboptimal. That's why, for example, we so often regret selling a stock too early (if the price continues to rise) or too late (if the price falls below what we sold it for); since there's only one perfect decision and many imperfect ones, it's much more likely you'll miss the perfect moment than hit it.

But in the newsvendor problem, we're not trying to predict the future because, as we've said, demand for *The Curious Gazette* is unpredictable. Instead, we're asking a different question: given that actual demand is so uncertain, how much should you order to maximize your profit? Or, to put it another way, how much should you order so that no matter what happens the next day, you'll know you made the best decision with the information that was available to you at the time? (Marina wishes she hadn't sold all her Apple stock in 1997, not long before AAPL began its rapid ascent, but logically she knows that given only what she knew then, she made the right decision. That's the kind of decision you want to make in the newsvendor problem.)

It turns out that there *is* a right answer to the newsvendor problem, and when every demand outcome is equally likely, this answer depends only on your unit cost and sale price. The basic reasoning goes like this: if your cost is high, you'll lose a lot of money on the units you cannot sell. Therefore, if your sale price isn't much higher than your cost (that is, if your margins are low), you should order a small number of copies. At the other extreme—if your margins are high—you should order a bunch of copies because in that situation the lost profits from understocking are much higher than the cost of overstocking.

In fact, there's a simple formula to tell you precisely how many copies to order, one that just about every MBA student learns:[6]

$$\frac{(\text{price} - \text{cost})}{\text{price}} \times \text{maximum demand}$$

For example, assume the sale price is 12 francs. (Many economic experiments, even in the United States, call their laboratory currency "francs.") As we've said, the maximum demand for *The Curious Gazette* is 100. If your cost is 9 francs, you should order exactly 25 copies. If your cost is only 3 francs, you should order much more—75 copies.

The same formula works on any demand spread. For example, suppose you're selling gizmos whose demand varies from 1 to 300; if the price is 12 and the cost is 9, you should order 75 (because $3/12 \times 300 = 75$), and if the cost is only 3 you should order 225 (or $9/12 \times 300$).

Not coincidentally, two researchers used these same two examples to study how people actually solve the newsvendor problem.[7] They asked MBA students at Duke University's Fuqua School of Business—very much the kinds of people who'll have to make such decisions in their future work—to choose the optimal stocking level under these price and cost conditions. The researchers, Maurice Schweitzer of the Wharton School and Gérard Cachon (then at Fuqua), didn't present the questions on a classroom problem set; rather, they ran a controlled experiment with real money at stake. How did the students do? Not as well as you'd hope from future business leaders. Most gave the wrong answers. More interestingly, their answers were off in a systematic way: the students ordered too few of the high-profit items and too many of the low-profit items. Those ordering items at a cost of 3 francs (who should have ordered 225) ordered, on average, about 178 units. Those ordering at a cost of 9 francs (who should have ordered 75) ordered, on average, about 140. If their decision was too high in one condition and too low in the other, what were they thinking?

By analyzing the data, the researchers concluded there were two reasons for this error. The first has to do with anchoring. Anchoring is the well-established tendency, discovered by psychologists Daniel Kahneman and Amos Tversky, to base our answers on a handy reference point, regardless of how arbitrary or irrelevant. For example, in one of their original studies of the anchoring bias, Kahneman and Tversky asked participants what percent of African countries are in the United Nations. The researchers spun a wheel of fortune, asked whether the UN percentage is higher or lower than the number the wheel landed on, and finally asked participants to name the actual percentage.[8]

Does the number on a wheel have anything to do with the actual percentage of African countries in the UN? Of course not, and no matter how superstitious you are, you won't think a random spin of the wheel predicts the correct answer, which, after all, doesn't change from one spin of the wheel to another. Participants realized this on a conscious level, invariably saying that the actual percentage is higher (or lower) than the number on the wheel, rather than saying that the percentage is the same. Nonetheless, their estimate of the actual number depended on the number on the wheel! For example, participants who saw the wheel land on 10 gave a median estimate of 25 for the percentage of African countries in the UN. The median estimate of participants who saw the wheel land on 65, on the other hand, was 45.

What people seem to be doing, Kahneman and Tversky concluded, is "anchoring" on a readily available number and then adjusting their estimate away from that anchor in the right direction—but not adjusting far enough. The anchor, though totally arbitrary in this case, tugged at their estimates.

Anchoring has an effect on many real-world outcomes. For example, in experiments of anchoring and negotiation, negotiated amounts tend to be anchored to the first number thrown out, strongly influencing the final outcome. (This is why, contrary to popular belief that you should never make the first offer, experts steeped in these research findings advise negotiators that it's often in their best interest to make the first offer, and to make a reasonably aggressive one.[9])

Likewise, when the MBA students chose a stocking level in the newsvendor problem, they appeared to anchor their answer to the average demand—150—and then adjust it up or down toward the optimal answer. But they didn't adjust enough, and therefore never quite reached that optimal answer.

There's a second effect, Schweitzer and Cachon concluded, that explains the participants' answers: the students seemed to want to reduce the absolute difference between the chosen quantity and actual demand. In other words, they seemed to care as much about minimizing inventory error as they did about maximizing profit. Think about it: if you care only about reducing the gap between the actual demand and your order amount, you'll order the average demand, 150. And if you care only about maximizing profit, you'll order much more in the high-margin case and much less in the low-margin case. But if you're trying to simultaneously optimize for both high profits and low inventory error, you'll order somewhere in between—just as participants in this experiment did.

The good news is that by knowing about this systematic bias, you can correct for it—if not in yourself, then in the people you're working with and managing. If you're managing buyers, the most obvious way to reduce their bias is to use a decision-support tool. In this simple case, even a formula in a spreadsheet will do. Our point is that even a simple problem leaves room for error, and using automation makes that error smaller.

Why merely smaller? Unless people have no discretion at all, decision-support tools don't eliminate human errors entirely; if for some reason people don't trust the tool, they may override its recommendations. For example, MetLife offers a handy Web-based tool, the MetLife Benefits Simplifier, to help people decide among their many available employee benefits options;[10] after you answer a short series of questions about your medical preferences, whether you have children, your plans for the future, and so on, the software makes several recommendations, including how much life insurance you should buy. All this is helpful and time-saving, but what if you don't trust MetLife to give you unbiased advice? ("Isn't it in their interest to sell you as much insurance as possible?" you might cynically wonder.) If so, you might discount the Simplifier's recommendations, purposely choosing less life insurance than it recommends. In that case, if the Simplifier's choice is optimal, then your choice is suboptimal, but insofar as you're anchoring your choice to MetLife's recommendation, your choice is better than it would be had you made it completely on your own.

Software isn't the only way to improve decisions. There's some evidence that training can reduce biases, too. Through extended experience, participants in a newsvendor experiment were able to achieve 90 percent profit potential[11]—again, not perfectly optimal, but better than they had done in Cachon and Schweitzer's studies. But training doesn't always eliminate suboptimal decision-making. For example, in one study researchers trained employees at seven companies about their companies' wonderful 401(k) plans, which included matching contributions from the employers and allowed participants to withdraw money for any reason.[12] Under these circumstances, no rational employee should contribute less than the amount eligible for the employer match since contributing less gives up free money. Yet despite the training, employee contribution rates didn't budge. If training doesn't solve a problem having the simple logic of a free lunch, one has to wonder what kind of training will be effective for problems that are more complicated and involve more people, a point we'll return to later in this chapter.[13]

Some problems rely so much on expert judgment that they don't lend themselves to computers or simple training. Computers are only good at following rules, and some problems don't have rules. How many units should you make when you launch a new product? A human being can make an educated guess, even if the answer proves to be way off. IBM's managers overestimated demand for ValuePoint by $700 million; the estimate was overly optimistic, but the number wasn't implausible. Now, IBM can make impressively sophisticated computers, ones that are better than humans at solving certain kinds of problems. Its Deep Blue system beat a world-champion chess player, Garry Kasparov, at a game Kasparov had been excelling in years before Deep Blue was even a twinkle in its designers' eyes. But chess is a much more straightforward game than intuiting customer tastes, anticipating competing manufacturers' plans, and making product judgments. If a computer had to throw out a number without benefit of human wisdom—say, from a random-number generator—it might easily err more than enough to break the bank if the company were to actually trust the computer's answer.

An experiment at HP illustrates this point. HP researchers had designed an intelligent computer system that would negotiate for goods that the company needed to buy on a regular basis. They called the system AutONA[14] (Automated One-to-one Negotiation Agent), and AutONA's goal was to take the place of human purchasing agents. AutONA's designers didn't think it could do a better job at negotiating with suppliers—unlike employees, however, it wouldn't expect a salary and benefits. But would AutONA at least perform as well as humans? Yes and no. Under some conditions, AutONA could negotiate as effectively as a human could. What's more, the machine passed a simple Turing Test: in some of the experiments, participants playing the roles of suppliers were fooled into thinking that AutONA was a human negotiator. However, when Kay-Yut introduced a shock to the system—sudden, unexpected changes to the supply-and-demand conditions—AutONA couldn't cope nearly as well as human negotiators.

That's not to say that it's theoretically impossible to program a machine to deal with abrupt market changes or any of the other challenges of negotiating with humans—only that there are some fields in which humans have an inherent edge. But when it comes to all sorts of precise optimization problems, like the next problem we look at, humans have trouble.

Choosing Your "Secretary"

Imagine you're hiring an assistant. You know how many applicants you'll be interviewing, and you know they'll be coming in one per day. Your goal is to find the best person for the job. There are two challenges, though. First, the applicants arrive in random order, so even after interviewing several candidates you have no idea whether the remaining applicants include a better choice. Second, you have to decide on the spot whether to make an offer. If you don't make an offer, the applicant won't be available the next day. In the real world, conditions vary a bit, but the basic idea remains: you don't know if a better candidate will come later, and there's a distinct chance of losing the best candidate if you wait too long in the process to make an offer. If you offer too soon or too late, you won't make the best decision. So when is the best time to settle on your choice?

Applied mathematicians have studied this so-called Secretary Problem since at least the 1960s (as you might guess from its *Mad Men*–esque name),[15] and they've long known the optimal solution. Think of choosing the ideal candidate as a decision of 100 percent quality, choosing the worst candidate as a decision of 0 percent quality, with other scores dispersed evenly in between. For example, if you have six candidates, choosing the second-best is a decision of 80 percent quality and choosing the third-best a decision of 60 percent quality.

Given all this, the optimal strategy goes something like this: since you can't call people back whom you've passed over, you need to get a sense of the quality of the applicant pool. That way you won't end up settling for candidates who are far worse than the best or rejecting candidates who are as good as you can reasonably expect. So your first step in tackling this problem is to sample the applicant pool by interviewing (but not hiring) the first few applicants. (Mathematicians have a way to figure out how many to sample, but we'll get to that later.) Once you've sampled these applicants and know how good the best one you've seen so far is, continue interviewing until you find the first candidate who's better than this. As soon as you encounter a candidate who is better than any of the ones you've seen, hire that person. However, don't hold out for the best for too long because the person might never appear. Therefore, if you don't find a suitable candidate after interviewing a fixed number of people, become a little less picky. (Here, too, there's a mathematical formula to tell you what that fixed number should be.) There's a specific rule for what it means to become a little less picky in this problem: instead of only hiring if you find someone better than all the candidates you've seen, now you hire the person even if he or she is second-best among all the candidates so far. If even the second-best doesn't appear after a certain number of candidates, lower your standard again by stopping at the third-best—and so on.

This solution makes sense once you hear it, but it's not obvious to most people. Even if they have some sense that they need to find out something about the applicant pool, they won't know how long to sample before going into hiring mode, nor will they know how long to hold out for the best before relaxing their criteria.[16] As a result, the decisions they make are not optimal: experiments show that when it costs nothing to keep searching, people typically settle too early, as if they're taking non-existent search costs into account. On the other hand, when researchers in another set of experiments imposed a search cost, the participants searched too much. It's not that people have it backward: they know they should search less when there's a cost to keep searching. It's just that they don't know how much less, and they tend to search a little longer than optimal, though less than they would if there were no cost.[17]

People aren't very good at figuring out what information to pay attention to. As experiments on the anchoring effect show, we're prone to take into account data that's completely irrelevant to the question we're trying to answer. But the problem occurs in other contexts. For example, suppose you've spent a long time standing in line for a busy ATM; how do you decide whether to give up or keep waiting? The only relevant factor (once you know how fast the line is moving) is how many people are in line ahead of you. But it turns out that many people also look *backward*: the more people behind them, the less likely they are to leave the line.[18] Along the same lines, telling people that other hotel guests had chosen to reuse their towels boosted the rate at which guests reused towels compared to just telling them that towel reuse is good for the environment. What's more, telling them that guests who'd stayed in this same room had reused towels boosted reuse rates even more.[19] None of this information should, by rights, affect someone's decision to get a fresh towel, but it does. When we're not sure what to do, we tend to take a cue from those around us.

But even when people understand on a conscious level what to pay attention to and what to ignore, they don't give proper weight to the relevant information. Consumers make cognitive errors like this all the time. Experiments have shown that when people compare the fake currencies of loyalty programs with real money, they overvalue the loyalty points.[20] People also pay too much attention to precision in prices. They're used to the fact that large numbers tend to be rounded off (to multiples of 10, 100, or 1,000) more often than are smaller numbers, so they take the fact that a number isn't round as a sign that it's small. In a set of studies that investigated this "price precision effect," one group of participants judged $395,425 to be smaller than a statistically identical group of participants judged $395,000; actual real estate buyers ended up paying more on average for houses whose asking price ended in a 0 than for other comparably priced houses.[21]

Memory sometimes plays a role in errors involving the overweighting and underweighting of information. For the participants in an experiment Kay-Yut conducted with a pair of colleagues from Stanford, participants evaluating all the possible choices for their next move put more weight on decisions they'd made in the past than on decisions they hadn't yet made. Similarly, in the newsvendor problem, if you know that a random number of customers between 10 and 20 will buy a paper, you need to consider the possibility of 14 customers just as likely as 15 customers or any other number in the range. However, if 12 customers showed up yesterday, people make decisions as though they're more likely to see 12 customers again, rather than 14 or 15 or any other number in the range. In Kay-Yut's experiments, people were trying to optimize for demand in the previous period.[22] This bias may be a consequence of a much more general mental shortcut: the availability heuristic, identified by Kahneman and Tversky.[23] Their experiments revealed that people judge the frequency of an event by how easily the event comes to mind. For example, which words are more common in English—those that start with the letter "k" or those in which "k" is the third letter? It's much harder to think of words where "k" is the third letter than it is to think of words like king, knight, knife, or key. Since these initial-k words are so much more readily "available" to our minds, we assume they're more frequent in the language than words with "k" in the third position, even though the opposite is true.

The failure to optimize happens in other decision problems. In one study, Neil Bearden, Ryan Murphy, and Amnon Rapoport found an interesting pattern when they asked participants to make decisions in a classical revenue management scenario: you have three weeks to sell a fixed number of widgets. Every day there is some likelihood a customer will give you an offer to buy. If you decide to accept the offer, you make money right away, but you lose the chance to sell it to someone else at a higher price later.

To find the optimal solution to this problem, you need to know four things: the number of widgets you still have, the number of days left, the chance of a customer showing up, and how likely a customer is to buy at each possible price. Knowing all this, a mathematician can figure out exactly when to accept and when to reject an offer.

But most of us aren't mathematicians; instead, participants in the experiment showed, as the researchers put it, "a clear pattern of being too demanding when holding higher levels of inventory and insufficiently demanding when holding lower levels." They took into account the number of widgets they still had left, just as they should have, but they didn't take it into account *enough*. The result was significant revenue loss.[24]

A different set of experiments looked at the quality of pricing decisions: how well do participants adjust prices in response to rising or falling demand for perishable items like fresh food and airline seats? Although participants moved their prices in the right direction—understanding that higher demand justifies higher prices, while lower demand calls for lower prices—they priced the perishable goods too high when demand was relatively high and too low when demand was relatively low.[25]

All these results have one thing in common: they show people overreacting to new or readily available information, a common theme in many economic experiments.

The Bullwhip Effect and the Beer Game

Years ago, executives at Procter & Gamble noticed a strange pattern in sales of their top-selling products: retail sales fluctuated a little, but retailers' orders fluctuated a lot. What's more, as the execs looked higher up the supply chain—up from the retailer to the wholesaler, from the wholesaler to the distributor—the swings in demand grew even wilder. When you plot the numbers, the resulting graph has an oscillating pattern that looks like a snapshot of a bullwhip in action. When order swings increase as orders move up the supply chain, it's the Bullwhip Effect.

The Bullwhip Effect is not limited to orders of soap and razor blades: it occurs wherever there's a multitiered supply chain. What causes this effect? Over the years researchers have found many contributing factors, such as lead times and lot sizes. But besides such process-related factors, there turns out to be an important, even overwhelming, behavioral reason, as shown in a clever experiment conducted at the MIT Sloan School of Management.[26] The experiment, which mimics real-world supply chains, has four participants playing the roles of the retailer, wholesaler, distributor, and manufacturer of a supply chain. (Their product is beer, so this experiment and its offshoots are sometimes called the Beer Distribution Game or simply "Beer Game.") The retailer is faced with end customer demand simulated by a computer. In each period, each player can place an order to his or her upstream partner (so the retailer can place an order to the wholesaler, the wholesaler to the distributor, and the distributor to the factory) and there is a delay before the order is sent out and received. Each player's goal is to minimize costs, which players incur when they have either too much inventory on hand or not enough.

What's interesting about this experiment is that the end customers' demand of the retailer is kept constant—a steady rate of 4 units per period, as announced to every player before the experiment starts. Logically, the Bullwhip Effect should not occur: since the retailer knows there's no fluctuation, he should always order 4 units. And if he always orders 4, the distributor should also always order 4—and so on to the other players. Everyone should always order the same amount of 4, incur no costs of excess inventory, and create no order swings at all. Simple, right?

But not only did the Bullwhip Effect show up—it did so in a big way. Some of the orders swung up to hundreds and even thousands of units! What were they thinking? Here's an answer from one distributor after the game was over: "I think the customer was making unreasonable demands and panicking, causing everyone else to do so also, so I could never be where I wanted to be."

What happened was that even if a player understood the optimal strategy, he or she didn't know whether the other players would understand the strategy and carry it out. Thinking that their downstream partners might order something other than 4, players changed their orders to buffer for the anticipated error. And this belief in other players' irrationality drives a systematic escalation of swinging orders: every swing, every deviation from the optimal order, is confirmation of the suspicion of "dumb" supply-chain partners and justification of a more varying ordering strategy, which, in turn, pushes the system further away from the efficient state of zero fluctuation.

Nobody likes this effect, which wreaks havoc on production planning, so researchers Diana Wu and Elena Katok ran experiments to see if they could reduce it. They tried training the participants by giving them hands-on experience with the problem and letting them see how much everyone in the supply chain was ordering—seemingly everything participants needed to know to make optimal ordering decisions—but the training proved not to be enough. What did work was combining this training with the opportunity for players to communicate with one another—for retailers, for example, to tell wholesalers how much they were ordering and *why*—and thus coordinate their strategies. Without such communication, people who had learned the optimal strategy didn't use it because of doubts about the other players' knowledge.

The Optimizer's Paradox

On one hand, traditional decision theory says that more options are always good—after all, you can always discard the additional options and do no worse. On the other hand, we know that too many options can be paralyzing, making it either harder to make the right choice or (because of fears of making the wrong choice) keeping us from making a choice at all. This "paradox of choice,"[27] as it's been called, shows up everywhere there's an overabundance of choices, from the frivolous to the consequential. In a famous study, more shoppers stopped to sample from a table of twenty-four varieties of jam than from one with just six varieties—but many more actually bought something from the latter.[28] In a more serious vein, senior citizens faced a great deal of confusion in choosing their prescription drug plan from the dizzying array in Medicare Part D. The eminent economist Daniel McFadden, who studied the issue, put it well when he said that "people appreciate having choices as long as they don't actually have to make one."[29]

One solution to the paradox of choice is to offer a default option, the choice that will go into effect if the decision maker makes no choice at all.[30] Another option, of course, is to reduce choices to a manageable number. But how many choices is best? If you can give any amount of freedom to decision makers, how much should you give?

It's probably safe to assume that the answer depends on the type of decision, so let's look at one in particular. Kay-Yut and Diana Wu investigated this question in the context of supply chains.

Imagine you are a retailer selling a single widget to consumers. During each time period, you need to make two decisions: deciding how many units to buy at a fixed cost from the manufacturer, and deciding on the price to charge your customers for that time period.

As you might expect, there's an element of uncertainty that makes it hard to know how many units to order: you simply don't know how many customers will want to buy the widget. But you do know the range of potential customers—and you can shift that range up and down by changing the price. For example, if you set a lower price, then you'll tend to get more takers, but, of course, lower prices mean lower profits for each unit sold.

Deciding how many units to order is tricky, too. If you order a lot, you may not be able to sell them all during the time period. (You can sell them later, but you'll pay an inventory cost for each unit staying on the shelf.) If you order too few, you lose the goodwill of those customers who have to wait until future periods for you to fill their orders; in this experiment, loss of goodwill due to back orders carries a "backlog cost." So whether you order too much or too little, you'll pay some cost for your error. By convention in such experiments, the researchers set the backlog costs at twice the inventory costs, making it less costly for participants to err by ordering too much than by ordering too little.

Instructions tell participants everything about the costs. Participants also know how demand is spread out (for example, that it ranges from 9 to 15 and that every number is equally likely). And in each period, participants are told about the actual demand and their resulting inventory and backlog costs.

Though the rules are fairly straightforward, this is a remarkably complex problem. Profit is a function of many variables: price, stocking level, inventory cost, and backlog cost. When you change the price, you change not only your unit profit but also your total profit because the price affects demand. What's more, your decisions in one period affect your profits not only in that period, but also in all subsequent periods.

But what makes the problem really complicated is that probabilities about demand get increasingly complicated to figure out from period to period. Again, it's a little like billiard balls on a pool table. Imagine a pair of them perfectly lined up with one of the corner pockets, the second ball just waiting to be sunk. It's a straight shot: if you hit the cue ball just so, it'll roll straight ahead and hit the second ball dead center, compelling it to roll forward into the corner pocket. But what happens if you make a tiny error on your first shot? For example, suppose you strike the cue ball not straight on but at a 3-degree angle to the right. The ball immediately rolls forward and ever so slightly to the left. As a result, it'll either miss the second ball entirely or it'll hit it so far on the left that the second ball will roll to the right, far away from the pocket you aimed at. The first error creates a larger second error, which creates a huge third error. These errors don't just add up—they compound in big ways. Something similar happens when you combine expectations about today's demand with tomorrow's; but that scenario is so much more complicated that most people can't even begin to understand the relationship between today and two days from now, let alone three or more. Because of this complexity, most people can't solve the problem without help from a computer.

Nonetheless, in running just about any retail business people must contend with this situation. Therefore, the problem of setting the right price and the right stock level has been studied thoroughly by decision scientists and applied mathematicians. As a result, the mathematics of this problem are very well understood, just as with the simpler news-vendor problem, so the goal of the experiments was not to determine the optimal solution, but to see how human decision makers fare in comparison.

The participants were undergraduates from the University of Kansas business school, all of whom were taking supply-chain management classes. That meant that they had at least some idea of how to set prices and balance inventories.

Since the experiment's purpose was to find out how people respond to different degrees of decision freedom, Kay-Yut and Diana tested and compared four different decision restrictions. The idea in all the conditions was for what happened at one point in time to reverberate through-out the game, just as in the real world. For example, a stocking decision in the first period affects what happens in the second period, which in turn affects the third period, and so on. To simulate these dynamics, the researchers had participants play the game for 36 periods—enough time for a clear and stable pattern of decision making to emerge.[31]

Here's what the researchers compared:

- In the first condition, the participants made both pricing and stocking decisions in each of the game's 36 periods.
- In the second condition, the researchers fixed the prices, so participants could make decisions only about the stocking level.[32]
- In the third condition, the stocking levels were fixed—participants could only change prices.
- The fourth condition was similar to the first, but participants had to make just one pricing and stocking decision, and to commit to it for the full length of the game.

Which condition would you expect to yield the best, most profitable decisions? Keep in mind that these students were paid in cash according to how much profit they generated in the game, just as though they were running their own business. So we can assume they wanted to come up with the best solutions; even so, they performed better when their choices were restricted. But in what ways?

To answer this question, the researchers calculated the participants' profit per period as a percentage of the maximum possible profit per period.[33] Using these percentages, they were able to compare the quality of decisions among the different conditions. The worst outcome was making both decisions in each period—participants' decisions yielded, on average, about 73 percent of the optimal profit. Having to make only one decision per period yielded better results, especially if participants had to make only stocking decisions (89 percent); making pricing decisions alone was harder for them than making stock decisions, as we can see from the fact that they got only about 77 percent of the possible profit when they had to decide on a price each period.

The most striking result, though, is what happened when participants had to make both pricing and stocking decisions just once, committing to them in the first period: these decisions yielded 88 percent of the optimal profit! So even though they had to decide about two things at once—price and stocking level—they did almost as well as when they had to make decisions only about stock alone.

You may be wondering why making both decisions just once, with no opportunity to correct them later, yielded higher profits than making both decisions each time. Let's make some educated guesses about the possible causes. For one thing, we know that participants acted short-sightedly: Kay-Yut and Diana estimated that they considered the next period only about a third as much as the current period, and subsequent periods after that mattered to them even less. The students acted as if thinking about the current period is hard enough without also trying to focus on the future. Although a dollar earned in the current period is no more valuable than a dollar earned in the last period, people focus much more attention on the current period than on the consequences of those decisions down the road. So perhaps they felt that their current decision didn't affect subsequent periods that much, or that they could correct their errors in subsequent periods. If so, then being forced to commit to both decisions in the first period—knowing that they wouldn't have a chance to make new decisions later—might have made the players think harder about the consequences of that one set of decisions.

Another possible explanation is that a onetime decision about two variables (price and stocking level) involves fewer choices than thirty-six decisions about one variable (price). Making choices takes effort and mental energy, so participants may simply have gotten tired and begun making sloppy choices as the experiment progressed. If too much free-dom yields suboptimal results, then it makes sense that having to make just two decisions could yield better results than having to make thirty-six decisions.[34]

Yet people like to feel in control; when faced with the opportunity to make frequent decisions, they often take it, overconfident of their ability to make consistently good decisions. Drivers, for example, like to change lanes whenever they feel stuck in a slow lane—even though changing lanes increases your risk of an accident without saving you much time.[35] Similarly, frequent stock traders underperform the market as a whole: in a famous study spanning 1991 to 1996, the most active stock traders earned 11.4 percent per year—not very impressive in a period when the annual market average was 17.9 percent.[36]

The takeaway from all this may seem obvious—make decisions less often—but it isn't so simple. First of all, it's not always true that making fewer decisions is better: as always, it depends on the situation. In fact, in cases where decisions don't ripple out and affect one another— when they're completely independent—you might get a risk-pooling effect from many decisions, with good decisions balancing out bad ones. Furthermore, even in those situations when too many decisions cause problems, you're left with the question of how often is just right? Once a minute is too often, but what about once a day? Once a month? That's an empirical question whose answer depends on your business. What we can say for sure is that you should at least consider the side effects of too-frequent decision making.

Some industries already seem to understand this. Clothing stores, for example, have the option to mark down products as often as they want, starting with high prices and lowering them little by little until they've captured as much revenue as possible. Most fashion retailers do it during only a few sales each year.[37] Resetting prices takes time and money, and figuring out how much to mark down each time is hard. By having only a few end-of-season sales each year, retailers greatly simplify the problem for themselves. They have to decide only when to have the sale, and once they've done that they only have to figure out how much to mark down each item.

In other industries, prices change much more often. The price of fuel at your corner gas station probably changes every day. Some car rental companies, especially at busy airports, have been known to change the price of a car four times in one day. In times of particularly heavy demand, Alamo and National (which are owned by the same company) change prices twenty or more times a day. Is that too often? It's hard to know for sure without testing. But our hunch is that several times per day is too often—not because each price is suboptimal (the prices are generated from computer data about what competitors are doing, how many cars are left on hand, and so on) but because any gains in more competitive prices might well be offset by other costs, especially in terms of newly confused and disgruntled customers.[38] Whatever industry you're in, if you suspect your decisions are too frequent, you might play around with how often you make them to see if revenues improve.

Making Problems Manageable:
An Example from HP

As of this writing, Kay-Yut is well into a project for HP's Corporate Treasury. The challenge is to optimize risk management of catastrophic events such as earthquakes. If a massive earthquake hit a facility, say a California warehouse housing critical inventory, business might be disrupted for weeks or even months—and the costs to the business would be on top of the loss of property. There are, of course, preventive measures that a company like HP can take to minimize its exposure. For example, the same inventory can be split, half of it stored in a warehouse in another state. The company could manage such a split in several possible ways, each with a different cost and a different risk profile. For example, putting another warehouse in Florida may reduce the exposure to an earthquake risk but increase exposure to the risk of a hurricane.

This problem may sound like an information-gathering exercise— finding out about potential exposures and the chances of each event happening—but it's more complicated than that. A global company like HP has many facilities all over the world: even if each facility has only three or four preventive measures to consider, the total number would be large. What's more, these measures cannot be considered in isolation. You need to study the *combinations* of these preventive measures. Just ten facilities with four options each would result in over 1 million combinations to consider—1,048,576 to be exact. And that's just the beginning: since no company can spend money on reducing every kind of risk, the challenge is to figure out which risk-reduction actions are worth taking.

Handling the complexity becomes a daunting task—not unlike the truck-route-optimization problem at the start of this chapter. But Kay-Yut and his colleagues designed an approach that radically reduces the decision's complexity. Their idea is to use mathematical optimization to narrow the dizzyingly long list of events and options down to a manageable set: rather than thinking about all the possible bad things that might happen, they focus on only those that the company really cares about. For example, if the decision maker is concerned about the worst case rather than about the average impact, there's no need to look at anything else. Knowing the limitations of the human mind helps design solutions that humans can use.

Contracting with the Fallible

In Kay-Yut's experiments with Diana, restricting decision freedom helped participants make better decisions. But it isn't always so easy. In that problem, you were managing your own company, but what if you want to influence decisions by outside partners, such as your buyers? You can't tell your external partners what they can and can't do—restricting decision freedom by setting the prices they can charge their customers, for example, is not an option. Instead, you must use a contract that gets your partners to freely choose to do what you want them to do. For example, contracts specify terms for the exchange of goods and services, such as how much a retailer must pay a wholesaler for ordering a certain volume of product. Built into each contract are incentives (in the form of price schedules, discounts, rebates, and the like) that influence the retailer's choices.

The question then becomes what kind of contract will achieve optimal results. Suppose you're the publisher of *The Curious Gazette*. Newsvendors all over the city are ordering the paper from you. A contract could spell out all kinds of terms for your relationships with the newsvendors. Do you sell the paper at a fixed price, and if so, how much? Do you give newsvendors a discount for ordering more than a certain amount, and if so, how much of a discount for what volume of orders? Should you give a buyback guarantee, and if so, under what terms? These are just some of the many ways you can tweak a contract to sway the newsvendors' behavior.

Contract theory says that if you design a contract just right—with exactly the right set of prices, rules, and penalties—you'll get your partner to do what you want even if the partner is only interested in his or her own gain. But there's a problem: for this to be true, your partner has to be able to optimize for his or her self-interest. The partner must take into account all the variables you've put into the contract—price, return policy, and so on—and combine them with knowledge about an uncertain world to make the most profitable decision. And, as we've seen over and over in this chapter, people aren't very good at reaching the optimal decision.

With that in mind, a good contract shouldn't assume that your partner is a perfect optimizer; it should somehow account for the person's computational limits and get the best possible results despite those limits. How do you do that? Through another series of experiments, Kay-Yut and Diana came up with some answers.

The basic setup was very similar to the Cachon and Schweitzer studies we looked at earlier. Participants played the role of newsvendors. Their task was to decide how many copies to order from the distributor in a situation where average sales are 100 units. Because of the cost and sale price, the optimal order quantity to the vendor, unbeknownst to the participants playing the vendors, was 125. Kay-Yut and Diana wanted to see the effect different types of contracts had on newsvendors' stocking decisions. Specifically, what happens if the contract gives some kind of discount for ordering above a certain number of copies?

You might guess that a volume discount will get people to order closer to the optimal amount. Indeed, rather than tending to anchor their orders to the only known number (100), players given a volume discount tended to anchor their order amounts to the number in the contract—125. For example, in the contract that gave an across-the-board cost break for ordering 125 or more newspapers, more participants ordered exactly 125 than any other quantity. Great—you got the buyers to do exactly what you wanted them to do, right? Yes, but at a pretty high cost to you: although they ordered the quantity you wanted, in this "all units" condition you had to pay them a good deal to do so. For example, if the original cost of the papers to the newsvendors was 9 francs each and you as the publisher gave a 1-franc discount for all the units, then if players ordered 125 units, you gave them a discount of 125 francs off a total of 1,125 francs.

Would a different approach work better at getting newsvendors to buy the optimal amount of 125? Kay-Yut and Diana tried an "incremental" discount: instead of discounting *all* the units as an incentive for ordering at or above a specified threshold, they discounted *only those units at or above* the threshold. For example, if the threshold was 100, and a player ordered 125 units, she'd get the discount for only units 100 through 125. The cost to you as the publisher under this contract is obviously lower than in the "all units" discount condition.

The incremental discount, though, encourages ordering above the threshold: the vendor wants to benefit from the discount as much as possible, so if the threshold is 70 (meaning the discount kicks in at order quantities of 70 or more), the vendor will tend to order more than 70 (because ordering 70 will discount only that last unit). For the same reason, if the threshold is 100 the vendor will order more than 100, and if the threshold is 125 the vendor will order more than 125. After all, a small cost to you also means a small gain to the vendor.

So there are obvious pros and cons to both the all-units contract and the incremental one. If you offer a more generous contract (the all-units one), you can better sway your partner's behavior, but it'll cost you. And if you want to save money on your influence tactics (by offering an incremental discount), you may get suboptimal ordering decisions. But here's what Kay-Yut and Diana found: on the whole, the incremental discount was better for the publisher than all the other discounts.[39] If the vendors are rational (able to see that the optimal order in both cases is 125), the two contracts would be equally good for the publisher. But if vendors aren't rational, like in this experiment, then the publisher is better off offering an incremental discount. Here's why. It's true that the vendors' decisions under the incremental-discount contract weren't quite as good (especially for the vendors) as they were under the all-units discount. But by setting the threshold at an attractive point, the publishers could get vendors to reach optimal decisions—and this swaying cost the publisher much less than the all-units discount would have. And although the decisions under the incremental discount weren't perfect, they were far better than under the original fixed-price contract. All in all, the incremental discount was the best value.

The economic theory of contracts, which assumes rational decision makers, says that several contracts (including the ones studied in this experiment) are equally good, capable of leading to optimum efficiency. But the experiments show otherwise: because people are not fully rational, some contracts work better than others for the same cost to the wholesaler—or, put another way, work just as well at a lower cost.[40]

The interesting upshot is that wholesalers who take retailers' bounded rationality into account can set higher prices than they could if the retailers made perfectly rational decisions.

Measuring Someone's Rationality

Okay, so you know that people aren't computer-like optimizers. And you get the idea that there are ways to make their decisions more optimal. But even though you know you need to take bounded rationality into account, it's not at all clear how much to do so. For example, if you know that the incremental contract works well when the target is set lower than perfectly rational people would respond to, you still don't know how much lower to set that target. Likewise, if you know that for most people less frequent decision making makes for better decisions, how much less often should people make their decisions? Complicating matters is the fact that, although everybody is at least a little irrational, different people have different levels of rationality. We know engineers who think through mathematical problems logically and unemotionally, coming up with answers not far off from what a computer would give. And, of course, there are more intuitive types (let's call them the poets) who rely more on gut feelings and vague rules of thumb, highly flawed though these methods may be. So there's no one-size-fits-all offset to use for adjusting for irrationality: the poet would need a bigger offset than the engineer. To properly correct for people's errors, you need to know the expected size of those errors; in other words, you need to measure each person's bounded rationality.

As reasonable as that sounds, doing it is harder than you might expect. That's because when you look at people's behavior, it's hard to know whether their optimization decisions come from irrationality or simply from a desire to optimize for something else. For example, a friend of Marina's who works as a pediatrician at a large clinic is puzzled by the behavior of some of her fellow doctors: under the clinic's employment contract, doctors earn a fixed salary for working a certain number of hours per year plus a bonus for every hour they work beyond that. As a result, many doctors get excited when they reach the threshold for bonus pay: they're eager to work overtime because they see the bonus for every additional hour they work as gravy. But Marina's friend has the opposite reaction: having done some simple arithmetic, she knows that every bonus hour pays significantly less than every hour of salary, and she doesn't want to work at a lower hourly rate. Not only that, she thinks it's strange that her colleagues are happy to do so. But are the other doctors being irrational? Possibly—but it's hard to say because it's also possible they're optimizing for total income rather than hourly rate. If so, it's perfectly rational to gladly take on a lower bonus (unless, of course, they could get other extra work that paid better elsewhere). In fact, if you're aiming to save up for a big purchase as quickly as possible, it would be irrational to turn down overtime just because of a preoccupation with your hourly rate. Unless we know a doctor's goals, we can't know whether the doctor is being irrational.

The same problem arises in the lottery studies we looked at in chapter 1 on uncertainty, when participants chose a less risky option even if the choice gave them a lower expected value: we can't conclude that most participants were unable to optimize with respect to expected value. We can only conclude that they were risk-averse—they were optimizing for lower risk.

To tease apart someone's bounded rationality from risk aversion, you need a different kind of experiment, one that looks at inconsistencies within an individual. For example, look at these two decisions

Kay-Yut and his colleague Tad Hogg asked participants to make in one experiment:

Decision One:

Option A (Very Risky Choice)	Option B (Safe Choice)
50% chance of receiving $1,000 and 50% chance of receiving $0	100% chance of receiving $400

Decision Two:

Option C (Moderately Risky Choice)	Option B (Safe Choice)
50% chance of receiving $650 and 50% chance of receiving $250	100% chance of receiving $400

Notice that the expected value of Option A (the very risky choice) is $500, whereas the expected value of Option C (the moderately risky choice) is $450. So both have a higher expected value than Option B (the safe choice), with an expected value of $400. So what would a rational person choose in each decision? Well, that depends on the person's risk aversion: it's rational for a highly risk-averse person to choose Option B in both decisions, and it's also rational for a highly risk-loving person to avoid Option B in both decisions.

Now let's look at what a moderately risk-averse person would do: she would choose the safe choice in Decision One (to avoid the very risky choice), and switch to the moderately risky choice in Decision Two. That could still be rational because it optimizes for the person's goal, which is as high an expected value as her level of risk aversion allows.

All these decisions wouldn't optimize for expected value, but not because the person is irrational. After all, there can be good reasons for a person to be risk-averse.

Here's what would be irrational, though: choosing the very risky choice for Decision One, but switching to the safe choice in Decision Two. That's because choosing Option A shows high risk-loving, whereas choosing Option C shows high risk aversion.

No rational decision maker would do that. And yet, out of the 108 participants tested, 18 did just that. They chose the very risky choice in Decision One and the safe choice in Decision Two.

Of course, we can't infer too much from people's choices in this one pair of decisions. Making one mistake on one pair of decisions doesn't mean the person is as irrational as can be. In fact, even consistency in making these two decisions could be a fluke. To get a measure of rationality, we need to test people on many pairs of decisions. What's more, these decisions can't be presented as pairs: that makes the problem too easy, drawing attention to the fact that, for example, Option B is the same in both decisions. Instead, the rationality test the economists developed presents many options and looks for inconsistent choices.[41] From these, one can gauge each person's "rationality index," a measure of how optimal the person's decisions are likely to be in many different types of problems.

Gauging someone's rationality promises tangible business benefits. One organization within HP, for example, is using the rationality index of each of its salespeople to interpret each salesperson's forecast. The idea, roughly speaking, is to pay more attention to forecasts from salespeople who tend to make consistent choices.

But does it seem odd to be measuring bounded rationality in terms of inconsistency? After all, we've said again and again that the mistakes people make are not random but systematic, even predictable. So why look for inconsistency? But think of it this way: if a person is rational, if she's optimizing for her objectives (whatever those may be), she should always make the same decision under the same circumstances. Yet experiments show that people aren't consistent. For example, in the contracting experiments Kay-Yut and Diana saw people making different decisions even when faced with the same problem time after time. These decisions aren't totally random—they're limited to a certain range—but they scatter over that range; they're not the same each time. The upshot is that the decisions aren't perfectly predictable, but they fall within a predictable range. So after watching a person's behavior over and over, you can spot patterns: you can predict how wide the spread is, as well as how likely you are to see one decision versus another. And identifying these patterns enables you to optimize contracts for these imperfect decision makers.

The Value Proposition

We've looked at a few ways to reduce the effects of people's bounded rationality. Some of our suggestions, like reducing how often you ask people to make decisions, are fairly straightforward and may be simpler than what you're already doing. But others may seem hopelessly cumbersome and hard to implement. Are the fixes worth it?

This is exactly the question every manager needs to ask before tinkering with processes and policies. Sometimes the answer is pretty clear: if millions of dollars are on the line, it's worth it to invest in technology, get training, or hire an expert. That's why the big companies we looked at earlier do many of these things. It's why, for example, HP continues to fund HP Labs: if scientists there can boost the company's profits by even half a percent, the savings amount to enough to fund the whole research organization.

Sometimes the opposite is clear: if the value of the decision is low, human errors are okay. That's why, for example, junior people are typically assigned small-stakes projects: even if they make mistakes, as beginners are likely to do, the cost to the business isn't as great. Similarly, if you run a small convenience store, it might not be worth your while to install expensive point-of-sale software that scans product bar codes for accurate prices. The cost of occasional cashier errors probably doesn't justify the expense of anything more than an old-fashioned cash register.

Often, the answer isn't obvious. If you're a restaurant manager with annual revenues of half a million dollars, and you've been winging it on a mix of rules of thumb and fudge factors passed down from your predecessor, is it worth it to buy software to help you set prices or manage your inventory? Does it make sense to hire a consultant to redesign your menu to help customers make better choices? It might or it might not, and that decision is itself a tough problem. That's why benchmarking is so popular: if you find that your peers running similar businesses are doing significantly better than you are, you can assume there's lots of room for you to improve. In that case, it's probably worth it to hire an expert.

You've seen how error-prone people can be, which means that even if they know what they want, they may well make poor choices and fail to reach their targets. Predicting people's behavior is hard for other reasons, too. We rarely act the same way in different contexts. For example, if we're swamped we tend to make decisions that are more rash than when we have plenty of time to consider our options. A woman who feels comfortable negotiating with another woman may refrain from negotiating with a man. And a person working alone sometimes works harder than in a group—though sometimes less hard, depending on a host of factors. So changes in our environment can greatly sway how we'll behave. What's more, though we all have much in common, each person is unique. (As the children's book has it, "We are all alike, we are all different.") Is it even possible to predict with any accuracy how a particular person or company will behave? This is the question we answer in the following chapter.

5

· · · · · · · · · · · ·

Reputation, Reputation, Reputation

In August of 2008, at the pinnacle of Michael Phelps's fame, the champion swimmer cashed in on his hard-earned Olympic glory with an endorsement deal with the Kellogg Company. It wasn't his first such deal—he'd long been paid to promote Omega watches and Speedo swimwear, among other products—but it caused some controversy since his face would appear on boxes of sugary Frosted Flakes. There was a chance that by trying to improve the cereal's image, Phelps would be damaging his own. New York's *Daily News* conducted an online "Flaking Out" poll, asking readers: "Will Michael Phelps's endorsement of sugary Frosted Flakes tarnish his reputation?" Only 9 percent of respondents said yes.[1]

Several months later, a widely circulated snapshot of Phelps holding up a marijuana bong (and wearing an Omega watch) forced him to admit that he had indeed inhaled. Kellogg swiftly announced it wouldn't renew the swimmer's contract, saying that "Michael's most recent behavior is not consistent with the image of Kellogg." That comment drew snickers from SNL's Seth Meyers, who sardonically pointed out that many of the company's cartoon mascots act like wild-eyed druggies. Proponents of legalizing marijuana called for a boycott of the cereal maker.

Soon it looked like Kellogg had miscalculated. Phelps's other big-name sponsors were standing by him. A little-known reputation-tracking company called Vanno reported that the reputation of Kellogg had actually gone down in the ranking of 5,000+ companies it tracks—from a recent high of No. 9 to No. 83. Leaving aside the question of how Vanno arrived at these numbers, the Vanno announcement gave the Phelps/Kellogg story new legs as the factoid itself became news on TV and in the blogosphere, temporarily boosting the reputation of Vanno in the process.

This story is a perfect example of the complex nature of reputation. Before we get into what reputation really is and how it works, though, we turn to a more basic question: why should you care about reputation in the first place?

Reputation's Payoff

Reputation pays off. That's easy to see in extreme cases like the star athlete who commands huge fees for endorsing a product or giving a motivational speech (or who, like Tiger Woods, suddenly loses huge fees after his reputation takes a nosedive). But you don't have to be one of a kind to profit from your reputation—it happens every day to ordinary people and companies that maintain a solid track record. Brand-name firms are able to charge more for their products than their lesser-known competitors. Plumbers and roofers with rosters of satisfied customers get jobs through repeat business and referrals, winning bids despite higher prices and often skipping the bidding process altogether. Recent grads from top schools command higher salaries and have an easier time getting hired. And companies with reputations for quality can collect licensing fees for letting third-party manufacturers use their name and logo; for a company like Disney, which earns about $30 billion per year through such licensing deals, capitalizing on its reputation in this way is, as a *Hollywood Reporter* headline quipped, like "a license to print money."[2]

Reputation pays off in even more remarkable ways. In 2005, when the iPhone was little more than a glimmer in the mind of Steve Jobs, the Apple CEO looked for a wireless carrier that would partner with Apple on the project. Thanks in large part to his reputation for making his bold visions a reality—think of the phenomenal success of the iPod and iTunes, Jobs-led projects that shook up the music industry—he was able to convince execs at Cingular (now AT&T Wireless) to partner with Apple long before he even had a crude prototype.[3] Admittedly, Jobs had to make significant concessions—including giving Cingular exclusive carrier rights—and he had a strong fallback in his willingness to become a de facto carrier by having Apple buy and resell wireless minutes. But Jobs was asking for something unprecedented in a wireless industry used to calling all the shots: Apple would have complete control over the iPhone's design, manufacturing, and marketing—and the wireless carrier wouldn't see a working prototype until well after the deal was done. Jobs's reputation (and Apple's) didn't guarantee a willing partner—in fact, Verizon flat out turned him down—but without it, he didn't stand a chance.

But we're interested in more than anecdotes. For hard evidence that reputations have measurable value and aren't just warm-and-fuzzy marketing fluff, consider a controlled experiment in one of the world's largest marketplaces, eBay, which has the biggest and best-known reputation system on the Internet.[4] As you know if you've ever shopped on eBay, buyers and sellers have an opportunity to rate each other. Over time, these ratings add up to a seller's (or buyer's) reputation, helping future users of the site decide with whom to do business.[5]

To run this particular eBay reputation experiment, the researchers worked with an established, highly rated eBay seller of vintage postcards. They asked the question: what is the effect of the seller's sterling reputation on buyers' willingness to pay for the postcards? To answer this question, the researchers had this seller create new identities—that is, the same seller offered the same goods while posing as someone with no reputation on eBay. The result: the difference in buyers' willingness to pay was 8.1 percent of the selling price. In other words, eBay shoppers were willing to pay significantly more to buy a product from a reputable seller—stark proof that establishing a reputation as an honest seller can pay off.

Why does a good reputation command a premium? When you're choosing whom to buy from, there's a lot of uncertainty. You don't know who will be honest and who will cheat, or who will even be capable of delivering on their promises. As a risk-averse buyer, you want to be sure of getting what you paid for. Because going with someone more reputable reduces the likelihood of being burned, you're willing to pay extra for this assurance. Something similar happens on the seller's side—if you're selling something to an unknown buyer and don't know whether the buyer will pay you, you may be more willing to sell the same product or service for less to a buyer with good credit—a reputation for paying on time.[6] In both cases, a good reputation commands a risk premium, sometimes called a reputation premium.

Put another way, reputation builds trust, helping people determine how trustworthy their would-be trading partners are. But while reputation is perhaps the main way to instill trust, there are others, which is why we devote a whole chapter to this broader concept.

But what happens when a reputation is neither positive (like the reputable eBay seller) nor neutral (like the new eBay seller) but downright negative? The cost can be tremendous. A famous example comes from the exploding-tires fiasco of a few years ago, when Bridgestone/ Firestone tires killed several people in Ford Explorer SUVs. Despite a long safety record from Ford and Firestone, both companies took a massive and lasting hit to their reputations—and to their market worth. Both companies had enormous direct costs, to be sure, including payments to the victims' families—and, in Ford's case, the cost to replace Firestone tires on all its cars, to the tune of $2.1 billion. But the financial impact of the crisis on both companies was much greater than the financial cost, with each company's market value dropping by about half. Ford's valuation before the crisis was $29 billion; afterward, it was $16 billion.[7] Since a drop this big can't be explained through direct costs, much of the drop comes from loss of reputation. We all know that reputation can turn on a dime: when Toyota's reputation fell following the terrible publicity surrounding the Prius crashes, Ford's sales picked up—and the newly profitable company suddenly seemed like a winner again.

More typically, though, a reputation is much harder to clean than to tarnish. Accordingly, companies that invest heavily in their brands also go to great lengths to protect their reputations from those who would harm them. Procter & Gamble, alleging that Amway distributors had spread false rumors of P&G profits going to Satanic cults, spent over a decade and untold legal expenses pursuing Amway in the courts. In the end, P&G won $19.25 million in a civil lawsuit. It may have been small compensation for the effort, let alone for the reputational damage, but for the company the case was a matter of principle. "This is about protecting our reputation," said Procter & Gamble's chief legal officer at the time. He added, as if to deter other would-be slanderers, "We will take appropriate legal measures when competitors unfairly undermine the reputation of our brands or our company."[8]

The Glue of Markets

Without information about reputation, markets can collapse. That may sound alarmist, but experiments and experience bear it out. For a dramatic example, let's look again at HP's reputation studies. Each time a buyer and seller completed a trade (or failed to fulfill a promise), that fact became part of the buyer's and seller's history, their reputations. Some traders maintained perfect reputations throughout the game's many rounds—except the last round. What happened in the last round? Just before it started, the person running the experiment (such as Kay-Yut) would announce that the upcoming round would be the final one. Once participants knew this, it made sense to cheat because honesty would no longer be rewarded. (After all, so what if they maintained a perfect reputation? There would be no future rounds in which to capitalize on it.) Therefore, even previously honest sellers would cheat. As a result, few successful trades took place in the last round—and in some experiments, not a single one did. Without the threat to reputation, the market had collapsed. Concerns about reputation, in other words, help keep people honest. Without concern for reputation, trade can break down completely.

"In the Market for a Lemon?"

For a deeper understanding of how reputation holds markets together, consider this curious fact: the moment a new car leaves the dealer's showroom, it loses an outsize chunk of its value. Why does a barely used

car cost so much less than a brand-new one? This is the question economist George Akerlof tackled in his famous "market for lemons" paper of
1970.[9] His answer was so insightful and had so many implications that it
eventually earned him a Nobel Prize—yet it was so unconventional (and
the ostensible topic so seemingly trivial) that several academic journals
rejected it.[10]

Akerlof's argument went something like this. Imagine you are a used-
car salesman, and you have good cars and bad cars (or "lemons"). You
know which cars are good and which ones are lemons, but a potential
buyer doesn't know which is which before buying the car. (Since one
side knows more than the other, economists say that the two sides have
asymmetric information about the cars on offer.[11]) The question for you,
the seller, is this: would you tell a potential buyer that a given car is a
lemon?

This is the Lemon Problem: it turns out that no matter which option
you choose, you lose. Here's why. If you decide to tell a buyer about the
glitches, he or she will choose another seller with a similar car unless
you offer a steep price break. (Even if other sellers don't disclose their
car problems, the buyer is still better off going with them because a
known problem is worse than merely some chance of a problem.) So it
appears that a better strategy is to keep your mouth shut.[12]

And that's true. Consider, however, what happens if you don't disclose
the lemons, just like everyone else. Since buyers can't tell between good
cars and bad cars, they always have to negotiate prices with the assumption that there is some chance that the car is a lemon. This means that
even good cars (which buyers don't know for certain to be good) don't
command a good price. Therefore, you as the seller lose out on the full
value of your good cars. This sounds bad enough, but it's actually just
the beginning of a terrible downward spiral. If good cars can't command
a good price, owners of good cars will be less likely to sell them, leaving
fewer good cars on the market; owners of lemons, on the other hand, will
be willing to part with them for a lower price. Therefore, the proportion
of cars on the market that are lemons will grow—and as it grows, so
does the risk of buying a lemon, further lowering car prices. The vicious
cycle continues until the lemons have driven all the good cars out of

the market! This is stunning considering that good used cars do exist. So why does even a slightly used car cost much less than a brand-new one? Because its price reflects the risk that it's a lemon.[13] Akerlof and other economists call this phenomenon, whereby asymmetric information about the quality of goods and services traded leads to a reduction in the average quality of items on the market, "adverse selection."

Are there any solutions to the lemon problem? Certainly, and in his paper Akerlof offered several ways in which markets respond to the problem. One solution is a lemon law, which most states have (although only some of them cover used cars). California's lemon law, for example, requires the seller to reimburse the buyer for a vehicle under warranty if the vehicle needs excessive repairs, as defined in the law. But enforcing such laws is costly. You may have to hire a lawyer—a cost only some lemon laws cover—and there's no guarantee you'll be able to collect even if you win. Furthermore, government intervention isn't practical for every situation. (Just imagine what would happen if the courts were responsible for overseeing the huge volume of transactions on eBay alone.) Another problem with legal solutions: finding an appropriate authority to regulate commerce across state and national boundaries. What's more, even without lemon laws, the market for used cars doesn't collapse. Reputation provides a solution.

Reputation to the Rescue

To see how this works in the used-car market, look at what happened when Marina tried to sell her car directly, rather than through a dealer. She posted an ad on Craigslist (anonymous, to protect her privacy), including a glowing description of the car and a set of photos showing off the car's sparkling exterior. To set a price, she looked up her model's year, mileage, and condition in Kelley Blue Book—and looked at how much similar cars were being offered for on Craigslist. (This last step was easy since she was selling a Toyota Camry—one of the most common cars on the market at the time.) Nearby dealerships also used Craigslist to advertise their used cars, and Marina hoped to sell hers for roughly the same price. After all, she knew she'd taken good care of her car, so why shouldn't it command top dollar?

Unfortunately, buyers didn't know this; unlike the local Toyota dealers, she had no reputation in car sales, and her anonymous ad didn't help matters, since she wasn't even putting her personal reputation on the line. Therefore, like other individual sellers, she had to price her car for several hundred dollars less than the dealerships did. Now, used-car dealers, especially fly-by-night operations, have a terrible reputation as a group—but authorized Toyota dealerships are another story. They stake their reputation on quality cars and reasonably honest dealings; at the very least, customers know they'll be able to go back if something goes wrong. An independent dealer with a long track record of selling used cars in the community would also be able to sell cars for more than an individual could.[14] This price premium may not seem fair (either to rival sellers or to buyers) until you consider both the cost of establishing a reputation and the insurance that buyers are in effect buying.[15] One way to think of reputation, then, is as a way to reduce the information asymmetry, balancing the scales by making buyers more informed about the sellers—and, therefore, about the cars themselves. Having to pay extra for reputation is a little inefficient, but it's more efficient than the alternative—which, without reputation information or other signals, is the potential collapse in trade.

One lesson in all this is to appreciate the value of reputation—that is, the value of having others know what we know about ourselves. Adults (unlike young children) understand that others don't know the same things we do, but we often act as if they do. Humans are notoriously bad at seeing things from another person's point of view: while we're rightly suspicious of others' private information, we forget that others are also suspicious of us. A more general version of this type of error has been called the Curse of Knowledge.[16] It's a curse because although you would think that private knowledge would give you an edge, it can also cost you by blinding you to what others don't know. For example, if we know the service we provide or the product we've developed is among the best on the market, we tend to assume prospective buyers do, too, or we think we just have to tell our customers about how great our product is and that will be that—they'll know what we know. Unfortunately, as the used-car example shows, telling isn't enough. Talk is cheap, and you need to show how you're different from the rest in more credible ways. Building a reputation—for both quality and good intentions—is one way; chapter 6, on trust, discusses several others.

How (and Why) Reputation Works

Everybody has a sense of what reputation is, but, as we've already suggested, reputation is trickier than most people realize. Even scholars from the different fields that have examined reputation define the concept in various ways.

We define reputation as a judgment or opinion based on a track record and held by an individual or a like-minded group. Apple, for example, is revered by its fans but is held in much lesser regard by fans of Microsoft. Microsoft has even more wildly divergent reputations depending on whom you talk to: shareholders love the company (for its solid financial performance) while many tech-savvy users resent the company's ability to get away with buggy software and high prices by dint of its near-monopolistic grip on the market.

Look at the polarized opinions about Whole Foods: as journalist Nick Paumgarten put it, "To some, Whole Foods is Whole Paycheck, an overpriced luxury for yuppie gastronomes and fussy label-readers. Or it is Holy Foods, the commercial embodiment of environmental and nutritional pieties."[17] So bear in mind that regardless of a target's overall reputation, individual people or groups may hold different judgments.

Your perspective can vary based not only on who you are, but also on what area of reputation you're looking at. For example, you don't have to be an Apple customer to know that Steve Jobs has a reputation as a genius at figuring out what consumers want in a technology product—nor do you have to be an Apple employee to think he's a tough boss to work for. Similarly, Apple has a good reputation for easy-to-use products (even when they aren't) and a poor reputation for pricing (even when their prices are actually lower). Reputation, therefore, isn't well captured in a single measure because it speaks both to what's being judged and who's doing the judging.

One lesson from this is not to assume that a good reputation in one area means the person or company is good in another area. Sometimes, though certainly not always, just the opposite is true. Perhaps, for example, you've had the misfortune of working for a company that bends over backward to please customers, but does so at the expense of its employees. Someone known for generous donations to charity may be covering up dubious business practices. Think not only of Bernard Madoff but also of the polluting oil companies that give money to environmental causes.[18]

This much seems straightforward. But there's one important distinction that people often blur, the one between two core types of reputation: reputation about *quality or ability* on the one hand and about *intention or motivation* on the other. Quality or ability speaks to whether a used car is a lemon or a peach, whether a vacuum cleaner is as durable as its maker says, whether the food at a restaurant is truly delectable, or whether a lawyer is a skilled negotiator. This type of reputation addresses the problem of *adverse selection*—the Lemon Problem—because it tells you about a track record when you can't discern quality or ability until after you buy the product or hire the person.

There's a second type of reputation, though, meant to address a different problem with asymmetric information—the problem of *moral hazard,* which we've touched on earlier. You may also have heard of moral hazard in the debate about the U.S. government's various bailouts—the fear that by absorbing the costs of risky behavior, the government encourages such behavior in the future. For the same reason, moral hazard is a major concern in the insurance industry: once insured, people have less reason to be cautious because it's the insurance companies—not the customers—who will pay for car repairs, doctor's visits, and property replacement. But moral hazard isn't just about bailouts and insurance—or even just about risk: moral hazard exists whenever one side (knowing more about its intentions than the other) doesn't have to bear the costs of its actions. A lawyer, for example, may be an excellent negotiator (a statement about quality) but may not *want* to negotiate hard if she gets the same fee either way (a statement about intention). However, if she doesn't negotiate hard, she hurts her reputation; and since a poor reputation carries a cost, reputation protects against moral hazard by suppressing the incentive to act on bad intentions. With threats to their reputation, even purely self-interested people and companies will consider it against their interests to cheat.[19]

This second type of reputation is much less stable because it's about intentions and motivation: whether an eBay seller will honor her promise of shipping the item in twenty-four hours, whether a business partner will adhere to the spirit of a contract (and not just the letter of it), or whether your celebrity spokesperson will maintain the image he had when he signed with you. All these people may have the ability to do these things, but whether they *want to* is another question.

Why should you care? Because the two different types of reputation suggest different responses. Reputations about quality and ability are more stable, less prone to changes. A good movie is a good movie: if many people you know enjoyed *Avatar* and they are people whose judgment you trust, chances are you'll enjoy the movie, too. The movie won't change from one showing to the next, so it's unlikely you'll be disappointed. It's a case of the past doing a good job predicting the future.

The same cannot be said about intention. Unlike quality or ability, intention is unstable and flaky, and it can be manipulated by changes in circumstances and incentives. A formerly up-and-up money manager absconds with his clients' assets. A longtime employee leaves to work for the competition. A once hardworking contractor starts to slack off. In all these cases, the past doesn't predict the future. Why the sudden changes? Perhaps the money manager faces a huge financial crisis at home, the employee receives an irresistible offer from your rival, and the contractor becomes so busy that he grows complacent about his relationship with you. Such changes in circumstances change the incentives for honest dealings—and can cause people with a good reputation for honesty to cheat. But these changes won't budge their ability to deliver a quality product or service when they want to.

Notice, too, our focus on track records: past events are matters of fact, not opinion, and are almost always the main drivers of reputation. So while reputation is often used to predict *the future* (will she fulfill her end of the deal?) and thus make decisions (should I do business with her?), it gets its power from information about *the past*. The Apple commercial that aired during Microsoft's launch of Windows 7 drives home this point. In these TV spots, PC, portrayed by John Hodgman, tells Mac, portrayed by Justin Long, "Windows 7 is out, and it's not going to have any of the problems my last operating system had. Trust me!" Mac, who feels he's heard this before, recalls the history of similar promises going all the way back to the 1980s, when PC wore a *Miami Vice*–inspired ensemble and promised that his latest operating system wouldn't have any of the problems Windows 2 had. The implication, of course, is that you can't inspire trust through promises about the future—rather, your past actions are the best predictor of your future actions. Or, as Henry Ford once put it, "You can't build a reputation on what you are going to do."

Smart companies have found lots of ways to collect information about customers' track records. You may know this as relationship marketing, customer relationship management (CRM), customer value management, or the like—but all these practices of recording and analyzing customers' behavior are really reputation tracking by another name. Using this information allows you to avoid one-size-fits-all policies, which (because customers are different) end up being unduly mistrustful of some and overly generous with others. Tracking your customers' history allows you to make worthwhile exceptions for your best (or worst) customers. At the extreme end, businesses have been known to blacklist customers who cost the company more than they bring in: for example, when a customer of Fairmont Hotels & Resorts who's failed to pay a bill or caused other serious trouble calls to make another booking, the high-end chain directs the caller to a special customer service agent to "discuss the issue."[20] This might be even more important at the other end of the spectrum, when a company gives preferential treatment to its most valuable customers. Good customers have earned a reputation and feel entitled to a reputation premium—and can get mighty angry if the company ignores their excellent track record and treats them like everybody else.

A nice case of recognizing customers' track records and treating them accordingly comes from Alaska Airlines, which goes beyond typical, impersonal loyalty programs to give its elite travelers their favorite cocktails when they're seated in economy class.[21] But you don't have to categorize your customers as starkly as "demons" and "angels"[22] to help you retain the ones you value. For example, the owner of Hyperfit USA, a popular gym in Michigan, keeps tabs on how often members come in for workouts; if a customer hasn't come in for three weeks, he sends the customer an e-mail.[23]

What trips many people up is the assumption that a reputation perfectly predicts someone's future actions, or that it doesn't predict anything at all. We want to steer you away from this kind of all-or-nothing thinking because the reality is more shaded: a reputation has some predictive power, but how strong a predictor it is can depend on the relative gain and loss of riding a good reputation: reputation can be used well or it can be exploited, as you'll soon see.

Reputational Erosion

What actually happens when a seller's reputation falters? At HP, Kay-Yut and his colleagues ran a series of reputation experiments that revealed several answers.[24] As you might recall from chapter 3, on reciprocity, participants played the roles of buyer and seller in a mock online marketplace. After the buyers ordered products from the sellers, the buyers had to pay for the products and the sellers had to ship them. At this point, each side had a short-term incentive to cheat: sellers could hope to keep the order fee without actually fulfilling the order, and buyers could hope to receive the goods without actually paying for them. However, even in the short term, cheating only paid off if the other side was honest. If both participants cheated, neither side would profit. When each side was finished making its choices, buyers and sellers saw the result on their computer monitors. Though there was a short-term incentive to cheat, the traders' dishonesty caught up with them in the long run as buyers learned which sellers didn't fill their orders and sellers learned which buyers didn't pay for the products.

The experiment was a greatly simplified model of the real world, of course: players could either pay or not pay, ship or not ship. The real world is more nuanced—and more complicated, often involving more people and subtler ways to cut corners. And yet the same trade-off is often at work, when the pursuit of a quick buck erodes one's reputation in the long run:

• The *Los Angeles Times,* a venerable newspaper with a hard-won reputation for honest reporting and an inviolable "Chinese wall" between its editorial and advertising departments, made a secret revenue-sharing deal with the Staples Center sports arena, the subject of a themed issue of the paper's Sunday magazine. When the story of this ethical violation broke, hundreds of the paper's reporters and editors protested that the deal raised public doubts about the paper's integrity. To end the internal strife and contain the reputational damage, the newspaper published a front-page apology and a detailed self-flagellating report.[25]

• To shore up profits, the oil company BP cut spending on maintenance and safety by more than 40 percent; the cuts contributed to a massive refinery explosion that killed fifteen people. The disaster made headlines around the world and led to the resignation of the company's CEO.[26]

• The law school of the University of Illinois admitted an academically unqualified but politically connected student in exchange for jobs for five of its otherwise unemployable current students.[27] Since a high job-placement rate helps a law school's rating, this kind of quid pro quo could temporarily boost the school's reputation, but the plan backfired with the ensuing scandal, ultimately forcing the resignation of the university's president to preserve the reputation of the university as a whole.[28] Even if the story never broke, however, lowering admissions or membership standards (for the sake of alumni donations or, in the case of a club or professional group, higher income from dues) gradually erodes an organization's reputation for selectivity.

So what happened in the experiment? You would expect players to stop doing business with the cheaters—and, indeed, they did. But buyers and sellers responded to cheating in another way, as well: retaliation. Rather than just ostracize the cheater (by not doing business with him or her), some participants made a point to cheat the cheater. Why does this happen? Most likely, retaliatory cheating was an act of righteous indignation, a positive sense of justice that spurs people to punish others even at a cost to themselves, as we saw in chapter 3, on reciprocity.[29] Perhaps participants who are tempted to cheat also feel less guilty about doing it to someone who's cheated them or someone else; in other words, they might be able to rationalize their own cheating behavior as "just deserts" for the other player's bad behavior. This wasn't a psychological study, so we can't know exactly what people were thinking or feeling. What we can say, though, is that the participants' behavior clearly showed that people cheat those with low reputations more.

Now, considering what we've already said about price premiums for a good reputation, you might expect that buyers in the HP experiment responded to cheating sellers by paying them less for the same goods. When a seller cheats consistently, paying even a lower price doesn't make sense; but when the seller has a spotty history—sometimes fulfilling orders and sometimes reneging—buyers might be willing to take a chance if the price is right. And yet the HP reputation experiments didn't show price discrimination. Players did less business with the cheater, or cheated the cheater more, but didn't hold out for lower prices. The reason for the lack of price discrimination against cheaters, we suspect, is that it's hard for buyers to figure out the right price given the interplay between the buyer's reputation and the seller's. When Kay-Yut and his colleagues looked at interest rates on the peer-to-peer lending site Prosper.com, they *did* find price discrimination based on reputation: borrowers with lower credit scores paid higher interest rates. On Prosper.com, only the borrowers have a reputation, so lenders can use just that one variable to decide on an appropriate interest rate to bid. But in a market where both sides have a reputation, these calculations aren't easy; it's much easier to just not do business with the disreputable buyer.

The Danger of Exploitation

We've made much ado about the ways reputation pays off. Unfortunately, there can be a dark side to this payoff: exploitation. In the HP experiment, as we already saw, many participants who'd built up reputations for fulfilling orders would, in the last round of the game, run off with the buyers' money without delivering. This "endgame effect," whereby reputation loses hold on people's behavior, occurs in many situations. In high schools, for example, we see this effect in the so-called senior slump: even the most hardworking students tend to slack off in the second semester of their senior year, after they've sent in their college applications; by this time they're not only exhausted, they also believe that their grade transcripts and teacher recommendations no longer count. And, in a sense, they're right: for all the hand-waving colleges do about the possibility of revoking admission offers after seeing the last semester's grades, students know that's not likely to happen. Why? Because colleges haven't built a reputation for following through with this threat except in extreme cases, when grades plummet. If a college actually starts rescinding offers of admission for grades merely slipping, word will spread and future threats will become credible.

Even without an endgame, a stellar reputation doesn't guarantee future performance. The most blatant recent example of such exploitation is Bernard Madoff, who capitalized not only on his reputation from his background (as former NASDAQ chairman, generous philanthropist, and pillar of the community) but also from his reputation for consistent returns. Of course, the returns were steady either only on paper or to the few individuals who got out early enough. When the economy tanked and forced many more investors to withdraw money, the whole fund was revealed to be a giant sham. It appears that Madoff was playing a reputation game because (unlike some others who've run Ponzi schemes) he disbursed his payments at fairly modest rates—10 percent, as opposed to, say, 50 percent. Furthermore, whereas he could have profited much sooner by taking all comers, he actually turned down prospective investors, suggesting in hindsight that he wasn't in it for a quick buck. By slowly building up his reputation, he made it likelier that people kept money with him longer, thus reducing the risk that the scheme would topple. In other words, his reputation wasn't just attracting investors—for a long time it actually kept the scheme from collapsing! In fact, if it weren't for the external shock of the economy, he might have been able to continue the scheme undetected indefinitely.

People exploit reputations in less spectacular ways, too. On eBay, a seller can build up a solid reputation from a string of small orders—only to cheat on a big order and bail out, leaving that online marketplace or starting over under a new identity. Similarly, a reputable seller in it for the long haul may be tempted to cheat on a few transactions and hope that her overall reputation won't suffer much. In fact, eBay sellers have been known to take a loss just to garner phony positive feedback, as economists Jennifer Brown and John Morgan have shown. Buying and selling feedback outright is against eBay's rules, so traders do it under the guise of selling something else. For example, a seller might advertise a "Positive Feedback E-book" that includes the promise of "Free Positive Feedback" for $0.01, including all shipping fees. Or the seller might offer a joke for a penny, embedding in the product description the words "positive feedback" and other clues to the nature of the sale. One seller's description (ostensibly of a digital photo) says, "100% feedback 100% need it, gotta have it, without it, how can they trust you???" Many sellers are more explicit, promising to leave positive feedback after you've paid and left five-star feedback. The point, of course, is to attract buyers whose real aim is to build an eBay reputation, and to do it while technically playing by eBay rules. Since eBay charges for BuyItNow sales, a 1-penny sale is a money-losing move—unless, say the researchers, the seller has "more lucrative business plans than the certain-loss market for online jokes."[30] In other words, although we can't prove that people are buying and selling reputations, the evidence strongly suggests it. In fact, since the study came out, eBay has attempted to close this loophole: it now requires BuyItNow items to be priced at least $1.00. But eBay traders can still buy and sell positive feedback; it's just that the transaction has to either use an auction or cost a dollar or more.

The bottom line is that reputation seems to promise something about the future, but in fact it is only about the past. The better someone's track record, the greater the opportunity for exploitation. Given the right incentives, even people with excellent reputations will fail to live up to what these reputations promise. For example, during the 2008 housing bust many borrowers with perfect payment histories "strategically defaulted" on their mortgages, abruptly stopping mortgage payments, knowing full well that their financial reputation—their credit scores—would suffer. In California, the rate of strategic defaults in 2008 was a stunning sixty-eight times higher than it was in 2005; in Florida, it was forty-six times higher. The strategic defaulters weren't subprime borrowers—on the contrary, these were people with an excellent track record for making payments, people who under new economic conditions appeared to be making a calculated decision to cut their losses on a house that was worth less than they owed on it. Even if their credit scores plummeted, they figured, they'd still come out ahead.[31]

Yet exploitation isn't always so calculated. This sometimes happens with licensing (as we've seen with Disney) and brand extensions, when companies who've built up an excellent reputation in one area branch out into other fields. Done carefully—not only through close monitoring of product quality, but selecting new products that are consistent with the core brand to begin with—this strategy can be enormously profitable even long-term. But when done less discriminatingly, it can dilute and damage the brand. Pierre Cardin has become a textbook case of this reputational pitfall. Celebrated in the 1950s for his avant-garde designs in high fashion, Cardin launched a ready-to-wear collection and branched out into perfumes and cosmetics by licensing his name to other companies. This is not unusual in the industry, as Coco Chanel and Christian Dior had already been doing the same thing. But Pierre Cardin didn't stop there. Seeing the profits in licensing, the company rented out the Cardin label to a slew of unrelated products—alarm clocks, baseball caps, cars, cigarettes, scuba gear, wine, and more. Over eight hundred different products bear the Pierre Cardin name under license (compared to fewer than three hundred each for Yves Saint Laurent and Christian Dior, and fewer than twenty each for newer designers like Ralph Lauren and Calvin Klein). Cardin's promiscuity in licensing has diluted both the meaning and the value of his brand reputation.[32] (Last year, Marina saw a four-piece set of Pierre Cardin luggage on sale for $100; given the uncertain quality associated with the Cardin name these days, this may have been no steal.)

The reputational slide from haute couture to the bargain basement may seem like a fine problem to have, since Pierre Cardin's licensing deals have generated over $1 billion in revenue per year. And that may be acceptable if you're okay with the reputational costs, which can erode the ability to capitalize on your reputation down the road. Wisely used, reputations can grow over time, much like principal does off compounding interest. But overexploiting your reputation is like living large off your principal—sooner or later, you'll have nothing left.

Think, too, of what happens when a company simply rests on its laurels while the rest of the industry keeps moving. That's what happened to Apple in the 1990s, when a lack of visionary leadership ground innovation to a near halt. While die-hard Mac loyalists continued to buy Apple products, Apple's share of the total PC market fell from 16 percent to 4 percent.[33]

Reputations and Reality

Reputations say something about real things in the world, but in themselves, reputations are not reality. Suppose you were an eyewitness to a crime or saw it replayed on the TV news. This way of gathering information is more reliable than hearing a secondhand report about what happened. Both help you form a judgment about what happened, but the first source of information is more closely tethered to reality. The same is true of reputations—there's a difference between firsthand experience and a combination of gossip, reviews on the Internet, or even ratings on eBay. Yet reputations get formed through a combination of all these sources. What's more, reputation oversimplifies complex information. Restaurant ratings, for example, often just give one measure that conflates multiple dimensions of the dining experience. Finally, all this information gets filtered through our far-from-perfect minds, which have a hard time making sense of loads of data. (When you think of organic produce, for example, which large retailer comes to mind? For many people, it's Whole Foods—but it turns out that the world's largest seller of organic food is none other than Walmart.) In short, reputation is just a proxy for the real thing: the link between reputation and reality isn't as solid as you may think.

To get a fuller picture about a person or a business, look at both anecdotes and statistics, if you can find them. On the Internet, it's easy to see horror stories (and glowing comments) about just about any major company; it's harder to find information that goes beyond isolated anecdotes. Depending on what you're looking for, you may have to turn to Dun & Bradstreet or Consumer Reports, for example. On the flip side, you may think that statistical ratings give you more accurate information, but even here you can do better by also looking at the anecdotal details. For example, when you see an imperfect score on eBay, you can go into the specific ratings to see what the negative reviews actually say. And if a large employer in your area attracts a great many applicants, talk to some employees to see why the company's great to work for. (You might learn, for example, that they treat people terribly—but pay exceptionally well.) Be like the college admissions officer who looks at both letters of recommendation *and* grades and test scores.

The Transparency Effect

If you've ever visited Los Angeles, you've probably seen letter-grade cards posted in restaurant windows. These are hygiene cards, and the A, B, or C shows the grade given to the restaurant by the latest Los Angeles County Department of Health Services inspection. Remarkably, most of these cards give the restaurant an "A" grade in hygiene. This seems hard to believe and makes cynical diners wonder if the restaurants that aren't up to snuff are bribing the health inspectors for a higher grade. You'd be right to be skeptical: when the hygiene-card program first went into effect in 1998, only 58 percent of restaurants had an A grade. But a pair of economists studying the situation, Ginger Jin and Phillip Leslie, found that the cards actually do improve hygiene quality. By 2003, not only did the number of restaurants with an A grade rise to 83 percent, hospital admissions in LA for food-related illnesses fell by 20 percent.[34] In other words, the threat of having a poor grade made public motivated restaurant managers to clean up their acts. This makes sense given the economic incentives for having a good (or bad) reputation:

the researchers found that the hygiene-card requirement boosted the revenues of grade-A restaurants by 5.7 percent, even after controlling for other variables. The revenues of grade-C restaurants, meanwhile, fell by 1 percent. New York City recently started a similar program, and though many restaurateurs resisted the change (quite understandably), those confident of their restaurants' cleanliness had reason to praise the new system. For example, Michael White, chef-owner of three upscale restaurants, told the *New York Times,* "I think it's great, because it will keep everyone on their toes."[35]

The hygiene report cards seem like a clear example of how reputational information affects economic behavior by both buyers and sellers. But is it an isolated case? Not at all. The same pattern emerged in Kay-Yut's reputation experiments. In one of them, he and his colleagues compared activity under two conditions. In one, participants would know about the outcome of every transaction; in another, they'd know only about their own transactions—in other words, who had cheated them personally. The effect on trading was remarkable: When a player could cheat with only one other player knowing, the average rate of fulfilled deals ranged from about 30 percent to about 70 percent, excluding the endgame rounds. But when the reputation spread far and wide to include all the players in the game, the average rate of fulfilled deals rose from a low of 75 percent to a high of 95 percent.[36]

But there are many ways to collect reputation information, and the inferences you make should be based on the way the reputation is built up. For example, on LinkedIn, the social networking site for professionals, users can build up a reputation by soliciting recommendations from former colleagues and bosses. What should you make of this information? Clearly, you should take it with a big grain of salt. For starters, notice the complete absence of negative references—all the site lets you do is recommend someone. A person who's had a checkered career that included both stellar performances and major screw-ups (as well as ethical lapses) may be able to obtain several glowing recommendations. But what about someone with no recommendations—what can you conclude from that? Not much. It's possible the person is hiding something—or she may just be sheepish about asking for recommendations, or may simply prefer to put her job-search efforts elsewhere. For all these reasons, the reputation system is weak.[37]

That said, people do make inferences based on the amount of information available. By making information about yourself or your company available, you can inspire trust. Put another way, once you develop a reputation for transparency, others have less reason to suspect you're hiding something.[38]

Rubbing Off, Selling, and Selling Out

We've already seen some of the many ways good reputations pay off. A more subtle point is that reputations *rub* off: the reputation of one entity affects the reputation of an associated entity. A company (or university, membership organization, or other group) builds its reputation from the reputations of its individual members, and members get reputations from the organizations to which they belong. A company's reputation boosts the reputation of its product brands, and those product brands boost the company's reputation. One of the most well-respected American companies is Johnson & Johnson, which many people associate with the baby products that bear this name—despite the fact that baby shampoo, diaper cream, and the like make up just a tiny sliver of Johnson & Johnson's vast offerings. The "baby halo," as it's been called, hovers over the entire Johnson & Johnson Family of Companies, including its less warm-and-fuzzy brands like Bengay, Rogaine, Sudafed, and Tylenol—as well as dozens of little-known subsidiaries. And while Johnson & Johnson typically holds the top spot in the *Wall Street Journal*/Harris Interactive ranking of the world's best corporate reputations, it was edged out in 2007 by, of all companies, Microsoft—apparently because of the generous philanthropic work of Bill Gates, who to many is synonymous with Microsoft.[39]

Because reputations can rub off, in extreme cases even a single individual can tarnish an entire organization's reputation. Think of the drunken captain of the *Exxon Valdez*—he may have been one bad apple within an otherwise decent company, but Exxon never recovered from the reputational damage of that disaster, not even after partly changing its name through the merger with Mobil. Companies and organizations can try to distance themselves from the offending individual, as we've seen with the resignations of the heads of the University of Illinois and of BP, but depending on the severity of the situation, firing one person may not be enough. Because reputations are so much harder to build than to ruin, it behooves organizations to screen applicants thoroughly on all the dimensions that matter, not just past accomplishments. Interestingly, the ability to do that is itself a function of the organization's reputation—a well-regarded organization can afford to be picky.[40]

If we put together the two ideas that reputations rub off and that they can pay off, it's easy to see why reputations can be bought and sold. We're not talking here about buying and selling positive feedback on eBay, but rather the way one person or organization can shine in the reflected luster of another's good name. For example, FDIC insurance helps Americans trust that they'll be able to withdraw their savings regardless of the reputation of their own bank. But that trust comes largely from the reputation of the U.S. government, not the FDIC itself (whose track record few citizens really know about). During the U.S. banking crisis of 2008, the federal government (worried that Americans' trust in the banking system was faltering) hired Suze Orman—who'd built a reputation for simple financial advice that millions of Americans listen to—to promote the FDIC in TV ads. Using whatever credibility she'd built up over the years, she informed listeners that "for seventy-five years, the FDIC has protected money you deposit in banks," adding that depositors haven't lost one penny in the history of the FDIC. She sold (or rented out) her own reputation to bolster that of the FDIC.

But even though reputation doesn't necessarily diminish through use, selling reputations isn't costless. For example, Disney must spend money to monitor who uses the Disney brand—not just preventing unauthorized use, but screening would-be licensees. If you're not discriminating enough in how you rent out your reputation and whom you endorse, you lose your credibility and hurt your own reputation. A-list celebrities usually understand this trap of "selling out" and carefully avoid it. Oprah Winfrey, for example, has said that she's turned down many offers to put her name on various products over the years. Of course, Oprah can afford to be choosy.[41] Celebrities who can no longer attract better opportunities sometimes capitalize on the remnants of their fame, even if they cheapen their image as a result. (William Shatner's self-mocking ads for Priceline come immediately to mind.)

Another way to buy reputation is through franchising: buying a McDonald's franchise, for example, rather than starting a fast-food restaurant from scratch. A less obvious way to buy reputation is the practice of "paying your dues"—working for a lower rate, especially at the beginning of one's career, in exchange for the opportunity to build work experience, especially at a prestigious firm.

But when someone buys a reputation, the potential for exploitation is great. What's to keep someone from buying a well-regarded restaurant, for example, and letting it go to pot, while counting on the restaurant's prior reputation to bring in customers? One answer is that while you, the buyer, may be able to exploit the reputation for some time, eventually you'll ruin the reputation—and have a hard time selling the restaurant when the time comes.[42]

In franchised businesses, however, the prospect of a future sale won't solve the problem because the individual franchise will continue to benefit from the reputation of the chain as a whole. Without other controls, individual franchisees can free ride on the chain's reputation forever—or until too much free-riding throughout the chain irreparably damages the whole chain's reputation. The potential for such free-riding exists whenever the party with a reputation enlists another party to act on its behalf. For example, decades ago Sears got in trouble with customers (and ultimately with the Federal Trade Commission) after some of its store managers used bait-and-switch advertising tactics to lure customers into their individual stores.[43] In effect, these managers used their employer's good name for personal gain, knowing that Sears would bear the costs of a tarnished reputation. Because so many managers were tempted into this kind of free-riding, the result was a tragedy of the commons for Sears as a whole. To prevent this problem, the parent company must provide clear rules and smart incentives—and monitor compliance. Doing that effectively has a cost, however.

Reputations as Self-Fulfilling Prophecies

Because reputations can be bought and sold, they can be self-fulfilling. For example, venture capital firms with good reputations for making companies successful not only get better deals but also end up with more successes because their connection with a start-up helps the start-up attract employees, customers, press coverage, and other resources that help the start-up succeed.[44] In this way, success breeds success.

Reputations can then snowball. For example, not only did Apple and Steve Jobs capitalize on their reputations to get the iPhone off the ground, but once the product succeeded, the reputations only grew—and, as of this writing, Apple tops the *Fortune* magazine list of the World's Most Admired Companies. Similarly, when you lend out your reputation, the reputation doesn't go away unless the borrower exploits it. Reputations grow through careful use.

Sometimes reputations snowball even when the original reputation wasn't well deserved—an oft-observed rich-get-richer effect. A Columbia University experiment on music popularity, for example, showed that the song listened to first (which the researchers had selected randomly) predicted which song would catch on among the study's participants.[45] People don't make decisions independently, but often follow the herd, so good reputations—earned through even a small edge in quality or ability—grow into better ones.

Improving the System

How can a reputation system be made stronger—and yield better results? Once again, eBay offers a great case study. As should be clear by now, having a reputation system is better for both buyers and sellers than not having one; it's also great for the marketplace where these buyers and sellers meet.

Once someone has built a reputation on eBay, switching to another marketplace (or going off to sell exclusively on your own Web site) becomes more expensive because you have to rebuild your reputation from scratch. So it makes sense for eBay to make the system as good as it can be.

Several years ago, eBay's executives faced this thorny problem: a sense that traders' scores didn't accurately reflect how well they were doing. If you looked at the sellers' scores, for example, you'd think buyers were thrilled with most transactions, since the average score was in the mid to high 90s. This seemed unlikely to reflect reality—so, in a very real sense, the feedback system itself was suffering from a bad reputation for validity. Having a weak reputation system is better than not having one at all, but not much better, since traders trying to make trading decisions can't place much trust in it. The cause of this problem, it turned out, was the threat of retaliation for giving a bad rating. Penn State economist Gary Bolton, part of a team of experts hired to solve the problem, summed it up this way: "There was a tendency for sellers, when they got negative feedback, to *give* negative feedback."[46] For example, if a buyer said that the item she ordered didn't show up on time and gave the seller a bad score, the seller might retaliate by giving the buyer a bad score. "This had a chilling effect on the site," Bolton says. As buyers came to know these retaliation effects, they tried to preserve their own reputations by not giving negative feedback to sellers: when they were happy with a transaction, they gave a high score, but when they were unhappy they simply stayed silent. As a result, sellers' scores skewed artificially high.

A double-blind feedback system solved this problem. Under the new system, sellers couldn't retaliate because they didn't know which buyers were giving them what feedback. When Bolton and his colleagues tested this new reputation system in the lab, they found that not only did retaliatory feedback disappear but feedback became more varied as well, suggesting that buyers felt freer under the new system to report their true experiences. Not only that, but sale prices and trading volume both went up—enough to justify implementing the change (called Feedback 2.0) in eBay's actual marketplace.[47] Although eBay doesn't report the effect on its business, there's good reason to believe it was positive.

As sellers with poor reputations lose business, they have less reason to stick around without changing their ways. And when buyers have more confidence in the eBay system, they're more likely to do business there. Think about what that says about the value of reputation: eBay already had a reputation system, but by improving that system the company was able to dramatically improve the market's efficiency and profitability.

Even under the new reputation system, eBay is not a paragon of virtue— a quick search of its user forums reveals plenty of horror stories about buyers being cheated by sellers, as well as buyers trying to extort money from sellers in exchange for not giving bad feedback. Sellers have complained that the new one-sided system is unfair, since buyers aren't all angels, and some sellers have gone so far as to sue buyers over allegedly defamatory feedback that buyers thought was merely honest. No reputation system is perfect, but considering its vast size and global reach, eBay does a far better job at facilitating commerce than it would without its reputation system.

What can we learn from all this? For starters, if you're in a position to design an online community, keep in mind the value of reputation, the potential for retaliation, the problem of anonymity, and similar dynamics. For example, the founders of Yelp understood the temptation for some users to shill for their friends' businesses; to reduce the effects of such gaming, the Yelp managers made sure the system demoted reviews written by users who'd only submitted one or two reviews.[48]

Second, realize that the way to collect reputation data depends on the environment. Because eBay buyers had to pay up front, the need for buyer reputations wasn't as pressing, since the worst that a buyer can typically do is not follow through upon winning an auction; a different trading system might call for a different reputation mechanism.

Third, if you have something to buy or sell, consider what kind of community is best for doing business. Furthermore, take reputation scores with a grain of salt. One careful analysis of eBay transactions disentangled traders' public reports from their private perceptions of transactions; the study found that if you listen to "the sound of silence," paying attention to when traders didn't leave feedback, you can infer that eBay buyers leave a transaction satisfied only about 79 percent of the

time, and sellers about 86 percent of the time.[49] But because dissatis-
fied traders are much less likely to leave feedback than satisfied ones (at
least before the rollout of Feedback 2.0), the reported averages are much
higher. When most users' reputation scores are 95 and above, as they are
on eBay, the scale isn't 0 to 100 but more like 95 to 100—so a feedback
score that's 95 percent positive is actually a *terrible* score. It's relative
reputation, not absolute, that matters.

This last is true in the brick-and-mortar world, as well. In this book
we usually refer to companies that are household names so that you'll
know what we're talking about. But sometimes a more obscure company
has a better reputation among a particular group than a well-known
one. Everybody's heard of Nikon and Canon, and among most people
these companies have excellent reputations for quality. Fewer people are
familiar with Hasselblad and Leica, but these companies make among
the best cameras in the world—and have sterling reputations among
professional photographers. What matters when you're judging quality
or ability (rather than intention or motivation) is how a person or product measures up among those who matter, not among the population at
large. And since there's a cost to building a reputation, it makes sense to
focus your reputation-building efforts on differentiating yourself among
your core audience, rather than trying to make a name for yourself with
the widest possible audience.

Reputation's Downsides

Throughout this chapter, we've hammered home the point that reputation has great value. But reputation is a double-edged sword. As you build
your reputation, you need to keep several potential pitfalls in mind.

First, the greater the reputation, the more vulnerable it is to market
fluctuations. In down markets, companies with the best reputations suffer the greatest falls in stock price.[50] These are the same companies that
do better than other companies when the market as a whole is rising.

Second, highly reputable people and companies are more vulnerable
to crises in general because they have more to lose. A study of car recalls

found that companies with good reputations before the recall suffered more as a result of the recall than companies with a poorer reputation to begin with.[51] Similarly, if a company's reputation is tied to that of one person, the whole company suffers when anything happens to the individual. Apple is nearly synonymous with Steve Jobs, so when Apple followers saw Jobs looking increasingly gaunt in 2008, they worried not only about his health but about that of Apple as well. And when the Tiger Woods scandal broke, no company was as vulnerable as Accenture, which had tied up its reputation with that of the golfer.

Third, because those with big reputations have more to lose, it's not in their best interests to take risks. That makes it harder for reputable businesses to innovate, sometimes leading them to coast on their reputations while smaller start-ups (with less to lose) outpace them. If you are that smaller rival, of course, you should recognize your relative lack of reputation as an opportunity—and jump on it.

Finally, even stellar reputations have limits as predictors of future actions, as we've shown with free-riding, coasting, endgame effects, changes in circumstances, and other opportunities for exploitation. So reputation isn't a silver bullet. In the next chapter, we'll tell you more about figuring out whom to trust and how to prove yourself trustworthy.

6

In Whom We Trust

On August 11, 2007, fifty-two-year-old Zhang Shuhong hanged himself inside the warehouse of one of his company's three factories. The Chinese company, Lee Der Industrial, had been an important vendor for the world's largest toy company, Mattel, and at its peak Lee Der employed over five thousand workers. Everything began to unravel, however, after Mattel discovered lead paint on toys based on Dora, Elmo, and other beloved characters. By the time Mattel found the problem, which affected eighty-three different products, almost a million tainted toys had gotten out to retailers and distribution centers, three hundred thousand of them actually reaching customers. This forced the infamous Mattel toy recall of 2007—not the company's first and not its last (with two more paint recalls within the next month), but certainly its costliest. Eventually, the Consumer Product Safety Commission ordered Mattel to pay a $2.3 million fine. In addition, Mattel incurred untold costs to its reputation—all on top of the $30 million cost of the recall itself. This was terrible news for Mattel, but a complete disaster for Zhang. Not only was he on the hook to Mattel, but the Chinese government revoked his firm's export license—a death sentence to a company with no domestic sales.

After Zhang's death, employees told reporters that Zhang was a good boss who paid well above the local minimum wage, gave workers a day off each week, and seemed to dedicate his life to the company. And nine days earlier, when news of the recall first broke, Mattel's CEO (at this point still cloaking Lee Der's identity) said Mattel had worked with the vendor for fifteen years. "This isn't somebody that just started making toys for us," he said. "They understand our regulations, they understand our program, and something went wrong."[1]

But what did go wrong? How could one of Mattel's most trusted suppliers, with a reputation built up over fifteen years, have made toys with toxic paint? It turns out that Zhang bought his paint from a company owned by his best friend—and that this paint supplier, in turn, relied on paint pigment he purchased from yet another supplier. It's this pigment supplier—three degrees of separation away from Mattel—that was the source of the problem, diluting paint powder with cheaper, lead-containing filler. Zhang didn't know about the subcontractor's misdeeds, and there's every reason to think that if he had known, he wouldn't have stood for it. But he hadn't tried to find out. Instead, Zhang had trusted his friend, and Mattel had trusted Zhang.

A chain of trust is only as strong as its weakest link. But this supply chain had more than one broken link: Mattel's letting the products out into the market without completing its own safety inspections was only the last in a long line of missteps by all the players in the supply chain. In some ways, it was the most damaging: instead of being able to quietly deal with the problem directly with the manufacturer, Mattel was forced into a public recall, which hurt the reputation not only of Mattel and Zhang Shuhong's factory, but also of the broader "Made in China" brand.[2]

Of course, not all stories of misplaced trust end this tragically. Nonetheless, not understanding how trust works—and therefore trusting too much or not enough—can spell the difference between flourishing, mutually beneficial relationships and big disappointments. To begin to unravel the notion of trust, we turn to a now-classic economic game.

The Trust Game

Some years ago, a trio of economists led by Joyce Berg of the University of Iowa devised a clever game—very much in the spirit of the Dictator Game and the Ultimatum Game—to test trust and trustworthiness. Variations of the so-called Trust Game have been used in hundreds of experiments since the original one, but let's start with the basic game.[3]

Here's how it works. When you show up to the lab, you're assigned one of two roles: the Investor (also called the Trustor) or the Trustee. Either way, you get $10 just for showing up—but you have an opportunity to increase your earnings with help from the other player. Unfortunately for you, you and the other player can't talk to each other. In fact, in the original experiment conducted in the 1990s, you're in separate rooms and remain anonymous to each other throughout the game. If you're the Investor, you have the option of sending part or all of your money to the Trustee in the other room. Whatever you send gets tripled before it reaches the Trustee—but you're totally dependent on the Trustee to give any of it back to you. And remember: you don't know each other (so you don't know how worthy the other player is of your trust), the Trustee makes a unilateral (Dictator-like) decision about how much to return to you, and you're playing the game only once (so there's no reputation threat to the Trustee for betraying your trust). If you entrust the other player with $1, the Trustee can send you back $3, $2, $1, or nothing at all. How much of your $10 you give the Trustee is a measure of your trust in that anonymous stranger; how much the Trustee sends back is a measure of that person's trustworthiness.

What should you do? And what do you think participants in this experiment did? Think about it: working together—with perfect trust on your part and perfect trustworthiness on the part of the Trustee, the two of you can increase your joint earnings from $20 (that is, $10 each) to $40 ($20 each, assuming an even split—your $10 investment tripled, plus the Trustee's original $10). If you're less trusting, you send less—but, of course, you also can't earn as much no matter how much the Trustee returns to you.

Relationship Between Trust and Payout

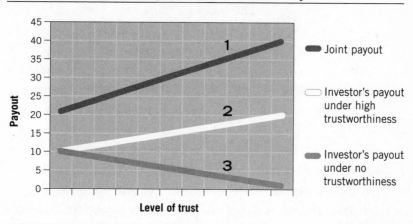

As the investor's trust increases, the joint payout increases (line 1). With a trustworthy trustee who shares the joint payout evenly, the investor's payout increases with increasing trust (line 2). However, without trustworthiness on the trustee's part (line 3), increasing trust decreases the investor's payout.

You can see that the game was set up to capture this key aspect of trust: the more trust in an economic exchange, the more wealth is created. At the extreme low end, if you don't trust the Trustee at all, you send nothing, so you get nothing—you're left with exactly what you started with.

That's not a recipe for prosperity, yet that's exactly what traditional game theory predicts you'll do. After all, a purely self-interested Trustee will pocket anything you send him (tripled or not), and knowing this, you'd be irrational to send anything at all.

If you remember the fairness chapter, this reasoning should sound familiar. And you should also suspect that it's wrong in predicting actual human behavior, which doesn't work quite the way theory predicts. (In a clever inversion, the twentieth-century philosopher Martin Hollis put it well when he said that trust "works in practice but not in theory."[4]) The original trust experiment had thirty-two Investor-Trustee pairs, and only two of the Investors sent nothing—almost the opposite of the "rational" prediction. Five players sent their full $10. The other Investors hedged their bets, with half of them sending between $4 and $7.

Given the absence of reputations, threat of punishment, or any other extrinsic motive for the Trustees to cooperate, this is a remarkably high level of trust. You might suspect this has something to do with the type of people who played the game—undergraduates at the University of Minnesota—but the Trust Game has since been played hundreds of times in dozens of settings, and although the results vary somewhat, one finding remains constant: Investors tend to trust the Trustees. So is this trust justified?

Sometimes. In the original Trust Game experiment, almost half of the Trustees sent back more money than the Investors had sent them. Some Trustees returned some money but less than the Investors had sent. And a handful of the Trustees kept all the money. Overall, whereas the average amount sent was $5.16, the average payback was only $4.66. In another version of the game, where Trustees were told how others had played, returns were better on the whole—but still, given the easy opportunity to take the money and run, some players betrayed their counterparts' trust.

Given all this, you might ask the question: why did the Investors put so much trust in the Trustees? Or, more generally, why does such intrinsic trust exist despite the risk of exploitation? For a clue, think back to the social dilemmas described in chapter 3, on reciprocity, such as the Prisoner's Dilemma.[5] These dilemmas show that if every individual acts out of rational self-interest, everybody is worse off. The prisoners fink on each other and both end up in jail. Sellers and buyers don't trust each other, so trade grinds to a halt. And shared resources like forests and lakes get overexploited until they have nothing left to give. Nobody can eat, nobody can trade, and pretty soon everybody dies. Put another way, groups with too many selfish types tend to become extinct. But if enough people act unselfishly, irrational though that may be, cooperation can continue and economic life can thrive. The people we're surrounded by are the survivors of a long process of winning and losing through various approaches to trust. Whatever the reason, at least some level of trust exists in all communities—some positive expectations about others' future behavior—even without reputations, warranties, contracts, legal systems, or other incentives. When you add these factors, trust usually increases because under these conditions we have a higher expectation that others will act trustworthy.

Trust and Prosperity

We can see the relationship between trust and economic prosperity on a global scale. Economists Paul Zak and Stephen Knack found that trust (that is, being trusting) is among the strongest predictors of a nation's wealth.[6] For example, when asked, "Do you think most people can be trusted?" fewer than 10 percent of respondents from Brazil, Uganda, and the Philippines said yes. Contrast that with the much wealthier countries of Norway and Denmark, where more than 60 percent of those surveyed answered yes. Admittedly, the question is vague ("Trusted to do what?" you might ask, or "Most people where?"). Yet it's the same question asked all over the world, with starkly different results. Zak argues that countries low in trust are poor because their citizens are reluctant to make the sorts of investments that create jobs and raise incomes. It's also possible that poverty makes people less trusting. If that's true, then poor, low-trust countries are caught in a vicious cycle, with low trust leading to poverty and vice versa.

But if trust leads to prosperity, that's not to say that *blind* trust does. After all, if people in the high-trust countries believe most people can be trusted, that may be because most people they've encountered (in their country) are trustworthy. And some of that trustworthy behavior likely comes from a culture that—through its norms, institutions, and social structures—rewards trustworthiness and punishes breaches of trust. In short, whereas trustworthiness leads to trust, trust alone does *not* lead to trustworthiness. For example, in the original Trust Game experiment, if you had sent $10, you were just as likely to get nothing back as you were to get back $20. A later study also suggests that people don't necessarily reciprocate trust with trustworthiness. This study compared results from a Trust Game with those of a "Faith Game." The Faith Game is very similar to the Trust Game, but with one crucial difference: the Trustees in the Faith Game don't know that the Investor is trusting them. Instead, the Trustees believe that the other player isn't an Investor at all but a Dictator simply choosing how much to share. The Investors, on the other hand, know the real setup, and they have to decide how much to send over based on their expectations of how the Trustee will respond. By comparing the results of this more nuanced game with the results of the Trust Game, the researchers can see whether Trustees' trustworthiness level has anything to do with their belief that they're being trusted. If it does—that is, if trust begets trustworthiness—then we would expect trustworthiness to be higher in the Trust Game than in the Faith Game. But the results of the two games are the same, further evidence that trust doesn't lead to trustworthy behavior.[7] In the lab, in the Mattel fiasco, in the Madoff scandal, and in countless run-of-the-mill betrayals, trust can lead to exploitation.

But while protecting yourself from exploitation, you don't want to be so distrustful that you avoid profitable deals or spend so much time and money protecting yourself that you cut too much into your profits. By greasing the wheels of commerce, trust reduces transaction costs: you spend less time performing extensive background checks, drafting ironclad contracts, and monitoring performance every step of the way. Without enough trust, you pay too high a price for doing business.

So there are problems with too little trust and with too much. But how do you figure out the optimal level of trust? There's no formula that incorporates all the possible factors, no software into which you can input everything you know about a particular business situation and get a precise answer, but this chapter will give you a few general principles to help guide your decisions.

Aspects of Trust

It would be hard enough to figure out the optimal level of trust if trust were just about one thing: will the person cheat me or not? But trust is about several things at once: intentions and ability in a specific domain.

In the previous chapter, we explained that reputation can reveal something about quality and ability or it can say something about intentions and motives. This important distinction applies to trust more generally. When people think about trust, though, they tend to focus only on intentions, just like the Trust Game does. They ask themselves, Will this vendor be honest and not cheat me? Will this employee work hard and not slack off? Does this agent have my best interests at heart? In short: is the person friend or foe?

Good intentions are important, of course, but they're only half the story—not of much use without the ability to deliver on them. For example, let's say you're playing the Trust Game with someone who genuinely wants to be unselfish and do the right thing. But suppose this player misunderstands the rules of the game or gets the math wrong; he might think, for example, that the right thing to do is to split the $30 that comes in, rather than the $40 that comes from his stake and your tripled stake, so he sends you $15 rather than the $20 you had hoped for when you entrusted your full $10. You still have a net gain, but you've been shortchanged. It's an honest mistake, but the result is the same as your partner having cheated you.

Our natural inclination is to assume malevolent motives in others—a tendency Stanford Graduate School of Business trust researcher Roderick Kramer has called the "Sinister Attribution Error." It's an error because bad actions could be due to circumstances beyond an individual's control—or they could indicate incompetence with no ill will. Have you ever had someone not respond to an important e-mail? You don't know why, so you naturally try to come up with an explanation. There are any number of explanations: your colleague might be on vacation and have forgotten to set up an auto-response, she may be attending to a crisis and unable to respond to any e-mail, or your message may have gotten caught in the company's spam filter, never making it to your recipient. The tendency to ignore all these possible explanations and instead assume she's intentionally blowing you off is the Sinister Attribution Error in action. This assumption doesn't really help you—in fact, it poisons relationships. As we've already suggested, giving people the benefit of the doubt prevents conflict and sustains relationships.

Conversely, don't assume that good intentions mean the person will be able to deliver. Family businesses are especially vulnerable to this problem. Wanting to keep the wealth in the family, and suspicious of outsiders, a business owner passes the reins on to his son, knowing that the young man will want the best for the business—but can Junior deliver on his good intentions? Sometimes the answer is no.[8]

The problem isn't limited to nepotism. Too often people judge each other's ability based on judgments of their intentions. If someone belongs to our church or sends her kids to the same school we send ours, we tend to think they'll want to do a good job for us—and that's not an unreasonable assumption. After all, anybody who plans to stick around in the community has to think about their reputation. But it's a mistake to assume that somebody who really wants to do a good job for you will actually do it. An incompetent accountant is likely to screw up your tax returns even if she means well. And your most diligent employee working nights and weekends to finish the job you've delegated to him could still miss an important deadline or turn in sloppy work.

It's a good idea to think about trustworthiness in terms of likelihoods, however imprecise. You might, for example, give someone a 70 on intentions and a 90 on ability (for a total likelihood of the desired outcome of 63 percent), and somebody else a 95 on intentions and a 60 on ability (for a combined probability of only 57 percent). This is a more nuanced and much more helpful way to see things than to simply ask, "Do I trust this person?" Also, notice that unless you're 100 percent certain on both counts, the combined likelihood of a good outcome is always lower than your assessment of ability or intentions alone. That's just Probability 101, and it helps explain why things are less likely to run flawlessly as more people enter the equation. The more complex the project and the more links in a supply chain (think Mattel), the less likely everyone's intentions and abilities will be up to the task.

Keep in mind, too, the element of luck. Even if you have a high level of trust in someone's ability and intentions, you can't be 100 percent certain that competent people will deliver on their good intentions. People get sick, a delivery truck breaks down, the computer crashes—however unlikely, events large and small can derail good plans. So when things don't go according to plan, don't be quick to infer either incompetence or ill will on the part of the person who let you down. How can you tell? One rule of thumb: if the bad outcome is really a fluke, a competent professional who values the relationship (or her reputation) should bend over backward to make amends—or at the very least provide a good explanation.

Beware the opposite mistake of assuming that someone who exudes warmth and good intentions can't be very smart or good at what they do. That may sound crazy, but psychological research attests to the fact that we sometimes think that intentions and ability are inversely related, particularly when we think of stereotyped groups. One study found, for example, that when working women become mothers, coworkers come to see them as warmer but less competent. (Men who become fathers, on the other hand, are seen as warmer but no less competent.)[9] Along the same lines, another set of experiments found that people perceive for-profit corporations as competent and nonprofits as warm but incompetent.[10]

So what is the relationship between the two types of trust? There really isn't one: good intentions say nothing about competence, good or bad, and competence says nothing about intentions. In determining trustworthiness, you need to judge them separately.

Then there's context. For simplicity's sake, we've been talking about intentions and ability in general. But separate judgments about someone's intentions and ability are only meaningful with respect to *something*, whether it's doing your taxes or making a sale or finishing a particular project on time. That means someone with high ability and motivation in one domain may be lacking either ability or motivation in another. Keep all three aspects of trust in mind as you figure out how much you can trust someone to do what you want.

The Force of Incentives

If ability and intentions in a particular context affect trustworthiness, then it stands to reason that anything that affects ability or intentions in a given context will also influence trustworthiness. Incentives can be a powerful force, but they can do only so much for ability: if you can't single-handedly lift a one-ton block of cement for $500, paying you $1 million won't get you to do it, either.[11] But not for lack of motivation. In fact, incentives are wonderful at swaying intentions, for good or ill.

Take the Mattel case. Because of the pressure to keep prices down, margins throughout the supply chain were low, so the temptation to cut corners was great. For the pigment supplier, that took the form of using cheaper, lead-filled pigment. The paint manufacturer, the factory owner's best friend, didn't do something quite as egregious, but he did fail to test the pigment before using it to make paint. Likewise, the toy factory didn't test the paint before applying it to the toys, and Mattel didn't test the final products before sending them out to warehouses and ultimately to customers. Had the same people been working in a different economic context—with a better set of incentives—none of this would have happened. What's more, given the same context, had Mattel or the manufacturer appreciated how strong the incentives were for cheating, the companies might have trusted less, done more testing, and discovered the problem before so much damage was done.

The incentives can be much more subtle. Consider a series of experiments conducted by Kay-Yut and UT-Dallas operations researcher Özalp Özer. Looking at a particular business context, they asked this question: how much can people be trusted to share information, and how much do their counterparts trust them?

Here's the business context. Imagine that you run a store for which you buy products from a manufacturer. The manufacturer needs to know how much product end customers will buy in the next three months so that she can plan capacity, especially in terms of parts it orders from its own suppliers. (As managers at the idle General Motors plants know too well, too much capacity costs money; but, as Nintendo has seen with its Wii console, not having enough capacity leaves earnings on the table.) Since you, the buyer, are closer to the end customers than the manufacturer is, you're in a better position to estimate future demand—and the manufacturer asks you for a demand forecast. What do you say?

Although planning for higher capacity costs the manufacturer money, giving too high a forecast costs you (the buyer) nothing. (Remember, you're only forecasting at this point, not placing an order.) In fact, it's in your best interest to err on the high side so that later, when you're ready to place orders, the manufacturer will always have enough product to fulfill your orders. Of course, you don't want to develop a reputation for overestimating demand—but suppose you're playing a one-shot game, so you know that if you lie about your private information, there'll be no negative consequences for you down the road. Economists describe this condition as *cheap talk* because the amount of information you reveal, or how honest it is, doesn't cost you anything. And under conditions of cheap talk, with only an upside to inflating demand, your best strategy is to do just that—to say you'll need a gazillion units. A shrewd manufacturer, for her part, knows that you have a strong incentive to exaggerate demand—and therefore won't believe you. That's the prediction from classical game theory, and economists have a cute name for it: *the babbling equilibrium*. The idea is that anything you communicate under conditions of cheap talk won't be believed at all—you might as well be babbling. There's no trust between parties, and no information is exchanged.[12]

As you already know, the real world rarely works that way: people often believe each other even when a game theorist says they shouldn't. Most of the time most people assume others are telling the truth, so we generally trust the information given to us.[13] We're persuaded by unverifiable promises and cowed by threats that, for all we know, may be idle. For example, in an experiment looking at cheap talk in the Ultimatum Game, Responders who threatened to reject low offers got higher offers, on average, than those who didn't.[14]

Interestingly, this truth bias, or the tendency to believe even in cheap talk, makes some sense. The fact is that most people *do* tell the truth most of the time, in part because most of us have some degree of aversion to lying.[15] For example, when you're selling a used car, you might not consider it your duty to advertise all of the car's defects—because you won't consider the omission entirely dishonest—but when asked point-blank whether it needs any repairs, you probably won't flat out lie to the prospective buyer. In fact, one experiment using the car-selling scenario found that asking direct questions does a good job of eliciting information left out through lies of omission.[16]

The aversion to boldfaced lying means that most of us are willing to give up some monetary gains so that we don't have to lie—just as, in the standard Ultimatum Game, many of us are willing to sacrifice money to keep someone else from getting an unfair share. The practical implication of all this is that if you know you'll be able to keep your word, making informal promises can pay off (and certainly doesn't hurt), even though the other party might be skeptical of your words because they're not binding. That's why letters of intent, though not legally binding, are so widespread: since people are loath to lie, especially in writing, such letters usually do mean something. They may not be as ironclad as a formal contract, but they're also faster and less expensive to draw up.

Similarly, cheap talk can help restore broken trust. One experiment investigated ways to restore cooperation following noncooperative behavior in a repeated Prisoner's Dilemma. You'll recall that if only one player doesn't cooperate in a Prisoner's Dilemma, that player comes out ahead, but if both fail to cooperate, then both are worse off. In this experiment, cooperation happened only when one player chose "Up" and the other player chose "Left." Choosing "Down" or "Right" meant noncooperation. The noncooperative player in the experiment was actually a computer; that way, the researchers could control that player's behavior. After each noncooperative move the computer sent a text message to the other player, who thought the messages were coming from another person. The researchers wanted to see the effects of different types of apologies on the human player on the other end. They found, not surprisingly, that substantive apologies were best at rebuilding cooperation. For example, offering to play Left while the other player played Down (and thus compensating the other player for a noncooperative move) worked better at restoring cooperation than merely saying, "I am sorry for doing this. I think we should go back to cooperation." But even an apology without penance sometimes worked if it involved a statement professing good intentions, such as "I was worried that you would choose Down this time, so I chose Right."[17] Although they're not as good as making amends, such verbal explanations for wrongdoing can, under some circumstances, be convincing enough to restore trust, even if they are technically cheap talk.

There are limits to lying aversion and truth bias, however. If the incentives to lie are high enough, they'll overcome the force of lying aversion, and people will be more likely to lie. Therefore, if we know that the incentives to lie are high, we should be more skeptical of what people tell us. As always, context is critical.

For example, here's what happened in the retail demand forecasting experiments: although the buyer does exaggerate somewhat, he also gives the manufacturer useful information; the manufacturer, in turn, trusts the buyer to some extent. This much isn't surprising, and it's consistent with the results of the Trust Game.

But here's where things get interesting. The experiments showed that the levels of trust and trustworthiness depend on a nonobvious factor: how much the buyer knows about future demand. When both sides know that demand is stable, the manufacturer trusts the buyer more. For example, rice has less demand fluctuation than video-game consoles. Because demand for rice is more stable, the buyer's knowledge of future demand for rice is more precise. As a result, the experiment found, he exaggerates less. Therefore, the buyer's forecasts are more trustworthy if he's selling something like rice than if he's selling something like a new video-game console. Therefore, the manufacturer also trusts the buyer more when demand is more stable. All of that makes sense: if you're the buyer, and you know that demand will be between 100 and 150 units, there's no point in telling the manufacturer that the demand is 600 units. After all, it's not as if you prefer to hurt the manufacturer; you just want to be on the safe side and you exaggerate only as much as you need to exaggerate to protect yourself. The manufacturer knows this, too, so when she knows that historically the demand is fairly stable, she'll trust you more than when demand can swing more wildly. Also helping matters in this situation is that your interests aren't in complete conflict: although the manufacturer incurs higher costs than you do from an inflated forecast, the manufacturer *wants* there to be enough supply to meet customer demand, just as you, the buyer, do. Because of this partial common interest, the two of you have some incentive for mutual trust. Besides, what's the alternative? With no better source of forecast information, it makes sense for the manufacturer to go with the information given by the buyer.[18]

Are we saying that people will always be this benevolent in sharing information that they believe to be accurate? No—only that people don't generally hurt others for no gain. In this experiment, which carefully manipulated only one variable at a time, the lower demand variability gave less incentive to exaggerate and improved the ability to make trustworthy forecasts. But there could be other incentives at work, and in the real world there usually are. The two parties might be competitors, for example, or the store owner might be competing for products against other buyers. Conversely, the two parties might have a long and fruitful history together, so they have an incentive for maintaining a good reputation. Or there might be other incentives built into a formal contract. You need to take all the incentives into account when deciding how much to trust. And as this example shows, the incentives to be trustworthy don't have to be obvious—they might be subtle and nonmonetary, like the effect of demand variability.

There's another interesting finding from these experiments. It turns out that one factor affecting the level of trust was cost. Specifically, when both sides knew that the cost of building extra capacity was low—in other words, when the downside of trusting an exaggerated forecast was smaller—manufacturers trusted the buyers more.

The point of all this is that two forces are at work in people's decisions about when to trust and when to act trustworthy: selfish economic interests and the desire to do the right thing. We're neither saints nor are we completely selfish. Small changes in incentives and other changes in the context can make the same person behave in very different ways. Put another way, given the same level of good intentions, different levels of ability to forecast accurately will yield different levels of trustworthiness. And given the same level of ability, different financial incentives will also yield more or less trustworthy behavior.

Keep that in mind as you decide whom to trust and how much: it's not just about the person, it's also about the situation the person is in. If you're dealing with a reasonably trustworthy person, you can increase trustworthiness by creating the right environments and incentives. On the flip side, if you can't change the environment or incentives, consider the effect these factors have on how much you can trust the person. And when someone acts in a way that seems untrustworthy, don't succumb to the Sinister Attribution Error. Instead, consider that the blame may belong on the situation—something about the environment and the incentives—rather than on the person. The relationship isn't necessarily in trouble if the outcome you get isn't the one you expect.

Trust in Different Cultures

What happens when people around the world play the Trust Game? It turns out that whether the game is played in China, Japan, Korea, or the United States, people's patterns of trust and trustworthiness change very little.[19] In all four places, as studied by economists Rachel Croson and Nancy Buchan, we see patterns similar to those in the original Trust Game experiment. This may seem unbelievable, especially given what we know from Paul Zak's survey, in which people from different countries had such starkly different responses to the question of whether most people can be trusted. How can we reconcile Zak's findings (and our commonsense intuitions about behavior in different countries) with Croson and Buchan's findings in the Trust Game? What appears to be going on is that the Trust Game strips away culture—including social norms, social structures, legal institutions, and reputation effects. What's left behind, we can assume, is human nature.

When we say "human nature," though, we don't mean that all people everywhere act the same way in the same situation. As we've already seen, individual participants in the Trust Game vary greatly in their trustworthiness and their propensity to trust: some send $1, others send all $10; some return half of the pie, others keep everything. Also, studies have found systematic differences between men and women: although the two sexes were equally trusting in the Trust Game, female Trustees all over the world sent back a noticeably higher portion of the money entrusted to them (37.4 percent on average) than did men (who sent back an average of 28.6 percent).[20]

The Distrust Penalty

One recurring pattern in many experiments is that even though trust doesn't beget trustworthiness, Trustees do seem to penalize *distrust*. One series of experiments investigated this question directly. In these experiments, Investors only benefited when they sent all or most of their money.[21] As the Investor, you may think that entrusting the Trustee with $2 out of a possible $10 shows some level of trust, but the Trustee likely sees the low percentage as a sign of distrust—and responds in kind. If you think back to chapter 3, on reciprocity, particularly the differences in how Dictators and Reciprocators judged the generosity of the same exact split, you'll begin to understand why this happens.

The emerging field of neuroeconomics offers another clue: in Trust Game experiments by Paul Zak and his colleagues, the researchers found that male participants responded to signs of distrust with an upsurge in a hormone associated with aggression, a form of testosterone called DHT.[22] Because DHT is associated with aggression, and perceiving distrust causes spikes in DHT, it seems likely that in sending back less in response to low-trust investments, men were punishing perceived distrust. (Women, we should add, also don't like being distrusted, but don't seem to respond as viscerally.) What also happens is that Trustees and Investors might see the same act differently because their perspectives on the situation aren't the same. The Investor knows her own intentions, but the Trustee can only guess.

What's more, the Investor is more dependent on the Trustee than the other way around, simply because the Investor has more to lose. This imbalance makes the Investor vulnerable and causes some counterintuitive behavior: while the rational way to build trust is a little at a time, vulnerable Trustors sometimes take big leaps of faith. They do less checking into a Trustee's trustworthiness or ignore red flags.[23] In the Madoff debacle, for example, individual investors weren't the only victims—some of the investors were professional financial analysts at feeder funds such as the Fairfield Greenwich Group (FGG). At one time, almost half of FGG's vast assets under management—$6.9 billion out of

$14.1 billion total capital—were invested with Madoff's firm,[24] yielding hundreds of millions of dollars in investors' fees for FGG. That's a high level of dependence. And whereas FGG staffers had the ability to do due diligence on Madoff, as long as they continued to collect hefty fees they didn't particularly want to.

Untangling Trust, Trustworthiness, and Reciprocity

Trusting and trustworthy behavior have more than one cause, even in the simple Trust Game. For starters, trust is a belief in future human behavior, in the other side's trustworthiness. And because other people's future behavior is inherently uncertain, trust always has some risk associated with it. This is especially true in the basic Trust Game, in which you have no information about how trustworthy the Trustee is. So how do we know that an Investor's caution in the Trust Game says something about trust and not just about her risk aversion? One piece of evidence comes from experiments led by economist Iris Bohnet. The experiments, conducted in several countries, show that most people entrust more when the returned amount is left completely to chance than if the decision depends on a Trustee. The researchers chalk this odd behavior up to "betrayal aversion"—although trusting a person and leaving the outcome to chance are both risky, there's just something about the prospect of being let down by another person that seems worse than getting the short straw in a random draw.[25]

Trustworthiness, too, can be explained through a combination of factors: part of it is pure altruism, the kind of unconditional generosity we saw in some players of the Dictator Game, participants who shared their money even though they didn't have to. The other reason for trustworthiness is reciprocity.[26] You as the Trustee might raise or lower the total you send back depending on the level of trust (or distrust) the Trustor has shown you.

In the real world your prospective partners aren't anonymous; there are things you can do to help you decide how trustworthy someone is.

Showing Trustworthiness and
Deciding Whom to Trust

All of us want to know whom to trust—but just as important is getting others to trust us. Being trustworthy, it turns out, reduces the cost of doing business just as much as having a trusted partner does. Consider a study of 344 automaker-supplier relationships in three countries: the United States, Japan, and Korea.[27] The researchers found that automakers with the lowest perceived trustworthiness had transaction costs *five times higher* than those with the highest perceived trustworthiness, spending far more of their face-to-face time with suppliers on haggling and ironing out contract details. It pays to be thought trustworthy.

So how do you prove yourself trustworthy—and, in turn, decide whom you can trust? We've already dealt with one way—reputation. Reputation, like all the other good signs of trustworthiness, hinges on the idea of "show, don't tell." Anyone can don a suit and a smile, just as anyone can say they're great at their job, but not everyone has a track record for keeping such promises. To tell who's trustworthy, you have to look beyond cheap talk. Likewise, to show you're trustworthy, you have to put your money where your mouth is. This section shows you how to do both.

Incentives and Warranties

EarthGrains is one of the largest bakeries in the United States, selling breads under such names as Rainbo, IronKids, Roman Meal, Country Hearth, and several others; on its own EarthGrains-branded bread, the company plays up its earth-friendliness. "We care about the earth so much," the slogan says, "it's in our name."

How much trust does this message inspire? Not much when you consider that any company can put the word "earth" in its name. The message is an example of cheap talk. Somewhat more meaningful is the company's pledge to give $100,000 next year to the Nature Conservancy (though even that may not mean much if you consider the company's annual revenues—over $2 billion before its sale to the much larger Sara Lee in 2001).

If we pay attention, we hear cheap talk all around us—and are wise to mistrust it.

We don't trust a supervisor's performance-review praise (cheap talk) if it's not accompanied by a good raise. Even if the praise is genuine, it's reasonable for us to be skeptical and to wonder if the supervisor is just manipulating us with costless flattery. Likewise, we don't trust a company's claim that we, its customers, are its greatest asset (cheap talk) because its actions (keeping us on hold) contradict its words. If a company really wants to show that it values its customers, it would staff up its call center so we didn't have to be on hold for so long. Of course, staffing up a call center costs a lot more than endless replays of a recorded platitude, but this cost actually makes the words more believable and makes you, the customer, able to distinguish the genuinely well-intentioned company from its cheap-talking rival.

The resulting short wait time inspires trust in another way: customers can conclude that the company cares a lot about customer service or that the company's products are so good that most users don't need technical support—or both.

Costly Signals

Warranties and other types of financial incentives for trustworthiness create trust by having the trustees put their money where their mouths are. But in the process, they're actually providing real value to the trustors—the call center really provides better customer service, and the warranty really ensures a better product. More surprisingly, though, a person or company can spend time or money to show trustworthiness without actually providing direct value. The only thing these expenses buy is a way to distinguish yourself from your inferior rivals. Welcome to the strange world of costly signaling.

The classic example is higher education, as first shown by Michael Spence, one of two economists who won the 2001 Nobel Prize with

George Akerlof. Like Akerlof, Spence was interested in markets with asymmetric information. And while Akerlof looked at the problem of car sellers knowing more about the quality of their cars than buyers, Spence sought to explain how job applicants (who know more about their ability than those on the hiring end) can distinguish themselves from less able candidates. Certainly, a degree from a prestigious university in a field directly related to the job would do it—say, an MD from Johns Hopkins, or an engineering degree from MIT—but those degrees aren't merely costly because they really do ensure high levels of useful skills. People get degrees that aren't particularly useful in the business world—think philosophy or medieval studies—yet do help them in the job market. What Spence realized is that degrees signal a worker's productivity not because of what the student learned in school but because they mark the student as productive in the first place. A student who's not a productive worker, the argument goes, wouldn't spend the time and money pursuing the degree. The degree is a costly signal that increases an employer's trust in the applicant's ability.[28]

There are many other examples of costly signaling in business. Many economists have noted that real estate agents drive expensive cars, lawyers use lavish office space, and large corporations spend hundreds of thousands of dollars to buy a thirty-second ad during the Super Bowl. Such extravagances provide so little value to their customers—and, in fact, actually drive up prices—that all these businesses might as well be burning money. Yet from the businesses' point of view, these are worthwhile investments insofar as they succeed in convincing customers, suppliers, and even rivals of some version of "You can trust me." They build trust because if a company can afford to buy a $5 million ad (or a lavish office), the company has enough resources to back up their products and services.

We're not suggesting that these extravagant expenditures serve no other purpose besides signaling. Super Bowl ads, for example, aim to build buzz and increase customers' emotional attachment to the product. But whenever the cost far exceeds any visible benefit, it's a good bet that part of the reason is signaling.

It can seem a little crazy to spend money on such signaling; particularly if your competitors are doing it, too, you can find yourself in an arms race that's costly indeed. If Coke spends $5 million on a TV ad campaign, Pepsi had better do something equally spectacular—with the net result that both beverage makers are, in effect, back where they started. That's the big problem with costly signals. But if your competitors are incapable of making costly signals, or simply aren't thinking along those lines, you can set yourself apart. For example, although large corporations all have spiffy Web sites and a professionally designed "corporate identity," a surprising number of small businesses simply slap something together. They believe that a Web site or business card is just a way to convey facts and make it easy for people to reach them, so they don't see the value in spending money on anything beyond that. They ignore the messages conveyed between the lines, including such signals of trustworthiness as high professional standards and the intention to stick around for the long haul.[29]

Costly spending doesn't always signal trustworthiness—nor is it always meant to. In fact, conspicuous consumption is often a signal of another sort: status. It's easy to say, "I have a high-powered job and a lot of money," but much harder to buy the trappings of this level of status. Because people without the high-paying job (or rich benefactor) wouldn't be able to drive a Lamborghini, the expensive car serves as a reliable signal of status—what we commonly call a status symbol. Similarly, luxury goods often signal their quality in frivolous but costly ways. Think of the tiny diamonds studding an expensive handbag. These aren't particularly decorative (since a less flashy motif might look better) but they do let buyers infer that if the purse-maker is willing to spend so much on the baubles, the company is also spending money on quality workmanship. Prices, too, can be a signal of quality, since people assume (all other things being equal) that a high-priced product is of higher quality than a cheaper one. There's a good reason for this: the producer of a lower-quality product who charges a high price will go out of business if customers come to see the prices as unjustified. Therefore, it stands to reason that a company that can manage to sell products for a high price for some time must indeed be providing products that are worth the price. In general, signaling is a way to communicate without reliance on words alone.[30]

Understanding costly signaling helps makes sense of a lot of peculiar phenomena, from fraternity hazing and religious ritual to criminals' tattoos. Hazing rituals' wackiness and danger are what make them reliable signals of your trustworthiness to the group—the harsher the rituals, the less likely someone without a genuine commitment to the group (like a mole or free rider) will wish to pay the price.

We can say the same of the Japanese business practice of spending night after night in smoky restaurants and karaoke bars. This all seems strange to many American visitors, who usually prefer to get down to business, but in light of costly signaling, this time-wasting practice makes sense.[31] Many religious groups also extract costly signals of loyalty and trustworthiness from their members.

The classic example is ultra-Orthodox Jewish men, who call themselves *haredi* and wear black coats, pants, and hats in every season and any climate. To outsiders, the custom of wearing these clothes may seem like nothing more than a throwback to life in a different time and place, like the old-fashioned garb worn by the Amish. The *haredi* men's clothes don't even seem to have anything to do with Judaism in particular. But to Richard Sosis, a University of Connecticut anthropologist and expert in signaling theory, the clothes' strangeness serves an important purpose:

> By donning several layers of clothing and standing out in the midday sun, ultraorthodox Jewish men are signaling to others: "Hey! Look, I'm a haredi Jew. If you are also a member of this group, you can trust me because why else would I be dressed like this? No one would do this unless they believed in the teachings of ultraorthodox Judaism and were fully committed to its ideals and goals."[32]

It's hard to know how committed someone is to a religion's ideals—anyone can say they are—so seeing a costly behavior is one solution. It doesn't have to be strange clothes, of course. Attending lengthy religious services that are boring to outsiders is another way of signaling your good intentions.

What about just wearing a Jewish symbol around your neck, like a *chai* pendant or a star of David? That kind of signal might be costly in a society with significant anti-Semitism, but today many places with a large

Jewish population don't face that problem—and, in fact, being thought Jewish might be a badge of honor—so a small trinket won't prove costly. Anybody can wear a pendant, after all, whether or not you're committed to Jewish ethics. Hence the persistence of the coats and hats.

So what does this have to do with business? Since trust reduces transaction costs, we should expect tight-knit religious groups with costly signals to have higher levels of trust and lower transaction costs. And that's just what Sosis and his colleagues found. Sosis, along with several other social scientists, has noted the remarkably high level of trust among *haredi* diamond merchants, handing over millions of dollars' worth of gemstones on what appear to be nothing more than handshakes.

How do we know the cause of such trust is costly signaling, and not, say, reputation within a tight-knit community? Well, reputation probably plays some role—in the real world, the various factors affecting trust work in concert. But if costly signaling weren't part of the story, then we would expect that within the same community signalers and non-signalers would have the same level of trust. And that's a question that can be tested with an experiment, which is exactly what Sosis did with economist Bradley Ruffle. The researchers had residents of two Israeli kibbutzim play a Prisoner's Dilemma–type game, a game in which high levels of mutual trust would be rewarded but where each player also had an incentive to cheat. They ran the experiment on a religious kibbutz as well as a secular one, and found much higher levels of trust and cooperation in the religious kibbutz. What's more, on the religious kibbutz men trusted and cooperated more than women did. The researchers concluded that this was because only men attended religious services—thus engaging in more costly signaling than women.[33]

Costly signaling happens in groups that aren't devoted to noble ideals as well. The sociologist Diego Gambetta argues that costly signaling explains why criminals are likely to be covered in tattoos: by making it hard for the tattoo-wearer to get a legitimate job, an outrageous tattoo (which would be too costly to a noncriminal) shows that the criminal is the bad guy he claims to be.[34] The economist Peter Leeson makes a similar argument about signaling in the age of pirate ships. Only real pirates routinely dared to hoist a Jolly Roger, the skull-and-crossbones flag meant to intimidate nearby ships into immediate surrender. Because piracy was illegal, authorities would shoot at ships carrying the pirate flag and could prosecute their sailors as pirates, subject to the maximum sentence of being hanged. But, flag or no flag, pirates were subject to the hangman's noose anyway, so using the Jolly Roger was cheaper for them than it was for privateers or other nonpirate ships. That's why the flag proved that you're an honest-to-goodness pirate.[35]

That's all interesting, but what does it really prove? After all, didn't Madoff also engage in costly signaling by giving millions of dollars to charitable causes and serving on the boards of several nonprofits? Indeed he did, and by focusing his largesse on Jewish causes, such as Yeshiva University and the United Jewish Appeal, he instilled trust within the Jewish community in particular. Although he was certainly not ultra-Orthodox like the diamond merchants, he did signal a commitment to at least secular Jewish values—and, indeed, a disproportionate number of his victims were Jewish, including Elie Wiesel, Steven Spielberg, and Hadassah.[36] So Madoff instilled trust in at least three ways—by exploiting his reputation, as we've said, by drawing attention to himself as a member of a particular ethnic group, and by engaging in costly signaling. So why were all these methods ultimately unreliable signs of his trustworthiness? The answer is in the balance of costs to benefits: what appears as a high cost (the millions he's donating and the hours he's giving) is small relative to his payoff; for Madoff, the generosity toward charities was apparently just another cost of doing business. To his victims it signaled trustworthiness, but in the wisdom of hindsight we can say that it wasn't a reliable signal. Costly signaling, like reputation and group membership, can be exploited when the stakes are high enough.

One lesson we can take away from costly signaling theory, though, is that your spending in the form of time or money does convey information about your intentions. For example, many people join trade associations or religious congregations to improve their professional networks. Most pay their modest dues and do little else—and gain little beyond the information in the member newsletter. More active members, who volunteer hours of their time for the benefit of the group, gain much more; they not only build relationships in the course of volunteering, but they also signal their trustworthiness as committed members of the profession.

Nothing Lasts Forever

As people respond to changing incentives, their behavior changes accordingly. The toy factory owner's best friend, for example, normally had his friend's interests in mind, but when the incentives changed, so did his intentions and behavior. Yet people sometimes act as if the rule were "once trusted, always trusted." The Mattel CEO's public statement of his bafflement on learning that Mattel's longtime manufacturer had been coating toys in lead paint is a case in point. Of course, a betrayal of trust is disappointing, and a betrayal of longtime trust can be devastating. But the possibility always lurks in the background. As times change, the temptation to be untrustworthy can change, too. That's why, for example, government clearance doesn't last forever—if you're given a high level of clearance, every few years the federal government reinvestigates to see if that clearance merits renewal. So keep in mind that even after you've decided someone is worthy of your trust, a little vigilance might still be necessary.

In this chapter, you saw something of human attitudes toward trust and learned some ways to establish trust and trustworthiness. You saw that, even with high levels of trust, you'll usually have to set up systems of rules, including rewards and penalties, to keep incentives from skewing trust. Whatever system you set up, many will try to game it, often subverting the system's actual intent. In the next chapter, we show some of the ways people have been known to game the system—and offer advice for avoiding similar pitfalls as you make up the rules for your own systems.

7

· · · · · · · · · · · ·

Playing to the Rules of the Game

Some years ago, a thirty-five-year-old civil engineer named David Phillips received a highly anticipated package: a box containing stacks and stacks of certificates for airline miles. Months earlier, Phillips had entered a special promotion, offered by Healthy Choice, to redeem product UPC labels in exchange for frequent-flyer miles. And after a marathon shopping spree and a frenzied bout of peeling off thousands of labels, Phillips earned more than 1.25 million miles—a number that's over five times the distance to the moon.

Though the tale reads like fiction (and, in fact, it inspired a plot point in the Adam Sandler movie *Punch-Drunk Love*), it's a true story, reported in the likes of the *Wall Street Journal* and the *Times* of London.[1] Here's what happened.

In early May of 1999, David Phillips, a married father of two, spotted the promotion on a frozen-dinner package. The promotion offered 500 miles for every ten Healthy Choice bar-code labels submitted by the end of the year. Carefully reading the rules, Phillips noticed an opportunity to double that reward: the company would grant 1,000 miles per ten labels if he sent them in by May 31. It's not clear why ConAgra, the packaged-food giant behind the Healthy Choice brand, offered this early-bird special. Perhaps they hoped to build up early excitement among consumers, or maybe they simply wanted to break up the torrent of entries into two waves. Whatever the company's intent, for Phillips the early deadline's double payoff had an unexpected effect: it put him in a buying frenzy. He began by buying household staples like soup and cereal. But soon enough, he struck pay dirt: a discount chain store called Grocery Outlet was selling Healthy Choice pudding cups for only 25 cents a piece. Each individual cup had a UPC label, and each would count toward the promotion. For every $2.50 he spent on pudding cups, he would earn 1,000 miles. It doesn't take an engineer to see this as an excellent exchange rate. Since 25,000 miles can buy a domestic ticket (and 50,000 miles buys a ticket overseas), those pudding cups translated into round-trip flights to most places in the world for just $125—or anywhere in the United States for half of that.

At that rate, it's well worth it to drive out of your way to stock up on pudding, even if that requires enlisting the help of your mother-in-law. And that's exactly what Phillips did, hitting every Grocery Outlet between his home in Davis, California, and Fresno, some two hundred miles away. The two cleared out the outlets' pudding shelves and, over several trips, filled their van with a total of 12,500 pudding cups. For these alone, he would earn 1,250,000 miles. The whole project cost $3,140 and between forty and eighty hours of work.

Though Healthy Choice ended up with plenty of publicity through Phillips's many media appearances, it's safe to say the labels-for-miles promotion didn't go quite as planned. The marketers clearly underestimated this shopper's zeal. Nor, apparently, had they taken into account the possibility of their products being available at cut-rate prices. There was nothing in the rules to disqualify the Grocery Outlet pudding cups or put a cap on the number of labels redeemed. Phillips had followed the rules to the letter, even if he may have ignored their spirit and intent. Phillips, whose ordinary job responsibilities included ensuring his employer's compliance with its environmental permits, was good at reading the fine print.

His gamesmanship didn't end there. With time running out before the May 31 deadline, he needed more hands to peel off the pudding labels than his own family had. So he turned to the Salvation Army, donating pudding if they'd remove the labels and return them to him.

This charitable donation earned Phillips a tax write-off, reducing his out-of-pocket costs to $2,325.

The man clearly understood the system. He first calculated the costs and benefits of participating—and later, in case of a dispute, he carefully photocopied his labels and videotaped all his Healthy Choice purchases. (This proved useful after the company initially claimed that they never received his entry.) Not everyone is quite as clever or methodical as Phillips, but there's a little bit of him in all of us. Given enough incentive, we will look for loopholes, subverting the intent of a rule for personal gain—if not for cold profit, then for the sheer fun of gaming the system.

This happens wherever rules exist, whether they be written or tacit, tax codes or company policies. Consider these examples:

• Companies wishing to save money on customer service use automated-response phone systems that answer frequently asked questions or route users to the right department. But customers hate listening to recorded messages and navigating a labyrinthine phone menu, so they learn how to bypass the different systems (press 3 and say "agent," or press 0# at each prompt, and so on) and publish these shortcuts on cheat sheets like DialAHuman.com and GetHuman.com.

• Pay-for-performance systems aim to reward quality: health insurers sometimes track doctors by patient outcomes, and the No Child Left Behind Act rewards schools for having students meet state standards. So to inflate their scores, schools push bad students to drop out while doctors turn away the sickest patients.[2]

• Congress, hoping to phase out the use of fossil fuels, gives a tax credit for mixing "alternative fuel," such as ethanol and other biofuels, into conventional fuel. Conventional paper companies had for decades been using "black liquor," a waste product of turning wood into pulp, to run their mills. Now, by mixing the black liquor in with conventional fuel, these companies get tens of millions of dollars in tax credits, while companies making recycled paper (and therefore not producing black liquor) don't qualify.[3]

As we'll see in this chapter, even small changes in the rules can create big opportunities for people to "game the system," following the rules but not creating the effects that the rule designers intended. In fact, sometimes the results of gaming create effects that are the *opposite* of what the rules were intended to do.

There's no end to the many ways rules can be gamed, so in this chapter we focus on just one type of rule that's common in many business (and nonbusiness) situations: what we call timing rules, or rules having to do with when something happens. Any kind of deadline or due date is a timing rule, as are start times or requirements stipulating minimum or maximum times for eligibility in a program.

For a sense of what we're talking about, consider an antipollution program created in Arizona in July 2000. The program, meant to give motorists an enticing tax credit for adding an alternative-fuel tank to their gas-guzzlers, inadvertently attracted many more applicants than planned. For one thing, the program failed to specify that the credit only applied to the purchase of a new car; moreover, the program didn't require motorists to actually use the second tank. As a result, the many people who already owned SUVs could spend less than $7,000 on a second tank to get $18,000 back in tax credits, all in a lump sum, without actually helping clear the state's smog. When, in September of that year, Arizona's governor saw the expected fiscal impact to the state—about $600 million, or 10 percent of the state's annual budget—she changed the rules, spreading the tax rebates out over five years. But here's the timing problem: these new rules wouldn't take effect for two weeks, so people now rushed to exploit the loophole before it closed. In the first nine days of October, the number of applications for the program jumped to 3,920—more than a tenfold rise from the same period in September.[4]

The Nick of Time

You've heard of this time and time again: after days, weeks, or even months of negotiations, unions and management narrowly avert a strike by reaching an agreement just before the deadline. Such eleventh-hour agreements happen in other types of negotiations as well. Lawyers, for example, often reach a settlement and avoid a costly trial even after a jury selection. In the Major League Baseball first-year player draft, which currently has a hard deadline for teams to sign each of their draft picks to a contract, most deals don't close until the day before the deadline, with a flurry happening in the final minutes before 12:01 a.m.[5]

Why do these things happen? Does it simply take a certain amount of time to reach an agreement, in which case a later deadline would enable an agreement to be reached before the eleventh hour, or does the mere presence of a deadline actually affect bargaining behavior?

For starters, we know that a deadline alone is not enough—if a deadline has no consequences, it often comes and goes with no agreement reached. You need only look at the history of failed peace talks to see that. But when the deadline has teeth—when negotiators know that not reaching agreement before the deadline will lead to a strike, or a legal trial, or the permanent loss of a deal—negotiations tend to drag on but suddenly end just before the deadline. Why is that?

To answer this question, economists Al Roth, Keith Murnighan, and Francoise Schoumaker analyzed several laboratory experiments that mimicked actual negotiations.[6] In these experiments, you and another player are negotiating over how to divide between yourselves 100 tickets for a kind of raffle, one in which each ticket represents a 1 percent chance of winning a large prize (of, say, $20). For example, having 60 tickets gives you a 60 percent chance of winning the large prize. The player who doesn't win the large prize automatically gets a smaller prize. But you have a chance of winning the large prize only if you and the other player can reach agreement about how to split the tickets. If you can't reach agreement, you both get the smaller prize. As a result of these rules, both players have incentives to cooperate (by reaching an agreement) and to compete (by fighting for the larger piece of the pie).

Each experiment tested multiple conditions, varying factors such as how much the two prizes are worth to each player and how much each player knows. For example, in one condition, the prizes are $36 and $4, while in another condition they are $20 and $5. In one condition, you know the size of your opponent's prize as well as your own, while in another you know only the value of your own prize; in one condition, you both know that *you* know your opponent's prize, and in another only you do. As you might expect, these variations affect the outcomes of the negotiations. For example, if you both know only the value of your own prize, you almost always split the tickets evenly, whereas if both parties know each other's prize value, the splits tend to take this additional information into consideration when deciding how to split the tickets. Although the experiments' tweaks and twists affected the substance of the actual agreements (that is, how to split the lottery tickets), one thing stayed constant across all experiments and conditions: the deadline effect. The researchers gave the participants a fixed amount of time to reach an agreement, such as 12 minutes. It was certainly possible to reach an agreement in that time—in fact, some players reached agreements just 1 or 2 minutes into the session. However, many agreements weren't reached until (quite literally) the last minute. For example, more than 30 percent of the agreements were reached in the last 30 seconds of each session. Whether the negotiation was to last at most 9 minutes or 12 minutes, and whether the fair split was obvious or more complicated, a good number of negotiating pairs reached agreement just before the deadline.[7]

Just shifting or redefining the deadline doesn't get rid of the effect, as we can see in Major League Baseball, where teams pick rookie players in a June draft, thus earning exclusive negotiating rights to those picks. Until 2007, teams had until one week before the next year's draft to sign the current year's draft picks. The economics and politics of the game are such that by failing to sign a star player, the team usually had more to lose than the player did. As a result, under these older rules, highly valued picks held out until close to June before signing. To prevent such season-long holdouts, Major League Baseball moved up the deadline, to mid-August, or just a couple of months after the draft. But this new deadline didn't give the teams the upper hand. The first year under the new deadline, players did, of course, sign up earlier than they would have under a later deadline, but a deadline is a deadline, and some players still waited until the eleventh hour. What's more, the second year after the deadline change, even more players held out until the deadline: they saw that those who'd waited last year had ended up with the best deals. In the 2009 draft, when super-agent Scott Boras negotiated a contract for pitcher Stephen Strasburg, the four-year $15.1 million deal was the biggest ever for a rookie—and team and player signed it 77 seconds before the deadline.[8]

Scott Boras is great at exploiting the many rules in Major League Baseball to get top dollar for his clients, incurring the wrath of team owners and fans alike. Even as star players flock to him, baseball fans blame him for ruining the sport because his knack for getting clients fantastic sums means that the most promising players end up on the teams with the most money to spend. Losing teams, who get first pick of players in the draft, end up passing over the top prospects because the teams likely won't be able to afford them when the time comes to sign. Instead, weaker teams use their first picks on players who are good and affordable (or "signable," in baseball lingo) and not the most sought after and beyond their budget. Yet fans want drafting based on ability, not signability. However you feel about Boras's influence on the sport—some call him a moneygrubbing shark and a bloodsucking Antichrist—he's only playing to the rules of the game, and if it weren't Boras it would be somebody else making the most of the system.

Part of the problem, of course, is that some teams have more money than others. But in theory, new draft rules could level that playing field. For example, most team owners would love a system of salary caps, which would benefit all but the richest teams. Although salary caps would also be popular with fans bemoaning the current system, players don't want to limit how much they can earn. The baseball players' union has a lot of clout, so such rule changes tend not to pass.

But some rules, including deadlines, have unintended consequences even when rule makers do have power to implement them—something Marina saw when booking a Princess cruise for her extended family. Many people book cruises a year or more in advance, so by the time Marina put down her deposit, many of the best cabins, including all those with balconies, were taken. Final payment is due sixty days prior to sailing, and naturally most people don't want to pay far before they have to—that's to be expected. But people don't want to miss the deadline, either: if you don't make your final payment you lose your reservation and your deposit. So a few days before the deadline, Marina called her travel agent with credit card in hand—and was surprised that the agent didn't want to take her money just yet. "I always tell my clients to wait until the day of the deadline," said the agent, who'd been specializing in cruises for twenty years. She explained that as the final-payment deadline approaches, some people who booked early and got a good cabin change their minds and forfeit their deposits; when this happens, cabins open up. So by waiting until the deadline, you up your chances of snagging one of these cabins. Of course, if other agents are giving their clients the same advice (or if the passengers figure it out themselves), then many people are competing for those few last-minute cancellations. The upshot of all this jockeying is that the cruise lines get their deposits quite late in the game from many passengers—but because most of the best cabins simply aren't available, very few passengers who wait until the last minute actually manage to get them. (In the end, Marina was not able to upgrade any of her group's cabins despite waiting until the last day to make her final payment.)

When you design a business process that seems to call for a deadline, be careful because the deadline is sure to affect people's behavior—and not always in ways that you want. The U.S. tax system has a classic example. Everyone knows you should generally postpone income and accelerate deductions, since doing so will obviously delay your tax burden. But the combination of progressive taxes (that is, higher tax rates for higher earnings brackets) and timing rules (the fact that income is taxed in the year in which it's received) sometimes creates an incentive to do the opposite. For example, if you expect to earn more next year, putting you in a higher tax bracket, you'll want to delay your business purchases, and perhaps even give your suppliers a price break for paying you now rather than next year.

All this seems harmless. But now consider a similar incentive in the business world. Suppose you're managing salespeople. To get them to make lots of sales you institute a system of nonlinear bonuses: the more units someone sells in a given quarter, the higher the rep's commission rate. For example, sales up to $10,000 earn you no commission, sales between $10,000 and $20,000 earn you 3 percent of that amount, sales between $20,000 and $30,000 earn you 4 percent of this bracket, and so on. Lots of sales-compensation systems work this way. But, as economist Ian Larkin discovered, this kind of system invites gaming *at the company's expense*.[9] Larkin looked at data from a large enterprise-software company that used this kind of sales compensation scheme, and through some clever statistical forensics he found that, not surprisingly, salespeople were manipulating when sales would register in much the way tax filers manipulate the timing of their income and expenses. Like the tax filers, they were doing nothing illegal. Yet they were costing their employer money, Larkin concluded. The reason is that salespeople at this company had some discretion to offer customers a discount; by comparing deals that were gamed through timing with similar deals that weren't, Larkin found that gaming led to excess discounts that cost the company 6 to 8 percent of revenue. Put another way, by offering discounts only to sway *when* customers placed their orders, not whether they placed them, the reps who gamed the system were using the company's money to increase their own commissions.

When Timing Is Everything

Here's another timing rule with economic consequences. If you're a regular bidder on eBay, you've probably noticed that many of the bids come close to the end of an auction. You may have even placed some of these last-minute bids yourself. It turns out that more than half of eBay auctions receive bids in the last ten minutes of the auction—and more than 10 percent receive bids in the last ten seconds. Although many buyers keep bidding up the item throughout the auction, savvy bidders swoop in just before the auction's about to end and snag the item when there's no time left to be outbid.

Such "bid sniping" doesn't even require sitting in front of your computer close to midnight—or whenever the auction is set to end. Sniping sites like AuctionSniper, BidNapper, and Cniper.com (to name just a few) will do it for you, and with a precision hard to achieve by hand. Many experienced eBay bidders don't even bother to bid earlier in the auction.

Yet sniping—whether manual or automated—isn't an inevitable part of Internet auctions. Amazon, which also runs auctions, has very little last-minute bidding, with only 11 percent of its auctions getting bids in the last ten minutes before their scheduled endings—only about a fifth of eBay's percentage.

What explains this difference? The answer, it turns out, is a rule about how an auction is to end. On eBay, each auction has a "hard close," a hard-and-fast ending time that's clearly publicized in advance. But Amazon has an extension rule, designed to give bidders a chance to respond to the competition. Amazon's rule is the electronic equivalent of the live auctioneer's call of "Going, Going . . . Gone." So even though Amazon posts a scheduled ending time for each auction, a bid close to that ending time extends the auction by ten minutes, enough time for counterbids. This rule is small only in the sense that it takes only a few words to express; a buyer or seller reading a list of rules on an auction site might easily gloss over it. Nonetheless, as people learn the rule and its implications, it ends up having important effects on bidding behavior and, ultimately, on sale prices.

How does the extension rule reduce sniping? (After all, you might expect that a firm deadline would encourage *early* bidding, as bidders make sure they don't miss the deadline.) And how does experience with each type of auction affect bidding behavior?

No one has explored these questions more than Al Roth. Working with Dan Ariely and Axel Ockenfels, Roth ran lab experiments with different auction stopping rules. Although it might be possible to draw some inferences from actual eBay and Amazon data, these inferences would be inconclusive: there are many differences between the sites besides the ending rule. For tighter controls, you need the lab.[10]

The researchers created a simplified version of eBay and Amazon in their lab. In one condition, the last round simulated the situation (on eBay) where you have only ten seconds left to submit one more bid. In the second condition, the auction is extended whenever there is a bid, just like on Amazon.

To make the experiment even more like the two auction sites, the researchers did something else. The Internet isn't always reliable, so submitting an eBay bid in the last ten seconds creates a chance that the bid won't go through; to simulate this reality, the researchers randomly chose 20 percent of these last-minute bids to fail.

These experiments replicated real-world bidding phenomena beautifully. First, they found that participants bid more in the last round under the eBay-style ending rule than under the Amazon ending rule, for reasons we'll get to in a minute. They also found that under the eBay ending rule, as participants gained experience, they were more likely to bid in the last round. Without experience, 40 percent of them bid in the last round—but after repeated play 80 percent did so. And completely the opposite happened on the Amazon-like site: the percentage of participants bidding in the last round *dropped* from 40 percent to less than 10 percent after they'd gotten the hang of that auction system.

The researchers also identified the main reason behind this remarkable difference. Even though eBay lets you hide your maximum bid, the site automatically bidding on your behalf up to this maximum, many users don't take advantage of this feature. Instead, they make incremental bids throughout the auction. Incremental bidding leaves room for more sophisticated bidders to bid-snipe, thus preventing the incremental bidders from responding with a last-minute bid. Because the incremental bidders never get a chance to put in their maximum bid, the winning bids from snipers aren't as high as they would otherwise have to be. As a result, the Amazon-style ending rule resulted in slightly higher revenue for the sellers, about 3 percent higher. Revenue-wise, this difference is slight, almost inconsequential—but in terms of profits it can be huge: when you're selling products with 6 percent margins, a revenue boost of 3 percent raises your profit by 50 percent.

If eBay and its sellers are leaving so much money on the table, why don't they curtail sniping? It might seem that there's a simple technological fix, like the use of CAPTCHA to keep out automated snipers. But while that would make it less easy to make last-second bids, it would not eliminate the overall incentive for late bidding: as long as there's a hard stop to the auction, many people will continue to bid late in the game, perhaps in the last minutes rather than the last ten seconds, and thus keep other would-be buyers from bidding their maximum value.

So why doesn't eBay switch to an Amazon-like ending rule? We can only guess that a rule change like that would be too disruptive for a site with millions of auctions in play at any time, and too costly for IT.[11] Some rule changes are so hard to implement that it's best to think through the rules before you implement them in the first place.

Of course, not all rules are hard to change; in fact, because small, seemingly insignificant changes to the rules can have a great impact, it often pays to tweak rules even when they seem to be working. They could work better still. Google and Yahoo!, which both use automated keyword auctions to sell billions of dollars in sponsored search results each year, run experiments to discover which sets of rules can make the auctions even more lucrative.[12]

Getting People to Follow the MAP

Now let's look at how timing rules played a key role in one of Kay-Yut's biggest successes at HP.

When you're in the market for a specific item—whether it's a particular model of computer, shoe, or sauté pan—competition among retailers is great. It promises to give you the lowest possible price for whatever it is you want to buy. If you comparison-shop online, most of the information is out there and your search costs are low. But very often, there's no real bargain to be had, as all the retailers sell the item at more or less the same price. That's because, unlike consumers, manufacturers actually don't like price competition among their retailers: price wars among retailers drive prices down to their cost. In fact, for big players and Internet merchants (who may be more interested in market share than immediate profits), prices can fall even below cost. If the retailers still pay the manufacturer its cost, you might think the manufacturer won't care, but it does care because if retailers see that manufacturer's products as unprofitable for them to sell, they won't want to carry them—and that's obviously something the manufacturer wants to avoid. To prevent that fate, the manufacturer might like to set a minimum price for all retailers to use, but there's one hitch: overt price-fixing (in this case "vertical price-fixing") is against the law.

The common workaround in many industries is for a manufacturer to set a Minimum Advertised Price (MAP): to be able to buy products from the manufacturer, the retailer agrees not to advertise the manufacturer's products below a certain minimum price. To sweeten the deal, the manufacturer typically throws in some advertising dollars, which the retailer can use to promote that manufacturer's products. In the United States, MAP agreements are legal because they don't mandate the actual price, only the advertised price.[13]

At least in theory, a retailer can turn down a MAP agreement. In practice, though, it can't afford to: not only would the renegade retailer lose promotional funding that its rivals are getting, but it would risk straining relations with the manufacturer.[14]

Still, MAP programs pose a problem for the manufacturer. Although retailers don't want their competitors lowering prices, each one would like the freedom to do so itself. In a way, MAP actually makes it even more attractive to lower prices because (if you get away with it) you can do it without starting a price war; if your competitors are sticking with MAP, you can violate it without worrying that your competitors will undercut you. So the incentives for cheating under MAP are high. Manufacturers, therefore, have to find ways to punish cheaters—to make cheating so costly that retailers won't want to do it.

Like so many other companies, HP has had penalties for MAP violations for years. But the penalties weren't working very well. The threatened penalty for violating a MAP agreement on, say, an HP printer was that HP wouldn't sell that printer to the violator again. This is a severe penalty and should be a real deterrent, but it also forces HP to punish itself: by depriving a big retailer of a top-selling printer, HP was shooting itself in the foot. That much is clear—but what's a better alternative? That was the challenge posed to Kay-Yut in 2000.

Working with Gary Charness, Kay-Yut tested several penalty systems.[15] Participants in the experiments role-played the different types of retailers HP was dealing with, including mass merchants and Internet retailers; these retailers differed in their goals, but regardless of their business model all of them had to order products, choose advertising budgets, and set prices for their end customers.

The experiments simulated the real world in another way, too: some products got phased out and were replaced with newer models, and retailers got notice of a phaseout several periods of play in advance.

In one set of rules, violating a MAP agreement for a product would cost the retailer its future advertising funds for that product. For example, a retailer who in one period of the game tried to grab market share by advertising a printer below the MAP level would lose that printer's ad funds for the next four periods.

Although these penalties are less severe than pulling a product completely, the system worked well overall. But experiments also revealed a serious shortcoming. Retailers quickly wised up to the fact that the closer they got to the end of a product's life cycle, the lower their penalty for a MAP violation would be. As a result, as a product was being phased out retailers made more and more MAP violations on it. For example, if the average number of MAP violations three periods before the end of a product life cycle was 8, the average would rise to 14 in the next period, and to 18 the period after that. In the final period—when no more ad dollars were at stake—violations were up to an average of 24, or three times the number just three periods earlier.

Nobody involved in designing this penalty system foresaw this effect—not HP's business managers, and not Gary and Kay-Yut. But the participants in the experiment, who were playing for money and were motivated to earn as much as the system allowed, did see this opportunity to game the system. It was only thanks to these experiments that the flaw with the forward-looking penalty became obvious. How would you fix it, though?

Unfortunately, getting rid of the end of a product life cycle is not an option—short life cycles are a reality of the high-tech industry. So Gary and Kay-Yut solved the problem a different way: by imposing a two-sided penalty. The first part of the penalty was retroactive, punishing retailers based on the shipment quantity *before* the MAP violation. The more the retailer ordered before the MAP violation, the harsher the penalty. The second part of the penalty was future-looking: the new policy penalized MAP violators in proportion to their sales immediately *after* the violation. That's because a MAP violation (which is a price cut) stimulates sales, so retailers tempted to generate sales through MAP violations will think twice, knowing that higher sales following a MAP violation will lead to stiffer penalties. Subsequent lab tests confirmed that this double-whammy of a penalty system reduced the rate of violations near the end of a product life cycle. It's this system that made its way into the standard contract between HP and U.S. retailers like Walmart and Best Buy, and remains part of it years later.

There's a general lesson from this particular experiment: timing issues are more important than you might expect. After all, the absolute size of the penalties didn't change, only the period in which the penalties applied. More generally, even a seemingly small change to the rules can have a big impact on people's behavior.

Despite knowing this, experienced game designers sometimes leave rules open to exploitation, as Kay-Yut learned the hard way. In 2001, he and his colleagues conducted a series of experiments to study incentives associated with market-development funds, or money that manufacturers give retailers for joint-promotion campaigns. In one experiment, these funds were 3 percent of how much retailers buy from the manufacturer. Participants played the role of retailers who order inventory from the manufacturer, receive market-development funds, and try to run a profitable business. As usual, the lab paid them according to how much money their retail business made. Of course, the researchers knew that people's behavior tends to change toward the end of a game; for example, in this game, if people know that the game will soon end, they have an incentive to ramp down their ordering so they're not left with unsold inventory. To reduce this endgame effect, Kay-Yut and his colleagues told participants that in the last period they'd be allowed to return any unsold inventory for a full refund.

So what's the problem? Consider what one clever player did: in the second-to-last period, this student ordered as much inventory as the software allowed—9,999 units. That's because he'd figured out a way to exploit the rules: whatever he ordered in the second-to-last period, he'd earn 3 percent of that minus a small inventory-carrying cost. (If he'd ordered that much any time before the second-to-last period, the inventory costs would have wiped out his profits.)

In hindsight, the loophole looks obvious. How could experienced researchers have forgotten about the 3 percent at the heart of the experiment—and not foreseen the incentive for gaming that it would provide during one period in the game? Yet out of fifteen sessions of experiments, involving more than one hundred participants, only this one person saw the trick—and made off with almost $1,000 for playing a three-hour game.

Ideally, we'd all be testing every important policy change in the lab rather than disrupting actual business operations by changing rules on the fly, but even HP doesn't test everything.

In lieu of a real experiment, you might try a thought experiment: put yourself in the shoes of the people you're dealing with, whether they be your suppliers, your resellers, or your employees, and try finding ways to exploit the system you're setting up for them, whether it's a supplier agreement, an employment contract, or a sales compensation scheme.

We've talked about designing rules and incentives to get the behavior we'd like. In the next chapter, you'll see this approach in use as we turn to ways of designing rules and incentives to solicit honest information for predicting the future.

8

. . . .

Predicting the Unpredictable

The Eighty-first Academy Awards ceremony, held on February 22, 2009, is now a hazy memory. Two days before the event, though, hundreds of thousands of Americans were engrossed in a pre-Oscar pastime: predicting the winners.

The message boards on Oscar.com were buzzing, and much of the debate swirled around the Best Actress category. The leading contenders were Meryl Streep in *Doubt* and Kate Winslet in *The Reader*. With little to go on besides subjective judgments of performance, all kinds of extra facts and opinions came in. "This is Kate's year," one moviegoer pronounced. Besides, this poster continued, "she already won a Golden Globe for this role, and she's due with five or six nominations, whereas Meryl already has two Oscars." Another poster gave a reason for the opposite conclusion: "From what I've read, Kate Winslet was much better in *Revolutionary Road* than *The Reader* so that could play a factor." And a few posters acknowledged the possibility that the award could go to a different actress altogether.

We can spend all day reading the chatter on message boards and listening to industry insiders—or we can take a quick look at Hollywood Stock Exchange (HSX.com), a trading market in which anyone can bet on Oscar outcomes, box office results, and the future values of individual actors and directors. It's a kind of NASDAQ for Tinseltown, with trading in Hollywood dollars (H$). In effect, HSX collapses all the information and noise into just a few neat numbers. At one point, shares of "Kate Winslet—*The Reader*" were trading at H$15.79, whereas you could buy "Meryl Streep—*Doubt*" for H$5.78 per share. Of the five nominees, Anne Hathaway was clearly the dark horse in this contest: shares of her role in *Rachel Getting Married* were selling for a mere H$1.10.

Nobody knew for certain that Kate Winslet would end up winning, but these prices served as an indicator of her prospects. In fact, each share price could be read as the likelihood of each outcome. There's no bookie setting the odds—the market does it automatically. And it seems to do it remarkably well. That year, HSX correctly predicted the winners of seven out of the eight top categories[1]—better than most movie critics—with similar prediction rates in prior years.

It's not just Oscar winners; users bet on the box office success of movies still in the making, for example. And their accuracy is striking. In one study by Harvard Business School professor Anita Elberse, the correlation between HSX prices and actual box-office receipts was .94[2]—a stunning degree of predictive accuracy for an industry that's notoriously unpredictable. Screenwriter William Goldman, whose screenplays included many hits (including *Butch Cassidy and the Sundance Kid* and *All the President's Men*) and relative disappointments (*The Hot Rock* and *Chaplin*) famously wrote in his Hollywood memoir that "nobody knows anything." No director, no studio head, no industry analyst knows what movie will make money, as any of a number of big-budget bombs shows. Goldman overreached a bit, though, when he wrote that "nobody, *nobody*—not now, not ever—knows the least goddamn thing about what is or isn't going to work at the box office."[3] The fact is that everybody, including Hollywood outsiders, knows a little something.[4] The problem HSX tries to solve is to pool together those little bits of information into a single prediction.

No money changes hands on the Hollywood Stock Exchange— users get several million Hollywood dollars for free when they sign up, and this money is worthless outside the game. Nonetheless, HSX is a for-profit operation. Owned by Cantor Fitzgerald, the Wall Street firm unfortunately known for its heavy death toll from the 9/11 attacks, HSX sells data to filmmakers, financiers, and others in the movie business.

Why would they want to buy data from HSX? Oscar night is just a onetime event, with those shares de-listed the next day. But the HSX operates continuously, with thousands of users trading shares of individual performers, directors, and movies in the making. With millions of dollars going into a film, Hollywood decision makers need to know how to spend it. After a few years out of the limelight, is Julia Roberts still worth $10 million a picture, or is her box office value falling? By tapping into the collective wisdom of the crowd through HSX, Hollywood decision makers can answer questions like this and offer clues to an otherwise unpredictable future.

HSX is a prediction market, and prediction markets, about which we'll have much more to say in this chapter, are a solution to one of the most important problems in business: predicting the future, or what most business people call forecasting. After all, it's not only Hollywood executives who want to find out what the future holds. In just about any industry, managers want to know how many widgets their division will sell next quarter or how much raw materials will cost a year from now. Accurate forecasts would help them budget perfectly, decide how many staffers to hire (or lay off), and how much inventory to order. But accurate forecasts are hard to come by, so managers settle for what they can get; unfortunately, inaccurate forecasts lead to either waste or unfulfilled demand. In the computer industry, for example, overly optimistic sales forecasts prompt companies to manufacture more product than they can sell before the product becomes obsolete. Erring on the side of caution, on the other hand, isn't safe either: that leads not only to temporary backorders, but also to customers taking their business elsewhere. These errors are costly even when demand forecasts aren't dead wrong.

Take the story of the Wii. Managers at Nintendo knew the long-awaited game console would be a big hit, but they didn't know just how big a hit until they launched the product in November 2006. The huge and drawn-out shortage left several million eager fans frustrated; these would-be buyers either delayed their purchase or, worse, impatiently opted for Sony's PlayStation or Microsoft's Xbox. As Nintendo left revenue and market share on the table, some of its loss became its rivals' gain. The fact that the Wii shortage continued for over a year—seemingly enough time for Nintendo to ramp up production—generated lots of suspicion. Was Nintendo creating an artificial scarcity to build up hype around the product? That line of thought exemplifies the Sinister Attribution Error, in this case customers and industry analysts blaming the manufacturer's marketing intentions rather than its inability to forecast demand or manage its supply chain. Naturally, Nintendo denied such ulterior motives. "A shortage just doesn't benefit us," said the president of Nintendo of America. Nintendo was not only losing sales—as much as $1.3 billion in the Christmas 2007 season[5]—but scalpers, not Nintendo or its retail partners, were profiting from the resulting inflated prices on the gray market.[6] Yet Nintendo was paying much of the price in ill will. Whether this damage was offset by positive buzz around the product is an open question. What we do know is that the shortage did entail costs. And if the shortage were for a less interesting product or service—say, laundry detergent or technical support—it's safe to say that any publicity for failing to satisfy demand wouldn't be what we'd call "buzz." Shortages for boring products don't tend to boost sales.

The Standbys: Guesstimation and Number Crunching

So forecasting errors can be a serious problem. Before we show two lab-tested solutions, let's look at how business forecasting is traditionally done. (The following table shows all the methods at a glance.)

The simplest, crudest method is guesstimation: using your feel for the situation to pull out a number.

Forecasting Method	Think of Ideas Popularized in . . .	Pros and Cons
Guesstimation	*Blink*[7] In some situations, a snap judgment gives better answers than a thorough analysis. By tapping into years of sometimes unconscious knowledge, and ignoring a multitude of irrelevant information, an art expert immediately recognizes a sculpture as a forgery.	• Easy but, unless done by experts, often inaccurate. • The fallback option when no data is available or a decision must be made in seconds.
Number crunching	*Super Crunchers*[8] By mining stores of historical data, number crunchers can tell which story lines will likely appeal to movie viewers and which vintage will produce the finest wine.	Good when abundant historical data shows a stable pattern.
Collective intelligence	*The Wisdom of Crowds*[9]	• Usually requires a large number of participants. • Participants must be diverse and have independent sources of information. • Is best when there is no hard data and information is spread out among many people.
Incentives and risk attitudes	*Secrets of the Moneylab*	Solves the problem of participants having some control over the outcomes they are trying to predict.

Different prediction problems call for different forecasting methods.

More sophisticated than guesswork is number crunching, which uses various forms of statistical analysis of historical data. This can start out simple—and, in some cases, stays simple. For example, if you notice that for the past several years your most popular product has sold three times as many units in October as it has in February, and you've seen this year's February numbers, it doesn't take much to predict sales for this October.

Number crunching is usually more complicated than that, though, relying on techniques such as regression analysis and Bayesian inference, as well as a slew of specialized quantitative methods (like bootstrapping, GARCH, conjoint analysis, and so on). With all these methods, the underlying assumption is that all the information you need is in the numbers, and all you need to find valuable patterns is the right math.

Obviously, if there is a lot of data, and if the data is informative, then quantitative methods are useful. And that's true in many situations. Consumables with steady demand are a great example. This includes food staples like milk and bread, as well as other products that people buy over and over, such as paper and ink cartridges.

But in many situations, there's either no historical data or the data contains no patterns useful for forecasting. A good example of this situation is the introduction of a new product. New product introduction—whether the product is a new gadget or a cultural product like a book or a movie—is a constant fact of life in many industries, from high tech to fashion. It's indispensable to growth, and without a steady flow of new products, companies in many fields would wither and die. The problem with new products, though, is that there's no past to look at for predicting demand.

So how do managers forecast demand for new products? Imperfectly. The most common practice is a meeting or series of meetings of people with some knowledge and interest in the product—representatives from product development, marketing, sales, manufacturing, and finance, for example. But anybody who's sat through such meetings knows the problems. Justin Wolfers, a professor at the Wharton School of Business, put it beautifully: "Think of what a meeting is," Wolfers told a reporter.[10] "It's some fat, obnoxious guy who talks for three minutes despite the fact that he knows nothing. In the meantime, there's a woman who sits in the back and says nothing because she may feel her opinion isn't taken into account. And then there's the brown-noser, who wants to be senior VP and will say anything the boss wants to hear."

We have nothing against fat guys, but Wolfers is dead-on: for a host of reasons, the opinion that carries the most weight in a meeting is not the one backed by the most information. The most articulate or opinionated participant has more sway than the quiet ones, no matter how knowledgeable, and all too often people tend to kowtow to the opinions of senior management or other high-powered, high-status group members. There are other group dynamics at work, too, that keep people from having their opinion heard and counted. In economic terms, though, the problem boils down to this: for many participants, the costs of speaking up for their views outweigh the incentives for doing so.

What about an anonymous democratic process? This would prevent some of the social-psychological problems of group decision-making, but it does nothing to give appropriate influence to people with the most information. In fact, the democratic ideal of "one person, one vote" ensures that (for example) a marketer's opinion counts for no more than the opinion of an accountant—or vice versa.

This seems like an intractable problem, but there's a solution.

Tapping into Collective Intelligence

The solution is to tap into the collective intelligence of many people: as we saw with the Hollywood Stock Exchange at the beginning of this chapter, many people together know more than most individuals alone. But although a prediction market is the most popular and simplest method of tapping into collective intelligence, it's one of several methods in information aggregation, as the field of study is called. All the methods are based on the same principle: having people put their money where their mouths are. For example, because traders in prediction markets bet more money when they're more confident, the prices reflect actual beliefs about outcomes—so the system weighs stronger beliefs more.

Prediction markets won't work every time: different situations call for different methods. For example, when you have only a few participants, a prediction market won't be sufficiently liquid, as we'll see. In that case, a different method of aggregating information might make more sense, and we describe one such method later in this chapter.

Prediction markets may sound more like a game than anything people outside Hollywood might want to use, but they're certainly a reality, albeit still not in the mainstream. Since 1988, the Iowa Electronic Markets have been used to predict the outcomes of U.S. elections, and have done so much better than polls. HP was the first company to run a corporate prediction market. After the explosion of interest in prediction markets set off by *The Wisdom of Crowds,* many other companies have used them as well. The largest provider of private prediction markets, NewsFutures, counts among its customers Eli Lilly, InterContinental Hotels Group, Johnson & Johnson, Pfizer, RAND Corporation, Renault, Siemens, USA Today, and Wells Fargo Bank, among others.[11] At least one of the Iowa markets—the Iowa Electronic Health Market, which predicts things like the spread of the swine flu—is now powered by NewsFutures.

Prediction markets seem to work by magic, but there are solid scientific principles behind the curtain. Let's look at several key principles that make prediction markets work—elements that, when missing, cause prediction markets to fail.

Large Numbers. The most basic principle that explains the magic of prediction markets is the Law of Large Numbers. Here's how it works. Everybody makes mistakes—experts and novices alike. But novices make bigger mistakes than experts. To use a simple example, suppose novices and experts are both asked to predict sales for a particular product. If actual sales are 100, the typical expert might predict sales of 95, 96, 97 or 103, 104, 105, and a typical novice might predict sales of 88, 89, 90 or 108, 109, 110. Individuals in both groups are off, but each novice is off by more. Put another way, the distribution of answers—and therefore of errors—is wider for novices than for experts. The average hovers around 100, but it's going to be off by a bit; the Law of Large Numbers, though, says that the more participants you have, the closer their average answer will be to the correct answer. And you're more likely to have a larger number of novices than experts. If you ask an individual novice, chances are his prediction will be less accurate than an individual expert's. But if you ask three experts and a thousand novices, the novices' average will actually be more accurate than that of the three experts!

Here's an analogy that shows how this is possible. Imagine that the information relevant to your prediction is sprinkled throughout a sea of knowledge—millions of tons of salt water containing little drops of relevant information. Experts and novices are both at sea trying to find the relevant information, but an expert is someone who can scoop out a bowlful of seawater, whereas a novice can scoop out only a cupful. The drops of relevant information are randomly distributed—nobody knows where they are, novices and experts alike. What they scoop up is completely random. So who has a better chance of having scooped some relevant information?

Clearly, the expert does. Now bring in five more experts with their bowls and five more novices with their coffee cups. What happens? The experts' edge continues to grow: they now have six bowls of seawater compared to the novices' six cups, so they're even more likely to have scooped up relevant information—or to have scooped up more of it.

But now suppose you've run out of experts and their big bowls. All you can do is keep sending novices out to sea. Can they, with their humble coffee cups, do better than the six experts with their bowls? Absolutely—sooner or later, cup by cup, the novices will scoop up more seawater (and more relevant information) than the experts did.

Something similar happens in prediction markets, with the market as a kind of centrifuge to separate the pertinent information from the rest of the seawater. In the real world, as in our thought experiment, you're much likelier to get a higher number of novices than of experts. After all, adding many experts is often impossible or unfeasible: there may not be enough experts available, or their time and expertise may be too expensive. But novices are plentiful and relatively cheap, so it's a lot easier to get ten novices than even one expert to participate.[12]

We should point out, however, an important way in which prediction markets differ from our seawater analogy. The aggregation of information in a prediction market isn't linear: the accuracy of predictions doesn't grow in proportion to the number of participants. For example, once you get to the point where the predictions are pretty good, adding more people won't help as much as it did when there were only a few participants and the predictions weren't nearly good enough.

There's another advantage to a large number of participants: liquidity. With plenty of traders, there are bound to be willing buyers available at any given moment.

Incentives. As we've said, meetings typically don't offer an incentive for revealing private information, let alone give proper weight to the opinions of the most informed individuals. Good prediction markets do. They don't reward status and power, instead letting any participant buy and sell shares anonymously. Since participants don't want to bid a high price for an outcome they believe is less likely, they won't—and the market price will thus reveal what most participants truly believe.

The problem with incentives, though, is they must be sufficiently high to motivate users. Because U.S. laws restrict gambling, most American prediction markets use play money, like the Hollywood dollars used in the HSX. (The Iowa markets, which are run by a university and have betting limits, have gotten special dispensation from the government.) How well does play money work? Since the premise of prediction markets is to get people to put their money where their mouths are, you would expect real money to work better than play money—and for markets that use real money to give better predictions than play-money markets. But is that true?

To answer this question, a team of researchers ran a controlled experiment that compared a play-money market with a real-money market in predicting the outcomes of 208 NFL football games.[13] The two markets—NewsFutures' Sports Exchange and Intrade's Ireland-based (and now-defunct) TradeSports.com—performed similarly well. TradeSports correctly predicted the winner in 135 of the games (or 65.9 percent), and SportsExchange did so in 139 of the games (or 66.8 percent).[14] Although these numbers aren't astounding, they're quite good compared to the performance of individual bettors. (In a competition against almost two thousand individuals, the two prediction markets ranked in sixth and eighth place.)

How can we explain that the play-money market did just about as well as the market that used real money? The researchers conclude that the two markets' different strengths and weaknesses offset one another. "Real-money markets may better motivate information discovery," they say, "while play-money markets may yield more efficient information aggregation." Put another way, to make enough money to make big bets in a play-money market, you need to be really good for a long time, whereas how much you bet in a real-money market may say more about how much of your own wealth you had to begin with—a factor that may have nothing to do with how good a predictor you are. In the case of football futures or HSX, people's inherent interest in football or show business seems to be enough of an incentive, particularly when combined with the thrill of competition. In more workaday forecasting problems, however, participants probably need real money to motivate them—and enough of it.

Price as a Unit of Measure. Information in the real world is messy. It's hard, for example, to combine a news story about a trend with an expert opinion about a specific product into a single prediction about demand. But share prices force different traders to express their individual predictions in one common measure.

What's more, through market-driven prices, prediction markets naturally put more weight on stronger, more informed opinions and encourage participants to capitalize on private information that's not reflected in the current market price. For example, suppose your company has set up a market to predict how many units of a new product will be sold in the first month of release. One of the stocks, corresponding to a prediction of 50,000 units, is called HIGH. Another, called LOW, gets bought by traders who believe the company will sell only 10,000 units of product. Let's say you have some information that makes you believe the company is likelier to sell 50,000 units than just 10,000 units; if so, you'll be willing to pay more for shares of HIGH than of LOW. Likewise, if more people value the HIGH shares more than the LOW shares, the price of HIGH stock will be that much higher. For these reasons, prices in prediction markets capture the latest available information about demand.

You might also wonder how prediction markets came about in the first place. Other financial markets (or exchanges) had been around for a long time, but their purpose was different. On the New York Stock Exchange, for example, people have been trading company stock since 1792. But although the main goal of NYSE and similar markets is to raise capital and enable individual investors to share the wealth, a natural by-product is information. A stock's performance on the NYSE tells you the company's value—quite literally, since the share price times the number of shares equals the company's market cap. A snapshot of the market at any moment is as good an indicator as any, capturing all the information available in earnings statements, product announcements, analyst reports, and news of acquisitions, layoffs, and management changes. Although trading activity can't predict everything—no one can know if, for example, a charismatic CEO will meet an untimely death on his next plane ride—it tells what people know and believe about the company's prospects.

In hindsight, it's a short mental leap from this type of market—where aggregated information is a by-product—to a prediction market whose main reason for being is to harvest collective information. Several economists had this insight.[15] Charlie Plott, the renowned experimentalist and Kay-Yut's teacher at Caltech, was one of them. In the 1980s, Plott and his colleague Shyam Sunder ran many experiments showing that a prediction market could work.[16]

Decision Markets: A Twist on Prediction Markets

Prediction markets aggregate information and put it in a forecast. But the output doesn't have to be a forecast. Instead, it can be a decision—not a prediction about the future, but a group-wide solution based on information aggregated from individuals. Consider the problem automakers faced after the U.S. government issued corporate average fuel economy (CAFÉ) regulations, which mandate a fleet-wide minimum gas mileage for cars sold in the United States. For example, during model year 1990 and beyond, the CAFÉ standard for passenger cars was 27.5 mpg, which means that across the entire fleet of passenger cars manufactured by a single automaker the average gas mileage per year can't exceed 27.5.[17] Some models can be less fuel-efficient, but only if other models make up for that through greater fuel efficiency. Sounds reasonable, right? But there's an implementation problem. Without resorting to Soviet-style central planning, how can an automaker ensure that its divisions collectively meet that standard, let alone do so in the most profitable way possible? For a decentralized company like Ford, each of whose business units looks out for its own bottom line, that's a particularly tricky problem. Ford enlisted the help of Charlie Plott, who used his know-how in prediction markets to find a market solution: an internal market for fuel-efficiency credits. In this market, divisions making vehicles whose gas mileage is higher (better) than the required average sell credits to fuel-inefficient divisions, raising the cost of producing a gas-guzzler—and thus revealing the optimal level of each type of car or truck.

Notice the parallels between this "decision market" and the prediction markets we've seen in this chapter. Each part of the company, each of which becomes a participant in the decision market, has different information: for example, each division knows better than any other how much it will cost the division to reduce fuel efficiency by one mile per gallon or how many cars of a particular efficiency they can expect to sell for a given price. Without the market, they don't have enough incentive to share this information with other divisions, and even if they did, the company as a whole has no way of weighting each division's input. As divisions trade in the market, though, information gets aggregated and the most profitable manufacturing plan emerges. Say what you will about Ford and its management, but adhering to CAFÉ standards is one problem they solved well.

When Prediction Markets Fail

Although the prediction market can be a powerful tool, it's prone to several pitfalls.

The Bloodless Stone

In 2003, after the U.S. forces took Baghdad, Saddam Hussein was on the run and managed to avoid capture for several months. During that time, Intrade (InTrade.com) conducted a prediction market on whether Saddam Hussein would be captured.[18] For a long time, the price of the bet[19] that Saddam would be "captured or neutralized" by the end of December hovered around 9 cents over the dollar; this means that if you bet 9 cents that Saddam would be captured and neutralized by the end of December—and you turned out to be right—you would earn $1.

In other words, the market deemed this outcome unlikely, with only a 9 percent chance of happening.

As we now know, Saddam was actually captured by the end of December—on December 13, 2003. Yet just two days earlier, the price had jumped from 9 cents to only 30 cents, meaning that the market was still predicting a strong chance (70 percent) that Saddam would *not* be captured by the end of December 2003. Compared to the resounding success of the Iowa Electronic Market in predicting U.S. elections, often weeks ahead and beating polls conducted at the same time, this prediction market had a dismal performance.

What happened? The simple answer is that you can't squeeze blood out of stone. If the players don't know anything, no method can get them to predict. Prediction markets don't have supernatural powers, and without crucial information, the market can be very wrong.

The second lesson from the Saddam Hussein story is that predictions can change very rapidly once new information becomes available and assimilated into the market—as they did two days before Hussein's capture.

Poor Liquidity

In general, prices in prediction markets capture all the information only if the markets are liquid. Think about what makes a market liquid: whenever a trader wants to buy or sell, he or she can find a taker. This liquidity ensures that his or her information is captured in the share prices. A higher level of trading activity captures more information more quickly. When the level of activity in the market is low, traders cannot always execute the trades they want, so the current price doesn't necessarily reflect private information of individuals. Traders' frustration at not being able to find buyers and sellers can reduce their activity in the market, making the problem snowball.

So even if you have enough participants for the Law of Large Numbers to work its magic, the numbers might not be high enough to create liquidity in the market.

Hewlett-Packard's experience with prediction markets illustrates this problem all too well. HP established a series of prediction markets from

1996 to 1999 to test whether the technology could help predict product sales. Unfortunately, the participant pool was too small: most participants were executives from marketing organizations, so the number of participants in each market ranged from only ten to thirty—minuscule numbers compared to the hundreds of players in the Iowa Electronic Market and potentially many more at markets run by TradeSports and the Hollywood Stock Exchange. Furthermore, the HP executives were too busy to pay enough attention to the markets, which were open at lunchtime and from 4 p.m. until 8 a.m. As a result, many of the HP prediction markets had very low levels of trading activity, averaging only a few trades per trader per market for the whole one-week session. Overall, the results were encouraging, beating official forecasts in accuracy six out of eight times, but these modest improvements were not worth the costs, which included participant training and their trading time.

There were other reasons for liquidity problems in HP's market. Unlike the Iowa Electronic Market in which traders bet their own money, for legal and business reasons the HP prediction markets were completely funded from the projects' budgets. And because of budgetary constraints, each participant, on average, received only a $50 stake. This obviously was not enough incentive for busy executives to trade more than a few times during a session. Compounding these problems was a steep learning curve. Although most participants had experience with trading securities and certainly understood the concept, they'd never used this particular trading software. Given this extra hurdle, participants were less willing to trade, particularly given the low stakes. To get around this problem, the manager of the HP prediction market project stepped in to become a stock agent, executing trades on behalf of some of the participants, but that didn't solve the motivation problem.

Bubbles

In most organizations, information flows anything but freely. As information moves up, down, and across the organizational chart, it gets filtered and distorted, leading to high ratios of noise to data. In a prediction market, on the other hand, even traders who work in the same organization can and do share independent information without these "game of telephone" effects. Traders' information isn't always independent, of course. In a prediction market run at Google, for example, employees who sat near one another or those belonging to the same social or work groups tended to make similar trading decisions.[20] But even if traders' information isn't independent, the market usually does a good job of sorting that out, such that those with better information profit from the errors of those who are merely following the pack.

Sometimes, however, markets create bubbles. In these unfortunate situations, rather than using private information to correct against errors in market prices, traders see prices going up and assume that other traders know more than they know themselves—so rather than selling, the new traders buy. This, of course, further inflates prices, which other traders see as more evidence that the stock is valuable, so they buy, further driving up the price—and so on, until the bubble bursts. While the bubble is growing, of course, most participants don't recognize it as a bubble—and during this time the market is a poor predictor. Why some markets create bubbles while others don't is a mystery. Many economists, however, believe that bubbles can arise whenever a disproportionate number of bullish participants enter the market.

On top of all this are practical problems, like some of the ones HP ran into. Intel has also experimented with prediction markets, running into other practical difficulties.[21] One was the question of how to integrate prediction markets' results with existing business processes, like production planning. For example, a market that predicts product demand a month from now in an organization that needs information about demand three months from now won't be useful no matter how accurate its forecasts.

The BRAIN Method

HP's research on prediction markets had reached a crossroads. On the one hand, asking people to bet money on their beliefs seemed like a good idea. On the other hand, in this particular business setting, the prediction market was plagued with problems. What was needed was a way to gather collective intelligence that didn't require many participants and took very little of their time.

With these goals in mind, in 2000 Kay-Yut and his colleagues at HP Labs designed a new method of aggregating information—an economic game that they affectionately dubbed BRAIN.[22] Instead of players trading with each other the way they would in a prediction market, players in the BRAIN game bet on outcomes directly with the "house," much as roulette players do in a casino.

Here's how BRAIN works. The game's organizer decides the possible outcomes, or "buckets"—such as ten possible ranges of sales figures for the following quarter. Each player gets 100 tickets to bet on these possible outcomes. Each player must use up all 100 tickets and must bet at least 1 ticket in each bucket. When time reveals the actual outcome, players get paid based on the number of tickets they bet correctly.[23]

In theory, these payment numbers would create the perfect balance between risk and rewards—prompting rational, risk-neutral individuals to reveal their true beliefs about the likelihood of the various outcomes. But, as we discussed in chapter 1, on uncertainty, people are not necessarily risk-neutral and rational. Some people are natural gamblers and some people hate to take risks. Therefore, even given the same information (such as 90 percent certainty of a particular outcome), they will bet differently: natural risk-takers will bet more aggressively than people who are very risk-averse. And between these extremes are many levels of risk aversion. That's why interpreting different people's bets and putting them together into one forecast is tricky.

Now, if we were dealing with prediction markets, these differences in risk attitude wouldn't be a problem. If the market is large enough and liquid enough, there will be enough of each type of trader that everything evens out. But BRAIN uses only ten to twenty bettors, not the hundreds or thousands of traders participating in a robust prediction market. So BRAIN must overcome a problem prediction markets deal with automatically: given that an individual bet says something about the individual's attitude toward risk as much as about his or her certainty in a specific outcome, how can you make sense of multiple bets, let alone synthesize them into a coherent forecast?

To solve this problem, the BRAIN team needed to separate each individual's risk attitude, which remains constant across situations, from the person's certainty about a specific outcome. To that end, the researchers developed a process to profile individuals about their attitude toward risk. With that information, and a little math, BRAIN can deduce information from bets. Then, once there's a common measure, BRAIN can compare apples to apples and roll up the bets into a single forecast.[24]

HP has successfully used BRAIN for a variety of predictions, including revenue forecasts and future prices of DRAM (an essential component of many HP products). Several HP customers have used BRAIN as well. A pharmaceutical company took internal bets on how many projects would get approved for a given period. A telecom customer used BRAIN to help predict the subscriber acquisition cost for a new service, that is, the cost of winning over one customer. And an insurance company used BRAIN to predict a department's costs for one fiscal quarter.[25]

Although BRAIN works superbly with small groups, it has some drawbacks. The main pitfall with adding up bets is the risk of counting the same information more than once. To prevent double counting, BRAIN relies on knowing how different bettors' information might be related. For example, if Alice, Bob, and John are participants in BRAIN, and BRAIN administrators know that Alice and Bob have similar sources of information, BRAIN can average their bets rather than adding both bets to John's. BRAIN has ways of coping with this problem—of understanding the underlying information structure—but these methods are imperfect. The resulting forecast is only as good as the system's formulas. A prediction market, on the other hand, does the math automatically—it "learns" the collective intelligence of the group and "agrees" on a forecast through the natural evolution of prices alone. Therefore, with enough motivated participants, the market may be a better choice because you won't run the risk that the math will be wrong.[26]

The Policy Analysis Market: A Cautionary Tale

After the 9/11 attacks, it became clear that members of the U.S. intelligence community were doing a poor job of sharing information. The CIA and FBI, for example, didn't know what the other agency knew. Organizational barriers made information sharing difficult, and staffers had no incentive to share information with "rival" agencies. A prediction market would seem the perfect solution to this problem. But the plan for the so-called Policy Analysis Market (PAM) never got off the ground, and the story of this abysmal, high-profile failure offers an important lesson for anyone thinking of setting up a prediction market.

The project had gotten off to a promising start. To prevent another 9/11, the Defense Advanced Research Projects Agency (DARPA), a research arm of the Department of Defense, was eager to try new methods of predicting events in the Middle East—not only terrorist attacks, but any geopolitical or economic events of interest to U.S. defense. To begin work on the market, they enlisted a company called NetExchange, run by people with expertise in prediction markets. (The company's president, Charles Polk, was a classmate of Kay-Yut's at Caltech.)

DARPA spent $750,000 to get started.

PAM might have remained an arcane research project if DARPA hadn't brought it before Congress by asking for more money. DARPA needed $8 million to fund PAM for another several years, at a time when the Bush administration was already under scrutiny for the war, especially the Terrorism Information Awareness Office (part of DARPA) and its plans for massive surveillance of U.S. citizens. Two senators were particularly outraged by the Policy Analysis Market and called a press conference to expose a project they deemed not only wasteful but also morally repugnant. One of the senators, Ron Wyden of Oregon, raised this question: "Why wouldn't terrorists just hop online and start betting if they couldn't either mislead American authorities about their plans or make money to fund more al Qaeda operations?"[27]

In the two days after the press conference, hundreds of news report ran about the strange project. In the swirl of controversy, the project was killed and DARPA director John Poindexter stepped down.

The project's supporters said the prediction market ended only for political reasons. It's possible that PAM would have addressed Senator Wyden's concerns about terrorists manipulating the market to advance the terrorist agenda. (For one thing, the market's designers could restrict access to trusted agents. Second, they could audit trading activity and flag suspicious trades, much the way the SEC does with the stock market.)

Nonetheless, the motive to manipulate the outcome to profit from the market is always a potential problem with insiders. So why doesn't it occur more often? That's because manipulation requires both *power* and *incentives*. In most markets, a single participant doesn't have enough power to sway the outcome. In the Iowa Election Market, for example, participants are individual voters, and they presumably know that one vote has almost no chance of swinging an election. Political insiders do have more power (although that power is not complete), but the market's stakes are far too low for insiders to profit from mercenary politicking. A campaign staffer could, in theory, leak a scandal to push down her candidate's price on the election market—but the market's financial incentives are too small to bother.

On the other hand, the market's incentives have to be high enough to get people to trade, as we've already said. The right incentive—not so low that people won't participate yet not so high that they'll be tempted to game the system—depends on the market.

A final lesson from the PAM debacle is to think about public perceptions. Even if you're planning an internal prediction market, people in the company may have misgivings about what you're doing. Try to anticipate people's objections and address them before the rollout. Along the same lines, set reasonable expectations, teaching the users of the market what it can and cannot do.

Self-Fulfilling Prophecies:
The Incentive Approach to Intentions

For information aggregation to work (whether through a prediction market, BRAIN, or similar method), participants must have some information about future events—but should have no power to affect the outcome. If they can affect the outcome, all hell can break loose.

And that's true not only of terrorist acts or election results. Take the more prosaic example of sales forecasting. Who would be most knowledgeable about future sales? Naturally, it's the salespeople themselves. Any forecasting processes should therefore include them. Suppose you give a salesperson—call him Sam—a big incentive to make an accurate sales forecast. That makes sense, right? Wrong. Here's why.

Sam understands that some deals are riskier than others: a prospect might become his biggest customer—or might order nothing at all. Going after a customer like that could bring in major business, but could also throw off Sam's forecasts. So Sam decides not to pursue risky deals, even if they are in the best interest of the company.

It quickly dawns on Sam that he can further improve the accuracy of his predictions by cutting back on sales efforts near the end of an accounting period. If he's reaching the end of the sales quarter and has hit his forecast, he'd only hurt his accuracy by closing more deals. So whatever forecast he makes becomes a self-fulfilling prophecy because he can sway sales up or down to match the forecast; furthermore, a lower forecast is obviously easier to fulfill than a higher one.

The upshot, of course, is that Sam's accurate forecast comes at a huge cost: lower sales. Incentives to make accurate forecasts create a perverse incentive for Sam not to do the job he was hired for. The fact that Sam the sales rep has an insider view into sales makes him the best person to make forecasts—and, in view of the bigger picture, the worst person for that job.

There seems to be an inherent trade-off between strong sales and forecast accuracy. But do you really have to sacrifice one for the other? Or is there a way to encourage accurate forecasts without discouraging sales efforts?

The problem might appear even more complex with a retailer or distributor. Unlike direct salespeople, these middle links in a supply chain buy products from the manufacturer and resell them to their own customers. A company like HP would love to know how much product a distributor will order in a given month, but that's hard for a distributor to predict because the distributor (call her Doris) doesn't know how much her end customers will buy. The underlying demand is random and can fluctuate greatly.

It turns out, though, that there is a way to encourage accurate forecasts from distributors without discouraging sales, and it requires completely reframing the problem. The word "forecasting" carries a lot of baggage—it evokes images of number crunching or possibly newer methods like prediction markets. But these methods don't work in all situations, so seeing the problem in terms of forecasting gets you to a dead end. If, on the other hand, you reframe the forecasting problem as another type of problem, you can let go of the baggage and see new avenues for solving the problem.

That's what Kay-Yut and his colleagues did with the seemingly impossible problem of getting distributors who don't know their underlying demand to tell the manufacturer how much product they'll order down the road. The key insight: instead of asking, "How can we improve the accuracy of a forecast?" they asked, "How can we get distributors to *stick* to the forecast they've made?" The solution to that problem requires some sort of *commitment device*—a way to get people to keep their promises. Prepayment is a kind of commitment device, and if you can get your customers to place preorders, you can greatly improve the accuracy of your forecasts—sometimes to 100 percent. Decades ago, before the Franklin Mint changed owners and branched out to miniature muscle cars and Jackie Kennedy faux-pearl earrings, the company was a class act. It sold limited-edition commemorative medals, limited only based on date and not quantity. Coin collectors would see an ad for these medals and had to place an order by the specified date; after the manufacturing run, the company would destroy the die. If an order came in after the deadline, the Mint would send the order and the check back to the customer, who'd learn to be early the next time. Yet because each limited edition wasn't based on quantity, the company wasn't putting a ceiling on profits.

This may sound like a gimmick, but Franklin Mint's founder, the serial entrepreneur Joseph Segel (who later went on to found QVC), insists the limited-edition concept had little to do with creating interest and everything to do with managing costs: because every medal was engraved only after all the orders had come in, the company knew exactly how many to make, with no worries about unsold goods and languishing inventory. "Almost every series I produced in those days was guaranteed to pay off," recalls Segel.[28] By getting exact order numbers before manufacturing, Segel was able to perfectly "predict" sales without putting a damper on them.

Kay-Yut used another commitment device: a down payment. We know that a down payment on a house enforces your promise to pay off the loan because if you fail to make your mortgage payments, you risk losing your down payment. HP's solution, which in lab tests created forecasts of remarkable accuracy, used a similar commitment device—a down payment on products the distributor commits to ordering by a particular date. For each unit in the commitment that the distributor fails to order, the distributor loses the down payment for that unit.

But how can Doris, our distributor, know how big a commitment to make? Her sales are unpredictable and, although she can make an effort to increase sales, these sales aren't a simple function of her efforts: many factors beyond her control affect how much Doris will sell. For example, Doris can't control a competing distributor who might undermine her efforts by offering an unbeatable deal to Doris's prospects. Likewise, if the overall economy is poor or if a specific customer has slashed its purchasing budget, the best distributor in the world won't do well.

But there is one thing very much under Doris's control: inventory management. If sales are low, she can keep more product in stock—and she can order more from the manufacturer knowing that she'll be able to hold on to a little excess inventory from month to month. Managing inventory helps Doris deal with fluctuating demand from her customers—and enables her to give good forecasts to the manufacturer without knowing exactly how much she'll sell by a certain date. She can do all this with or without the down payment—but without having made a down payment she has little incentive to do so.

The down payment is not enough, however. It encourages sticking to the forecast but gives no incentive for additional sales. So HP also put in a reward for meeting the commitment—a discount that kicks in once the distributor places the actual order. Each unit the distributor actually orders (up to the commitment amount) will trigger this discount.

Here is an example to illustrate this scheme (also shown in the table below). Assume the distributor, Doris, is selling a product at $50 per unit, and that her cost to buy it from the manufacturer is $40 per unit. Without any kind of special incentives, therefore, her profit is $10 per unit. Under the manufacturer's double-sided incentive scheme, however, she pays $1 per unit for down payment and receives an additional discount of $2 per unit actually ordered. Expecting sales of 100 units, she "commits" to 100 units.

When the time comes, if Doris orders 80 units, lower than her commitment, she will receive the additional discount on the 80 units ($2 × 80 = $160) but will lose the down payment on 20 units ($1 × 20 = $20) with a net incentive of $140 or $1.75 per unit. If she orders the full

Actual Order	80 Units	100 Units	120 Units
Commitment (or advance order)	100 units	100 units	100 units
Down payment ($1/unit committed)	$100	$100	$100
Discount ($2/unit ordered up to the commitment)	$160	$200	$200
Down payment lost (for not meeting the commitment)	$20	$0	$0
Net incentive (discount − payment lost)	$140	$200	$200
Net incentive per unit ordered	$1.75	$2	$1.67
Profit per unit ($10 + net incentive)	$11.75	$12.00	$11.67
Total profit (profit per unit × units ordered and sold)	$940	$1,200	$1,400.40

Given the same advance order (100 units), the system rewards forecast accuracy without penalizing additional sales.

100 units, she gets $2 per unit in incentives, and forfeits no part of the down payment. If she orders 120 units—more than her commitment—she will receive the discount for only 100 units at the total of $200, or $1.67 per unit. Her profit margin (per unit) is highest when she hits her commitment exactly. However, because she earns revenue (and profits) from each additional sale, her bottom line continues to grow.

The incentive, on a per-unit basis, is highest when the distributor hits her commitment. Therefore, it behooves her to commit to this sales level as much as possible. The additional discount is pushing the distributor to commit as much as possible, and the potential loss of the down payment is pushing her to commit as little as possible. This balance provides a strong incentive for her to be accurate—to match her commitment to actual future sales.

Furthermore, this system does not discourage the distributor from selling more; that's because she continues to make money off each additional unit of sales, even after she meets her commitment.

Experiments at HP Labs showed the effectiveness of this scheme. In the experiments, students who played the roles of distributors received cash according to how much money they made in the game. (The game also included important elements from the real world—for example, the students competed with one another for customers.) This system resulted in astounding forecast accuracy (of 80 to 90 percent) and beat a competing system not only in accuracy but in total sales.

The double-sided incentive, which came from seeing the forecasting problem as a commitment problem, was the key to the solution. But this insight was only the first step: there's no general answer to the optimal level of each type of incentive. Coming up with the best levels required trial and error—rigorous experiments safely confined to the lab.

We wish we could give you a general formula to help solve prediction problems in your business. But there's a good reason we won't, which we might call the Dear Abby Dilemma. When people wrote to the popular advice columnist with a small personal problem—seeking her thoughts on a parenting question or a sticky social situation, for example—she'd write back a few words of homespun wisdom that neatly solved the problem. But when someone had a really juicy story or sought advice on a soul-wrenching problem, Abby invariably told the troubled reader to see a therapist or talk to a trusted clergy person. This answer sounds like a cop-out, unsatisfying at best. ("I wrote to you for advice, not a referral," we can hear the poor reader saying.) But Abby was right. Some problems are too complex to resolve in a few glib sentences. A responsible advice-giver needs to know much more about the person and her situation, and may well need some back-and-forth to find a solution that fits. That's what a therapist can provide.

We won't send you to a therapist for your economic prediction problems (let alone a priest or a rabbi), but we won't endorse one-size-fits-all solutions, either. Throughout this chapter we've pointed out the pros and cons of different approaches to predicting the unpredictable and have shown that some work better for some situations than others. And the toughest prediction problems require individual help. Sometimes, you need an experimental economist.

Conclusion

During the summer of 1941, the great physicist Richard Feynman took a break from his PhD studies at Princeton to join the war effort, having passed up a job at Bell Labs to work at an arsenal in Philadelphia. At first, the army underused his talents, having him check gear drawings for accuracy. Yet when, near the end of the summer, Feynman was finally given an actual design task, his physics training wasn't quite enough: applying a knowledge of physics was the work of an engineer, not a scientist. Somewhat clueless and frightened, Feynman went to a mechanical engineer for help.

"There's nothin' to it," the engineer told him, and quickly explained everything Feynman needed to know. One of the keys to a good design is to pick the right pair of gears. For example, any number of gear pairings have a gear ratio of 2 to 1—you can choose a 10-toothed gear with 5-toothed gear, or you can opt for 24 and 12, or 48 and 24, and so on. In theory, all these pairs could work, so which one should you choose? Is there one combination that's more likely than others to work best in practice? The engineer had a simple solution: "You look in the Boston Gear Catalogue, and select those gears that are in the middle of the list," he told Feynman. "The ones at the high end have so many teeth they're hard to make," he explained. "The gears at the low end of the list have so few teeth they break easy. So the best design uses gears from the middle of the list."[1]

Feynman never tells us the name of this engineer. Unlike Feynman, the engineer never became famous, never made lasting contributions to science or engineering. In all likelihood, he hadn't majored in physics in college. He didn't need to. With an understanding of the relevant basics (torque, friction, motors, and the like) and an orientation toward the practical and efficient, the engineer had everything it took to do his job. He might even have had an edge over the scientist. Whereas a physicist (or at least the caricature of a physicist) might have needed to run many controlled experiments comparing different gear pairs before finding a useful pattern, the engineer made do with his on-the-job experience to tell him what happens when the proverbial rubber meets the road.

We want you to be like that anonymous engineer. Throughout this book you've read about many of the forces that drive behavior. Some are straightforward: it's easy to apply the notion that, while everyone wants a fair deal, two people may have different ideas of what's fair. Other forces work in considerably more complicated ways—the ways, for example, that different types of contracts lead to different kinds of stocking errors. But all these insights can be applied in one way or another, and as you go about putting them into action, you'll do well to keep in mind this dictum: *Learn the science, but be the engineer.*

Of course, this isn't to say you need to be a trained engineer of any sort to apply many of the principles in this book. True, if you want to optimize your profits to the last dollar, you may need to hire someone to perform the arcane work of behavioral modeling and mathematical analysis. But most of the insights in this book will help get you close enough to the solution for all practical purposes. For example, our chapter on trust (chapter 6) tells you that market uncertainty keeps people from sharing accurate information; merely knowing this is enough to suggest better information-gathering strategies—when the market is more volatile, rely on information shared by partners less. Similarly, you may not know the precise minimum number of people to make an internal prediction market work—a question even scientists can't yet answer— but you'll have a pretty good sense that if only five people have insight into a question, that's not enough to build a prediction market around. You'll know to try a different prediction strategy.

In this way, each chapter should give you several fresh approaches to the problems in your business—perhaps even in ways we haven't envisioned. Kay-Yut's understanding of rationality (chapter 4), for example, sparked in him a creative approach to the difficult and seemingly unrelated problem of managing catastrophic risk without breaking the bank. We hope you'll look at the biggest problems in your business in a way a behavioral economist might—and find clues for engineering solutions that work on real people.

The Scientist in You

But let's return to the science. Experiments are the stock in trade of economists like Kay-Yut, and we don't want to dismiss them as impractical, even in the crisis-driven world many businesses inhabit. Even so, experiments are not the be-all and end-all of good decision-making: as you've seen, even academic economists routinely draw informed conclusions from field tests and careful analyses of historical data. And inside corporations, market researchers have long used these methods to learn about their customers. At HP and a handful of other companies, Kay-Yut and his colleagues have gone a step further to use all the methods in a scientist's toolbox to learn about other types of relationships, particularly those among manufacturers and retailers. Can you do some of the same for the important relationships in your business? We've provided general principles and insights, and you can go far by applying these principles no matter what industry you're in. But we hope that some of you, at least, won't stop there—that this book has inspired you to be more systematic in gathering and analyzing new data to glean fresh insights particular to your business. Behavioral economics is a rich and fertile field whose cultivation enriches us all. We hope to see you there.

ACKNOWLEDGMENTS

....

This is the part of a book where authors run the greatest risk of falling into a pit of platitudes. We are no different, starting with the perilous observation that people working well together can accomplish far more than all of them working alone. In any case, our first thanks are to each other (Kay-Yut and Marina) for managing to complement the other's strengths with suitable weaknesses.

Though talk is cheap, both of us have an aversion to lying, so you should believe us when we say that we're sincere in our appreciation for our entire editorial team, especially our editor David Moldawer, who has shown himself to be both keen of eye and quick of mind. Thank you, David, for your guidance and insightful suggestions. We're also thankful to everyone else at Portfolio who helped polish our prose and take our thoughts retail: Emily Angell, Laura Clark, Maureen Cole, Sharon Gonzalez, Victoria Hartman, Mirko Ilic, Muriel Jorgensen, Richard Lennon, Joseph Perez, and Fabiana Van Arsdell.

We are grateful to all the scientists whose research we draw on, especially (in alphabetical order) George Akerlof, Dan Ariely, Linda Babcock, Neil Bearden, Yoella Bereby-Meyer, Joyce Berg, Gary Bolton, Gérard Cachon, Colin Camerer, Gary Charness, Rachel Croson, John Dickhaut, Karen Donohue, Feryal Erhun, Armin Falk, Ernst Fehr, Shelly Fisk, Robert Forsythe, Simon Gächter, Uri Gneezy, Jerald Greenberg,

Werner Güth, Teck Ho, Tad Hogg, Charles Holt, Bernardo Huberman, Ginger Jin, Daniel Kahneman, Elena Katok, Boaz Keysar, Roderick Kramer, Sebastian Kube, Ian Larkin, Susan Laury, Phillip Leslie, John List, Christoph Loch, George Loewenstein, Kevin McCabe, Keith Murnighan, Axel Ockenfels, Özalp Özer, Jeffrey Pfeffer, Charlie Plott, Amnon Rapoport, Al Roth, Bradley Ruffle, Francoise Schoumaker, Maurice Schweitzer, Uri Simonsohn, Richard Sosis, John Sterman, Richard Thaler, Justin Wolfers, Diana Wu, and Paul Zak.

To the many people at HP who have championed Kay-Yut's work over the years and supported this book, especially Shelen Jain, Bernardo Huberman, Jaap Supmont, and Cecile Savy. Though some may see support of employees' personal projects on company time as evidence of corporate irrationality, in our case it's undoubtedly a good business decision.

To Kay-Yut's teachers and mentors, especially Charlie Plott and John Ledyard of Caltech.

To the magazine editors who've given Marina space to write about experimental economics in business, especially Philip Yam of *Scientific American* and Nelson Wang when he was at Portfolio.com.

To Ted Weinstein for his superb representation—and especially for the savvy to spot a book waiting to bust out of a magazine article. Ted, your reputation among writers is well deserved.

We're almost through, so please indulge us in a final unoriginal sentiment: our deepest appreciation is for our families, starting with our parents, to whom this book is dedicated. In a predictable symmetry, both of us have the good fortune of a loving spouse and a pair of lovable children. Kay-Yut thanks his wife, Li-Chih, and his sons, Jun-Li and Jun-Yuan. Marina thanks her own better fourths: Ephrem, Sarah, and Nathan.

NOTES

········

Introduction

1 In truth, Marina doesn't remember exactly how much she earned that day, only that it was more than $70 but less than $100. But Kay-Yut recently told her that, on average, players in that game make $75. Marina would like to think she earned more than that.

2 After several reorganizations at HP Labs, Kay-Yut's job remains the same—but he now works in a group called Business Optimization Lab.

3 Rana Foroohar, "An Experimental Mind," *Newsweek,* October 6, 2003. Marina Krakovsky, "Experiments at Work," *Scientific American,* March 2006. Marina Krakovsky, "The Not-So-Dismal Science," Portfolio.com, June 26, 2008 (http://www.portfolio .com/executives/features/2008/06/26/HPs-Kay-Yut-Chen/).

4 Kay-Yut never published these results, but more recently a paper by academic researchers reported similar effects from both a lab experiment and a field study. See Noah Lim, Michael Ahearne, and Sung Ham, "Designing Sales Contests: Does the Prize Structure Matter?" *Journal of Marketing Research,* vol. 46, no. 3 (2009): 325–45.

5 About Capital One, see Charles Fishman, "This Is a Marketing Revolution," *Fast Company,* April 1999. About Harrah's, see Christina Binkley, "Lucky Numbers: Casino Chain Mines Data on Its Gamblers, and Strikes Pay Dirt," *Wall Street Journal,* May 4, 2000.

6 For an example, see the work of a company called MarketingExperiments.com.

7 Hal Weitzman, "An Experimental Approach to the Right Answers," *Financial Times,* April 20, 2009.

8 A list of labs, with links to pages about participating in an experiment, appears at http://leem.lameta.univ-montp1.fr/index.php?page=liste_labos&lang=eng.

9 J. C. Cox et al., "Competition *for* Versus *on* the Rails: A Laboratory Experiment," *International Economic Review,* vol. 43, no. 3 (August 2002): 709–36.

10 Kelleher has been quoted saying this in many sources, and the saying has become something of a cliché in the industry, even among rivals. Yet the renegade strategy of avoiding hubs can't be easily replicated: its success depends on its going against

the grain, since if others redirected flights to smaller airports, those airports would become overly congested as well.

11 The athletic coach analogy also comes from Charlie Plott.

Chapter 1. Capitalizing on Uncertainty

1 Casanova's account comes from Jacques Casanova de Seingalt, *The Memoirs of Casanova, Volume 2 of 6: To Paris and Prison* (Teddington, UK: The Echo Library, 1997). The story is retold in many books about the history of gambling, including William Poundstone, *Fortune's Formula: the Untold Story of the Scientific Betting System That Beat the Casinos and Wall Street* (New York: Hill and Wang, 2005), and David G. Schwartz, *Roll the Bones: The History of Gambling* (New York: Gotham Books, 2006).

2 In roulette, for example, the house edge comes from the two green squares along with the eighteen reds and eighteen blacks. A player betting $1 on red, for example, has an 18/38 likelihood of winning $1. The casino wins the player's dollar whenever the ball stops on anything other than red—so it has a 20/38 likelihood of winning the $1. That difference between the casino's expected winnings and the player's is the house edge.

3 Charles Holt and Susan Laury, "Risk Aversion and Incentive Effects," *American Economic Review,* vol. 92, no. 5 (December 2002): 1644–55.

4 Because the expected payoff of A is $1.64 and the expected payoff of B is only $0.475, the difference in expected payoff is $1.17.

5 In the Holt and Laury experiments, about two-thirds of participants were risk-averse to some extent, continuing to choose A past the point of risk neutrality. And some people are erratic, switching not only from A to B, but sometimes back to A again for no apparent reason.

6 Steven J. Kachelmeier and Mohamed Shehata, "Examining Risk Preferences Under High Monetary Incentives: Experimental Evidence from the People's Republic of China," *American Economic Review,* vol. 82, no. 5 (December 1992): 1120–41.

7 Kay-Yut Chen and Suzhou Huang, "Durable Goods Lease Contracts and Used-Good Market Behavior: An Experimental Study," in *Experimental Business Research: Economic and Managerial Perspectives,* ed. Amnon Rapoport and Rami Zwick, vol. 2 (New York: Springer, 2005).

8 Kay-Yut Chen and Charles Plott, "Nonlinear Behavior in First Price Sealed Bid Auctions," *Games and Economic Behavior,* vol. 25, no. 1 (October 1998): 34–78.

9 Other researchers studying sealed-bid, first-price auctions have explained overbidding using not risk aversion, but a related behavioral tendency called ambiguity aversion. Both risk aversion and ambiguity aversion are aversions to uncertainty. See Ahti Salo and Martin Weber, "Ambiguity Aversion in First-Price Sealed-Bid Auctions," *Journal of Risk and Uncertainty,* vol. 11, no. 2 (September 1995): 123–37.

10 J. Berg, J. Dickhaut, and K. McCabe, "Risk Preference Instability Across Institutions: A Dilemma," *Proceedings of the National Academy of Sciences,* vol. 102, no. 11 (2005): 4209–14.

11 L. Barseghyan, J. T. Prince, and J. C. Teitelbaum, "Are Risk Preferences Stable Across Contexts?: Evidence from Insurance Data" (December 2009). Forthcoming from *American Economic Review.*

12 Brian J. Zikmund-Fisher and Andrew M. Parker, "Demand for Rent-to-Own Contracts: A Behavioral Economic Explanation," *Journal of Economic Behavior and Organization,* vol. 38, no. 2 (February 1, 1999): 199–216.

13 The certificates had a restriction—they had to be used within two weeks—so that it wouldn't be obvious to participants that they were, in effect, buying money. See U. Gneezy, J. A. List, and G. Wu, "The Uncertainty Effect: When a Risky Prospect Is Valued Less Than Its Worst Possible Outcome," *Quarterly Journal of Economics*, vol. 121, no. 4 (November 2006): 1283–1309.

14 This so-called between-subjects design was meant to keep the "correct" answer from being obvious. In fact, when the researchers conducted the experiment using a with-in-subjects design—that is, having the same people choose a price for each of the three options—participants did the sensible thing and paid for the lottery a price somewhere between that of the two certain prizes.

15 U. Simonsohn, "Direct-Risk-Aversion: Evidence from Risky Prospects Valued Below Their Worst Outcome," *Psychological Science*, vol. 20, no. 6 (2009): 686–92.

16 Tao Chen, Ajay Kalra, and Baohong Sun, "Why Do Consumers Buy Extended Service Contracts?" *Journal of Consumer Research*, vol. 36, no. 4 (December 2009): 611–23.

17 Alice M. Isen and Robert Patrick, "The Effect of Positive Feelings on Risk Taking: When the Chips are Down," *Organizational Behavior and Human Performance*, vol. 31, no. 2 (1983): 194–202.

18 Another vivid example of how variance can kill, this one from Sam Savage, is of a drunk walking down the highway. (On average, the drunk is moving along the cen-terline—but of course he is actually staggering and zigzagging across the line, and is soon dead.) Savage dubs the error of ignoring the variance "the flaw of averages," and has written a book about the business implications of this error. See Sam Savage, *The Flaw of Averages: Why We Underestimate Risk in the Face of Uncertainty* (Hoboken, N.J.: Wiley, 2009).

19 Animal studies, computer simulations, and experiments using robots have shown the evolution of risk-averse behavior. Biologists argue that attitudes toward risk depend on participants' ancestral environments. For some creatures, natural selection favors a risk-averse strategy: this happens for so-called stable species, or those whose envi-ronment is predictable. In other words, if you know where your next meal is coming from, there's no need to take undue risks to get it. For other species, risk-seeking is more adaptive. For example, a study of chimpanzees and bonobos, both close relatives of humans, found that whereas bonobos are risk-averse (preferring a certain payoff of four grapes over an uncertain payoff of either one or seven grapes), chimpanzees were the opposite, perhaps because the environment in which they evolved forced them to be risk takers. See Sarah R. Heilbronner, Alexandra G. Rosati, Jeffrey R. Stevens, Brian Hare, and Marc D. Hauser, "A Fruit in the Hand or Two in the Bush?: Divergent Risk Preferences in Chimpanzees and Bonobos," *Biology Letters*, vol. 4, no. 3 (June 23, 2008): 246–49. Even among humans, though, males are, on average, less risk-averse than women, apparently because risk-loving men enjoy more reproductive success than their risk-averse brethren. (Women prefer risk-loving partners.) See Susan Kelly and Robin Dunbar, "Who Dares, Wins: Heroism Versus Altruism in Women's Mate Choice," *Human Nature*, vol. 12, no. 2 (June 2001): 89–105. For evolution of risk aversion in computerized agents, see J. Neil Bearden, "Evolution of Risk Aversion in Adaptive Learning Agents," in *Computing in Economics and Finance 2001*, no. 253 (2001), Society for Computational Economics. See also Y. Niv, D. Joel, I. Meilijson, and E. Ruppin, "Evolution of Reinforcement Learning in Uncertain Environments: Emergence of Risk Aversion and Matching," in *Proceedings of the Sixth European Con-ference on Artificial Life*, ed. J. Kelemen and P. Sosik, pp. 252–61 (Berlin: Springer-Verlag, 2001).

20   Of course, there are other reasons people prefer to work for someone else, from access to group health insurance to the feeling of being part of a team.

21   The decision of whether and for how much to settle depends on many factors, particularly how the lawyer is paid. See Steven M. Shavell, "Suit, Settlement, and Trial: A Theoretical Analysis Under Alternative Methods for the Allocation of Legal Costs," *Journal of Legal Studies,* vol. 11, no. 1 (January 1982): 55–82.

22   Tom Davis, "Effective Supply Chain Management," *Sloan Management Review,* vol. 34, no. 4 (Summer 1993): 35–46.

23   This is true only as long as the risks aren't correlated, that is, as long as they don't tend to swing in the same direction.

24   Assuming that the probability of one plane crashing is p, that the probability of a second plane crashing is the same as that of the first (p), and that the two events are independent, then the probability of at least one plane crashing is $1 - (1 - p)^2 = 2p - p^2$. Since p^2 is a very small number, the chance of at least one plane crashing is almost $2p$.

25   Quoted in Daryl-Lynn Carlson, "Recessions Breed New Generation of Entrepreneurs," *Financial Post,* March 20, 2009.

26   Insurance companies have other sources of profit, most notably from the tremendous float they accrue by holding and investing policyholders' premiums before paying out claims.

27   Claire Poole, "Don't Get Mad, Get Rich," *Forbes,* May 24, 1993.

28   Margo Baldwin, "Zero-Waste Publishing: While Going to Recycled Paper Is an Essential First Step, Real Change Will Only Come When Book Sales Become Nonreturnable," *Publishers Weekly,* August 14, 2006. See also Jim Milliot, "Who's Footing the Bill for the Price Wars?: $8.98 Bestsellers Bring an ABA Letter and Suspicions About Extra Discounts," *Publishers Weekly,* October 26, 2009.

29   Eric T. Anderson, Karsten Hansen, and Duncan Simester, "The Option Value of Returns: Theory and Empirical Evidence," *Marketing Science,* vol. 28, no. 3 (May–June 2009):, pp. 405-4-23.

30   "2009 Holiday Return Policies," ConsumerWorld.org, http://www.consumerworld .org/pages/returns.htm.

31   Darren Rovell, "Playoff-or-Payoff Guarantees Back After Layoff," ESPN.com, October 25, 2002.

32   In fact, it did rain during this period, and Tourism Victoria had to pay up. See Shannon Moneo, "No Rain, No Gain: Teacher Cashes In on Victoria's Sunshine Pledge," *Globe and Mail,* April 15, 2009.

33   Sarah Bernard, "The New Style Merchants: Small Boutiques Run by Young Women with Very Decided Tastes Are Guiding the Look of the City," *New York,* August 20, 2007.

34   Paula Paul, "Sales Staff Has Choice of Pay Plans," *Automotive News,* February 5, 2001.

35   Tad Hogg and Bernardo Huberman, "Taking Risk Away from Risk Taking: Decision Insurance in Organizations" (HP Labs working paper, April 13, 2006).

36   J. D. Cummins, R. Phillips, and M. Weiss, "The Incentive Effects of No-Fault Automobile Insurance," *Journal of Law and Economics,* vol. 44, no. 2 (2001): 427–64.

37   Audie Cornish, "Zappos Proves Shoes Do Sell Online," NPR's *Weekend Edition Saturday,* July 14, 2007.

38   Alexandra Jacobs, "Happy Feet," *New Yorker,* September 14, 2009.

39   Mark Israel, "Do We Drive More Safely When Accidents Are More Expensive?: Identifying Moral Hazard from Experience Rating Schemes," CSIO Working Paper #0043, 2004, Center for the Study of Industrial Organization at Northwestern University.

40   Diana Burrell of The Renegade Writer Blog (http://therenegadewriter.com/2008/05/27/lets-kill-the-kill-fee/).

41   Jennifer Howland, "'Kill' fees," *Folio: the Magazine for Magazine Management,* January 1984.

42   See, for example, E. Fram and A. Callahan, "Do You Know What the Customer You Penalized Yesterday Is Doing Today?: A Pilot Analysis," *Journal of Services Marketing,* vol. 15, no. 6 (2001): 496–509.

43   These and many other foibles are well documented in academic literature and popular writings alike. The classic academic collection is Daniel Kahneman, Paul Slovic, and Amos Tversky, eds., *Judgment Under Uncertainty: Heuristics and Biases* (Cambridge, UK: Cambridge University Press, 1982). One excellent recent treatment is Leonard Mlodinow, *The Drunkard's Walk: How Randomness Rules Our Lives* (New York: Pantheon Books, 2008).

Chapter 2. Fair's Fair

1   The account of the Washington Ballet Company fiasco comes from articles in the *Washington Post* and the *Washington Times.* See Sarah Kaufman, "Ballet's Italy Tour Canceled Over Dancers' Meal Ticket," *Washington Post,* April 13, 2005; Daniel Williams and Sarah Kaufman, "Washington Ballet's Italian Faux Pas De Deux," *Washington Post,* May 3, 2005; and Jean Battey Lewis, "Clumsy Steps," *Washington Times,* May 34, 2005.

2   More sophisticated negotiators can try to increase the size of the pie so that both sides get more, but the Ultimatum Game keeps things simple with a zero-sum negotiation. Furthermore, in the standard Ultimatum Game both sides know the size of the pie.

3   W. Güth, R. Schmittberger, and B. Schwarze, "An Experimental Analysis of Ultimatum Bargaining," *Journal of Economic Behavior and Organization,* vol. 3, no. 2–3 (1982): 367–88.

4   M. M. Pillutla and J. K. Murnighan, "Unfairness, Anger, and Spite: Emotional Rejections of Ultimatum Offers," *Organizational Behavior and Human Decision Processes,* vol. 68, no. 3 (December 1996): 208–24.

5   Alan G. Sanfey, James K. Rilling, Jessica A. Aaronson, Leigh E. Nystrom, and Jonathan D. Cohen, "The Neural Basis of Economic Decision-Making in the Ultimatum Game," *Science,* vol. 300, no. 5626 (June 13, 2003): 1755–58.

6   R. Forsythe, J. Horowitz, N. E. Savin, and M. Sefton, "Fairness in Simple Bargaining Experiments," *Games and Economic Behavior,* vol. 6, no. 3 (May 1994): 347–69. The lead author, Robert Forsythe, is also the creator of the Iowa Electronic Markets, a set of betting markets for predicting election results and other future outcomes, one we discuss in a later chapter, "Predicting the Unpredictable."

7   This result and many others appear in Colin Camerer, *Behavioral Game Theory: Experiments in Strategic Interaction* (Princeton, N.J.: Princeton University Press, 2003).

8   John A. List, "On the Interpretation of Giving in Dictator Games," *Journal of Political Economy,* vol. 115, no. 3 (2007): 482–93.

9   You might notice that the control group in this study gave at a higher rate (71 percent) than in past Dictator studies (an average of 60 percent). The rate of giving varies somewhat from study to study, but whether it's 71, 50, or 61 percent, the rate of giving is far higher in the standard Dictator game than in the variation List tested (where, given the option to take as well as give, only 10 percent gave anything at all).

10 Edward P. Lazear, Ulrike Malmendier, and Roberto A. Weber, "Sorting, Prices, and Social Preferences" (NBER Working Paper No. 12041, April 2010).

11 D. Kahneman, J. L. Knetsch, and R. Thaler, "Fairness as a Constraint on Profit Seeking: Entitlements in the Market," *American Economic Review,* vol. 76, no. 4 (1986): 728–41.

12 Eric T. Anderson and Duncan I. Simester, "Does Demand Fall When Customers Perceive That Prices Are Unfair? The Case of Premium Pricing for Large Sizes," *Marketing Science,* vol. 27, no. 3 (May–June 2008): 492–500.

13 Peter Fishman and Devin G. Pope, "The Long-Run Effects of Penalizing Customers: Evidence from the Video-Rental Market" (University of California at Berkeley Department of Economics working paper, June 2007).

14 Alyssa Abkowitz, "How Netflix Got Started," *Fortune,* January 28, 2009.

15 Though Blockbuster officially did away with late fees, the company replaced them with a fee for replacing the movie after a certain number of days late. In some cases, the replacement fees were based on a higher price than what the movie was currently retailing for. These hidden fees prompted several lawsuits by state attorney generals and district attorneys, at least one on the grounds of "unfair business practices," forcing costly settlements. Of course, the company also incurred the wrath of countless customers, many of whom undoubtedly switched to Netflix.

16 The example of sibling rivalry comes from Teck-Hua Ho and Xuanming Su, "Peer-Induced Fairness in Games," *American Economic Review,* vol. 99, no. 5 (2009): 2047–77.

17 Ernst Fehr, Helen Bernhard, and Bettina Rockenbach, "Egalitarianism in Young Children," *Nature,* vol. 454, no. 7208 (August 28, 2008): 1079–83.

18 Teck-Hua Ho and Xuanming Su, "Peer-Induced Fairness in Games." According to another paper, half of responders demand more when they know other responders are being offered more. See Marc Knez and Colin Camerer, "Outside Options and Social Comparison in Three-Player Ultimatum Game Experiments," *Games and Economic Behavior,* vol. 10, no. 1 (July 1995): 65–94.

19 Sarah F. Brosnan and Frans B. M. de Waal, "Animal Behaviour: Fair Refusal by Capuchin Monkeys," *Nature,* vol. 428, no. 6979 (March 11, 2004): 140.

20 Rachel Croson and Jen Shang, "The Impact of Downward Social Information on Contribution Decisions," *Experimental Economics,* vol. 11, no. 3 (2008): 221–33.

21 Sara J. Solnick and David Hemenway, "Is More Always Better?: A Survey on Positional Concerns," *Journal of Economic Behavior and Organization,* vol. 37, no. 3 (1998): 373–83.

22 L. Babcock and G. Loewenstein, "Explaining Bargaining Impasse: The Role of Self-Serving Biases," *Journal of Economic Perspectives,* vol. 11, no. 1 (1997): 109–26.

23 A good account of the Amazon fiasco is David Streitfeld's "On the Web, Price Tags Blur; What You Pay Could Depend on Who You Are," *Washington Post,* September 27, 2000.

24 "Making Loyal Customers Pay," *Washington Post* blog The Checkout, August 7, 2006.

25 A good discussion of the incident and its implications for pricing is David Leonhardt's "Why Variable Pricing Fails at the Vending Machine," *New York Times,* June 27, 2005 (http://www.nytimes.com/2005/06/27/business/27consuming.html?ex=1277524800 &en=72ef44cbd51eac99&ei=5090).

26 R. Thaler, "Mental Accounting and Consumer Choice," *Marketing Science,* vol. 4, no. 3 (1985): 199–214.

27 Since the study was conducted in the 1980s, the prices in today's dollars would be significantly higher. In any case, what's important is the relative price at the two locations.

28 A whole book has been written about the art and science of fair pricing—Sarah Maxwell, *The Price Is Wrong: Understanding What Makes a Price Seem Fair and the True Cost of Unfair Pricing* (Hoboken, N.J.: John Wiley and Sons, 2008).

29 Alvin Roth, Vesna Prasnikar, Masahiro Okuno-Fujiwara, and Shmuel Zamir, "Bargaining and Market Behavior in Jerusalem, Ljubljana, Pittsburgh, and Tokyo: An Experimental Study," *American Economic Review*, vol. 81, no. 5 (1991): 1068–95.

30 J. Henrich, R. Boyd, S. Bowles, H. Gintis, E. Fehr, C. Camerer, et al., "'Economic Man' in Cross-Cultural Perspective: Ethnography and Experiments from 15 Small-Scale Societies," *Behavioral and Brain Sciences*, vol. 28, no. 6 (2005): 795–855.

31 A. E. Roth, "Bargaining Experiments," in *The Handbook of Experimental Economics*, ed. J. H. Kagel and A. E. Roth, pp. 253–326 (Princeton, N.J.: Princeton University Press, 1995).

32 Several experiments have shown that when people precede their negotiations with some rapport-building chitchat, they're more likely to reach agreement. See, for example, Michael Morris, Janice Nadler, Terri Kurtzberg, and Leigh Thompson, "Schmooze or Lose: Social Friction and Lubrication in E-Mail Negotiations," *Group Dynamics: Theory Research, and Practice*, vol. 6, no. 1 (2002): 89–100. For a discussion of these effects, see Kathleen L. Valley, Leigh Thompson, Robert Gibbons, and Max H. Bazerman, "How Communication Improves Efficiency in Bargaining Games," *Games and Economic Behavior*, vol. 38, no. 1 (January 2002): 127–55. For a discussion of e-mail in negotiations, see Kathleen L. McGinn and Rachel Croson, "What Do Communication Media Mean for Negotiations?: A Question of Social Awareness," in *The Handbook of Negotiation and Culture*, ed. Michele J. Gelfand and Jeanne M. Brett, pp. 334–49 (Stanford, Calif.: Stanford Business Books, 2004).

33 Quoted in "Stressing Value of Face-to-Face Communication," *Wall Street Journal*, August 17, 2009.

34 Yoella Bereby-Meyer and Shelly Fisk, "Is Homo Economicus a Five-Year-Old?" (SSRN working paper, August 24, 2009), http://ssrn.com/abstract=1460482.

35 J. C. Cox, "How to Identify Trust and Reciprocity," *Games and Economic Behavior*, vol. 46, no. 2 (February 2004): 260–81.

36 B. Huberman, C. Loch, and A. Önçüler, "Status as a Valued Resource," *Social Psychology Quarterly*, vol. 67, no. 1 (2004): 103–14.

37 This table, along with other ideas in this section, was adapted from Christoph H. Loch, D. Charles Galunic, and Susan Schneider, "Balancing Cooperation and Competition in Human Groups: The Role of Emotional Algorithms and Evolution," *Managerial and Decision Economics*, vol. 27, no. 2–3 (2006): 217–33. The authors call these forces "emotional algorithms" because they see them as rules that govern when a person's response will be more competitive or cooperative. The four forces here also map to categories developed by anthropologist Alan Page Fiske in A. P. Fiske, "The Four Elementary Forms of Sociality: A Framework for a Unified Theory of Social Relations," *Psychological Review*, vol. 99, no. 4 (October 1992): 689–723.

38 Notice that these preferences are also in our own self-interest, just not in our immediate material interest.

39 See, for example, I. Bohnet, B. S. Frey, and S. Huck, "More Order with Less Law: On Contract Enforcement, Trust, and Crowding," *American Political Science Review*, vol. 95, no. 1 (2001): 131–144. Also, see Ernst Fehr and Urs Fischbacher, "Why Social

Preferences Matter: The Impact of Non-selfish Motives on Competition, Cooperation, and Incentives," *Economic Journal*, vol. 112, no. 478 (March 2002): C1–C33.

40   See, for example, F. Warneken B. Hare, A. P. Melis, D. Hanus, and M. Tomasello,
"Spontaneous Altruism by Chimpanzees and Young Children," *PLoS Biology*, vol. 5,
no. 7 (2007): e184.

Chapter 3. What Goes Around: Reciprocity

1   Information about SAS comes from several sources. David A. Kaplan, "SAS: A New
No. 1 Best Employer," *Fortune*, January 22, 2010; Charles A. O'Reilly III and Jeffrey
Pfeffer, *Hidden Value: How Great Companies Achieve Extraordinary Results with Ordi-
nary People* (Boston: Harvard Business School Press, 2000); Rebecca Leung, "Work-
ing the Good Life," *60 Minutes*, April 20, 2003; "Doing Well by Being Rather Nice,"
The Economist, December 1, 2007.

2   Although the company is not altruistic in the usual sense of the word, managers and
employees are in fact practicing one form of altruism: the you-scratch-my-back-and-
I'll-scratch-yours variety that biologists call "reciprocal altruism." Economists distinguish this sort of "weak reciprocity" from a "strong reciprocity," whereby people
act kind toward others even when they have nothing material to gain, even in the
long term. This chapter deals with both types of reciprocity. See Samuel Bowles and
Herbert Gintis, "The Evolution of Strong Reciprocity: Cooperation in Heterogeneous
Populations," *Theoretical Population Biology*, vol. 65, no. 1 (2004): 17–28.

3   George A. Akerlof, "Labor Contracts as Partial Gift Exchange," *Quarterly Journal of
Economics*, vol. 97, no. 4 (November 1982): 543–69.

4   Ernst Fehr, G. Kirchsteiger, and A. Riedl, "Does Fairness Prevent Market Clearing?"
Quarterly Journal of Economics, vol. 108, no. 2 (May 1993): 437–79. See also E. Fehr,
G. Kirchsteiger, and A. Riedl, "Gift Exchange and Reciprocity in Competitive Experi-
mental Markets," *European Economic Review*, vol. 42, no. 1 (January 1998): 1–34.

5   Minimum-wage laws throw a monkey wrench in this argument because wages cannot
legally fall below the minimum wage, but without the minimum wage the argument
makes sense. What's more, in many labor markets (such as the market for professionals), wages are too far above the minimum wage for that to explain labor costs—
and yet job shortages continue because salaries don't fall with the rising supply of
workers.

6   George A. Akerlof and Janet L. Yellen, "The Fair Wage-Effort Hypothesis and Unemployment," *Quarterly Journal of Economics*, vol. 105, no. 2 (May 1990): 255–83.

7   Fehr, Kirchsteiger, and Riedl, "Gift Exchange and Reciprocity in Competitive Experimental Markets."

8   For a discussion of the use of field experiments in economics, see G. W. Harrison and
J. A. List, "Field Experiments," *Journal of Economic Literature*, vol. 42, no. 4 (December 2004): 1009–55.

9   Sebastian Kube, Michel André Maréchal, and Clemens Puppe, "The Currency of
Reciprocity—Gift-Exchange in the Workplace" (working paper no. 377, University of
Zurich Institute for Empirical Research in Economics, July 15, 2008).

10 Gary Charness, "Attribution and Reciprocity in an Experimental Labor Market," *Journal of Labor Economics*, vol. 22, no. 3 (2004): 665–88.

11 Armin Falk, "Gift Exchange in the Field," *Econometrica*, vol. 75, no. 5 (September
2007): 1501–11.

12   Bruno S. Frey and Felix Oberholzer-Gee, "The Cost of Price Incentives: An Empirical Analysis of Motivation Crowding-Out," *American Economic Review,* vol. 87, no. 4 (September 1997): 746–55; and Bruno S. Frey and Reto Jegen, "Motivation Crowding Theory: A Survey of Empirical Evidence," *Journal of Economic Surveys,* vol. 15, no. 5 (2001): 589–611.

13   U. Gneezy and A. Rustichini, "A Fine Is a Price," *Journal of Legal Studies,* vol. 29, no. 1 (January 2000): 1–18.

14   Interview with Uri Gneezy, August 25, 2008.

15   U. Gneezy and A. Rustichini, "Pay Enough or Don't Pay at All," *Quarterly Journal of Economics,* vol. 115, no. 3 (August 2000): 791–810.

16   Natalie Glance and Bernardo Huberman, "The Dynamics of Social Dilemmas," *Scientific American,* vol. 270, no. 3 (March 1994): 76–81.

17   The term "tragedy of the commons" has entered the English language, but it originated with an academic paper. See Garrett Hardin, "The Tragedy of the Commons," *Science,* vol. 162, no. 3859 (December 13, 1968): 1243–48.

18   U. Gneezy, E. Haruvy, and H. Yafe, "The Inefficiency of Splitting the Bill: A Lesson in Institution Design," *Economic Journal,* vol. 114, no. 495 (2004): 265–80.

19   Ernst Fehr and Simon Gächter, "Altruistic Punishment in Humans," *Nature,* vol. 415, no. 6868 (January 10, 2002): 137–40.

20   We say "not *always* rational" because whether the player gets a material reward for punishing freeloaders depends on the size of the punishment relative to the reward. Under some conditions and some punishment strategies, a player can be better off by punishing a cheater.

21   The word "breeder" shows vividly the subjectivity of judgments of "selfishness" in human societies, where people have simultaneous allegiances to multiple groups. (The same person can be a hard worker at the office and a slacker at home, or vice versa.) According to UrbanDictionary.com, a second definition for "breeders" is heterosexual couples "who have a significantly higher risk of contributing to the population increase than the homosexuals do."

22   That's why costly punishment is sometimes called a "second-order public good" or "second-order altruism," to contrast it with the first-order generosity of people who cooperate by doing their share in the first place. Some players are first-order altruists but not second-order altruists—that is, they give to the group, but don't bother punishing those who don't. These are the bystanders, who don't directly harm the group but who also don't protect it from those who do harm. The most interesting players are first-order cheaters who are nonetheless second-order altruists. These are the hypocrites, who don't do their share in the first place but nonetheless punish other cheaters, thus keeping more resources to themselves. For an analysis of these dynamics in biological systems, see Omar Eldakar and David Sloan Wilson, "Selfishness as Second-Order Altruism," *Proceedings of the National Academy of Sciences,* vol. 105, no. 105 (2008): 6982–86.

23   Kay-Yut Chen, Scott Golder, Tad Hogg, and Cecilia Zenteno, "How Do People Respond to Reputation: Ostracize, Price Discriminate or Punish?" In *Proceedings of the 2nd International Workshop on Hot Topics in Web Systems and Technologies,* ed. V. Padmanabhan and F. E. Bustamante, (IEEE, 2008): 31–36.

24   Jerald Greenberg, "Employee Theft as a Reaction to Underpayment Inequity: The Hidden Cost of Pay Cuts," *Journal of Applied Psychology,* vol. 75, no. 5 (1990): 561–68.

25   http://www.planetfeedback.com/best+buy/price/value/price+gouging+at+best+buy/ 307383.

26   Boaz Keysar, Benjamin A. Converse, Jiunwen Wang, and Nicholas Epley, "Reciprocity Is Not Give and Take," *Psychological Science,* vol. 19, no. 12 (2008): 1280–86.

27   Some readers may wonder whether this is the endowment effect at work—the tendency to value something more once you own it. But one of the experiments by Keysar and colleagues ruled out this explanation. For examples of the endowment effect in the lab, see D. Kahneman, J. L. Knetsch, and R. Thaler, "Experimental Tests of the Endowment Effect and the Coase Theorem," *Journal of Political Economy,* vol. 98, no. 6 (1990): 1325–48.

28   Armin Falk and Urs Fischbacher have developed a theory of reciprocity that takes both intentions and outcomes into account. For more about how misinterpretations of intentions become self-fulfilling prophecies, see Armin Falk and Urs Fischbacher, "A Theory of Reciprocity," *Games and Economic Behavior,* vol. 54, no. 2 (2006): 293–315.

29   This approach to de-escalating conflict echoes a decades-old strategy called GRIT (graduated and reciprocated initiatives in tension reduction), the essence of which is for one side in a conflict to make a small concession and ask the other side to do the same. (In most conflicts, in contrast, neither party typically wants to make a concession, with each expecting concessions from the other side first.) For more information, see Svenn Lindskold, "Trust Development, the GRIT Proposal, and the Effects of Conciliatory Acts on Conflict and Cooperation," *Psychological Bulletin,* vol. 85, no. 4 (July 1978): 772–93.

Chapter 4. Crossing the Bounds of Reason: Rationality

1   Descriptions of optimization in modern trucking come from David Diamond, "The Trucker and the Professor," *Wired,* vol. 9, no. 12 (December 2001): 164–73.

2   One factor the system typically doesn't optimize for is safety, as the tight schedules force most drivers to use their on-board dispatching computers while driving instead of taking the time to pull over. (See Matt Richtel, "Truckers Insist on Keeping Computers in the Cab," *New York Times,* September 27, 2009.) Put another way, the systems ignore one obvious cognitive limitation in humans: the inability to properly attend to both the road and the screen. To tackle this problem, trucking companies could require their drivers to pull over when they get a new message—but four fifteen-minute stops per day would take a full hour, thus reducing efficiency by about 1/8. A compromise between that and the current system might be to use shorter messages delivered by voice, just as many cars' navigation systems do.

3   The idea that because of cognitive limitations humans aren't able to optimize (or maximize utility) comes from the Nobel Prize–winning economist Herbert Simon. Simon argued that rather than being rational, people are better thought of as "bounded rational"—as rational as possible given the bounds of the brain, of finite time, and so on. Instead of maximizing, people "satisfice," settling for a solution that, while not perfect, is good enough under the given constraints.

4   See, for example, Hossam Sadek and Zach Henderson, "It's All in the Details," *Pharmaceutical Executive,* October 1, 2004, http://www.pharmexec.com/pharmexec/article/articleDetail.jsp?id=129291. The use of such profit maximization software ensures that doctors who take samples but don't go on to write prescriptions for that drug won't get many samples in the future. So doctors can't give too many samples away to their poor and uninsured patients—or, if they do, they must eventually prescribe these pricey drugs to other patients. As a result, "free" samples end up being quite expensive.

decisions than they would in the same two hours on the job. But that doesn't seem to explain the effect. Even near the beginning of the experiment, before exhaustion can set in, people repeatedly making more complex decisions fare worse than those who make simpler decisions.

35 See D. Redelmeier and R. Tibshirani, "Why Cars in the Next Lane Seem to Go Faster," *Nature*, vol. 401, no. 6748 (September 2, 1999): 35–36. See also D. Huang, "Lane-Changing Behavior on Highways," *Physical Review E*, vol. 66, no. 2 (August 2002): 1–5.

36 Brad M. Barber and Terrance Odean, "Trading Is Hazardous to Your Wealth: The Common Stock Investment Performance of Individual Investors," *Journal of Finance*, vol. 55, no. 2 (April 2000): 773–806.

37 Youyi Feng and Guillermo Gallego, "Optimal Starting Times for End-of-Season Sales and Optimal Stopping Times for Promotional Fares," *Management Science*, vol. 41, no. 8 (August 1995): 1371–91.

38 Gary Stoller, "Car Rental Prices Can Change in a Heartbeat," *USA Today*, March 14, 2007.

39 The researchers also looked at the effect of another common type of contract—the rebate contract—and found that it worked nearly as well as the incremental-discount contract.

40 This result about contracts and bounded rationality is analogous to what's been found about auctions and risk aversion: although different types of auctions should give equivalent results, risk aversion tends to raise prices in sealed-bid auctions above what they'd be in, say, English clock auctions.

41 This isn't the only way to measure bounded rationality. Another team of economists, who think of bounded rationality in terms of how people behave in strategic interactions with other players, measure bounded rationality as the number of steps of thinking a player uses in making decisions in a game with another player. A perfectly rational player would think an infinite number of steps ahead, but most people think fewer than two steps ahead. See C. F. Camerer, T.-H. Ho, and J. K. Chong, "A Cognitive Hierarchy Model of Games," *Quarterly Journal of Economics*, vol. 119, no. 3 (August 2004): pp. 861–98.

Chapter 5. Reputation, Reputation, Reputation

1 You can see the poll (now closed) at http://www.nydailynews.com/sports/2008olymp ics/2008/08/19/2008-08-19_breakfast_of_a_champion_frosted_flakes_p.html.

2 Georg Szalai, "License to Print Money for Disney," *Hollywood Reporter*, June 10, 2008.

3 For a detailed account, see Fred Vogelstein, "The Untold Story: How the iPhone Blew Up the Wireless Industry," *Wired*, vol. 16, no. 2 (February 2008).

4 Paul Resnick, Richard Zeckhauser, John Swanson, and Kate Lockwood, "The Value of Reputation on eBay: A Controlled Experiment," *Experimental Economics*, vol. 9, no. 2 (June 2006): 79–101.

5 As this study's authors point out, eBay gives no direct incentive for rating your trading partners, and giving feedback takes at least a little bit of time and effort; therefore, doing so seems irrational in the economic sense. Yet millions of users do take the time to give ratings. One interpretation of this behavior is reciprocity—the desire to punish traders who've treated you poorly and to reward those who've treated you well. Reciprocity drives reputation systems online and off. You may be afraid to confront a

backstabbing colleague, for example, but it's easy, satisfying, and relatively risk-free to hurt the colleague's reputation through the office grapevine; in fact, listeners may even thank you for the information.

6   This is a nonissue on eBay, where buyers pay before orders ship; however, it happens in other markets whenever sellers give preferential treatment to customers with a good track record.

7   Charles J. Fombrun and Cees B. M. van Riel, *Fame and Fortune: How Successful Companies Build Winning Reputations* (Upper Saddle River, N.J.: Pearson Education, Financial Times, 2004).

8   "Procter & Gamble Wins $19 Million in Satanism Suit," *New York Times,* March 20, 2007.

9   G. A. Akerlof, "The Market for 'Lemons': Quality Uncertainty and the Market Mechanism," *Quarterly Journal of Economics,* vol. 84, no. 3 (August 1970): 488–500; for an experimental study of the effect of lemons, see M. Lynch, R. Miller, C. Plott, and R. Porter, "Product quality, consumer information and 'lemons' in experimental markets," in *Empirical Approaches to Consumer Protection Economics,* ed. P. M. Ippolito and D. T. Schefman, pp. 251–306 (Washington, DC: Federal Trade Commission, Bureau of Economics, 1986).

10   For Akerlof's own account of the paper's history, see "Writing 'The Market for "Lemons"': A Personal and Interpretive Essay," Nobelprize.org, November 14, 2003.

11   In the cars example, it's the sellers who have more information. But in two important cases of asymmetric information—insurance and credit markets—the buyers have more information than the sellers. And in many situations, both types of asymmetry exist: buyers know more than sellers about one thing, and sellers know more than buyers about something else.

12   That is, if you don't feel bad about lying or don't think of withholding this information as a lie. In chapter 6, we explore the notion that some people are just averse to lying.

13   Notice that the Lemon Principle, as Akerlof calls it, doesn't hold in the market for new cars. That's because although some new cars are lemons, there's no information asymmetry: the seller knows no better than the buyer which cars are lemons. And without information asymmetry, there's no adverse selection.

14   An individual can get a high price for a used car by selling to someone who already knows and trusts her, such as a friend or coworker; however, the odds of finding such a buyer just when she wants to sell are against her—and her narrower options (relative to a dealer) give her less bargaining power in the price negotiation.

15   In fact, Kelley Blue Book lists three separate prices for each car, in ascending order: Trade-in Value, Private Party Value, and Suggested Retail Price. By selling your own car to a stranger, you'll earn much more than through a trade-in, but the sale price will be lower than what a dealer would charge the same stranger.

16   The term "Curse of Knowledge" was most recently popularized by Chip and Dan Heath in *Made to Stick.* Its economic implications were noted years earlier in C. Camerer, G. Loewenstein, and M. Weber, "The Curse of Knowledge in Economic Settings: An Experimental Analysis," *Journal of Political Economy,* vol. 97, no. 5 (1989): 1232–54.

17   Nick Paumgarten, "Food Fighter," *New Yorker,* January 4, 2010.

18   One study suggests that charitable giving does dupe many people. The study shows evidence that while breaking environmental and worker-safety rules tarnishes corporate reputations—and contributing to charitable causes improves reputations—charitable giving can diminish the negative reputation of companies that break the rules. See Robert J. Williams and J. Douglas Barrett, "Corporate Philanthropy,

Criminal Activity, and Firm Reputation: Is There a Link?" *Journal of Business Ethics,* vol. 26, no. 4 (August 2000): 341–50.

19 Most people are motivated by other forces, too, and may not need extrinsic incentives to be good—only classical economics assumes we're all inherently selfish. But even in this more nuanced, behavioral model of economic behavior, the reputation effect helps, by distinguishing between the people who cheat only when the payoff is worth it and those who never cheat.

20 Kitty Bean Yancey, "When Irate Guests Pounce: Should Hotels Have a Blacklist?" *USA Today,* September 15, 2006.

21 Scott McCartney, "Your Airline Wants to Get to Know You," *Wall Street Journal,* March 24, 2009.

22 The terms were popularized by Columbia Business School economist Larry Selden. See Larry Selden and Geoffrey Colvin, *Angel Customers and Demon Customers: Discover Which Is Which and Turbo-Charge Your Stock* (New York: Portfolio, 2003).

23 Justin Martin, "Do Your Customers Love You?" *FSB,* October 2007.

24 These experiments, as well as analyses of Prosper.com interest rates, are in Kay-Yut Chen, Scott Golder, Tad Hogg, and Cecilia Zenteno, "How Do People Respond to Reputation: Ostracize, Price Discriminate or Punish?" *Proceedings of the 2nd International Workshop on Hot Topics in Web Systems and Technologies,* ed. V. Padmanabhan and F. E. Bustamante (IEEE, 2008), 31–36.

25 Felicity Barringer, "*Los Angeles Times* Issues Unsparing Report on Itself," *New York Times,* December 21, 1999.

26 Steven Mufson, "BP Failed on Safety, Report Says," *Washington Post,* January 17, 2007. Time will tell the effect on BP of the Gulf of Mexico disaster of 2010, and it's not yet clear what role cutting corners may have led to this explosion and the resulting environmental catastrophe.

27 Jodi S. Cohen, Tara Malone, and Robert Becker, "U. of I. Jobs-for-Entry Scheme," *Chicago Tribune,* June 26, 2009.

28 The Illinois governor, while calling the resignation voluntary, said he thought the move was designed to "make sure that everyone in our state, in our country, our whole world, knows that the University of Illinois and its excellent reputation and its scholarship will continue." See Amanda Paulson, "Admissions Scandal Brings Down University of Illinois President," *Christian Science Monitor,* September 23, 2009.

29 We've already seen a clear example of costly punishment in the Ultimatum Game. In this experiment, the cost of punishing the other player was less direct—by cheating the person who cheated you, you tarnished your own reputation with other traders, thus potentially hurting your future payoffs. In this setup, other traders didn't know why you cheated—only that you did—so your reputation took a hit; you can imagine a different set of rules, though, where other players learn the circumstances under which you cheated; under these rules, retaliatory cheating would actually earn you a good reputation—as someone not to mess with.

30 Jennifer Brown and John Morgan, "Reputation in Online Auctions: The Market for Trust," *California Management Review,* vol. 49, no. 1 (2006): 61–81.

31 Kenneth R. Harney, "Homeowners Who 'Strategically Default' on Loans a Growing Problem," *Los Angeles Times,* September 20, 2009.

32 For more on Pierre Cardin's reputational slide, see Charles J. Fombrun, *Reputation: Realizing Value from the Corporate Image* (Boston: Harvard Business School Press, 1996), and Leyland Pitt and Michael Parent, "Stretching the Luxury Brand," *Financial Post,* October 24, 2008.

33 From Apple company history on FundingUniverse.com. See http://www.fundinguni verse.com/company-histories/Apple-Computer-Inc-Company-History.html.

34 G. Jin and P. Leslie, "The Effect of Information on Product Quality: Evidence from Res- taurant Hygiene Grade Cards," *Quarterly Journal of Economics,* vol. 118, no. 2 (2003): 409–51, and G. Z. Jin and P. Leslie, "Reputation Incentives for Restaurant Hygiene," *American Economic Journal: Microeconomics,* vol. 1, no. 1 (February 2009): 237–67. Interestingly, the introduction of posted grade cards also reduces the competitive advan- tage of chain restaurants, which derive their reputation from being part of a well-known chain. The authors also note that popular tourist areas, like Venice Beach and the Santa Monica Pier, tend to have restaurants with poor hygiene because most customers don't have a chance to learn about the restaurant's reputation through repeat visits: because the restaurants don't have a strong incentive to build a reputation for good hygiene, poor hygiene persists in the absence of posted grades. Although posted grade cards are still a rarity in the United States, one way of disseminating reputation information is catching on all over: user ratings on sites like Yelp and TripAdvisor. As more and more tourists can access these sites through smartphones, we can expect quality to rise.

35 Glenn Collins, "City Restaurants Required to Post Cleanliness Grades," *New York Times,* March 16, 2010.

36 K.-Y. Chen, T. Hogg, and N. Wozny, "Experimental Study of Market Reputation Mechanisms," *Proceedings of the 5th ACM Conference on Electronic Commerce* (2004): 234–35.

37 On the other hand, LinkedIn does a clever job of using reputational incentives to get users to contribute content to the site. By answering other users' questions on LinkedIn Answers, users can gain a reputation for being knowledgeable and helpful in their field.

38 Based on their analyses of companies with good and bad reputations, the authors of *Fame and Fortune* identify this kind of transparency as one mark of a company with a good reputation. Of course, this is merely a correlation; it's possible, for example, that a company with a good reputation has less to hide and therefore makes itself transparent—rather than the other way around.

39 Ronald Alsop, "How Boss's Deeds Buff a Firm's Reputation," *Wall Street Journal,* Janu- ary 31, 2007.

40 It seems like a catch-22—if you don't have enough members, you might be tempted to lower your membership standards, but lowering your standards further hurts your ability to attract good members; at some point, there is no way to reverse this downward spiral.

41 Oprah has been far less choosy in who and what she endorses informally. Though her intentions are good in publicizing controversial medical treatments through her show, for example, such implicit endorsements have hurt her image in the eyes of some doctors.

42 Steven Tadelis, "The Market for Reputations as an Incentive Mechanism," *Journal of Political Economy,* vol. 110, no. 4 (August 2002): 854–82.

43 We learned about this case from Gary J. Miller, *Managerial Dilemmas: The Political Economy of Hierarchy* (Cambridge, UK: Cambridge University Press, 1992).

44 See, for example, D. H. Hsu, "What Do Entrepreneurs Pay for Venture Capital Affili- ation?" *Journal of Finance,* vol. 59, no. 4 (2004): 1805–44.

45 M. J. Salganik, P. S. Dodds, and D. J. Watts, "Experimental Study of Inequality and Unpredictability in an Artificial Cultural Market," *Science,* vol. 311, no. 5762 (Febru- ary 10, 2006): 854–56.

46 Phone interview with Gary Bolton, May 27, 2008.

47 Gary Bolton, Ben Greiner, and Axel Ockenfels, "Engineering Trust: Reciprocity in the Production of Reputation Information" (SSRN working paper, April 2010).

48 Anya Kamenetz, "The Perils and Promise of the Reputation Economy," *Fast Company,* November 2008.

49 C. Dellarocas and C. A. Wood, "The Sound of Silence in Online Feedback: Estimating Trading Risks in the Presence of Reporting Bias," *Management Science,* vol. 54, no. 3 (March 2008): 460–76.

50 Fombrun and van Riel, *Fame and Fortune.*

51 Mooweon Rhee and Pamela R. Haunschild, "The Liability of Good Reputation: A Study of Product Recalls in the U.S. Automobile Industry," *Organization Science,* vol. 17, no. 1 (January–February 2006): 101–17.

Chapter 6. In Whom We Trust

1 Louise Story, "Lead Paint Prompts Mattel to Recall 967,000 Toys," *New York Times,* August 2, 2007.

2 In the following weeks, as consumers became wary of all sorts of products manufactured in China, Mattel found itself in the odd position of publicly apologizing to China's chief of product safety and to the Chinese people for Mattel's own weak safety controls. See Jyoti Thottam, "Why Mattel Apologized to China," *Time,* September 21, 2007.

3 The Trust Game is sometimes called the Investment Game. See Joyce Berg, John Dickhaut, and Kevin McCabe, "Trust, Reciprocity, and Social History," *Games and Economic Behavior,* vol. 10, no. 1 (July 1995): 122–42.

4 Martin Hollis, *Trust Within Reason* (Cambridge, UK: Cambridge University Press, 1998).

5 In fact, the Trust Game is a sequential Prisoner's Dilemma. Although players don't act simultaneously (and the Trustee knows how much the Investor trusts him), the Trust Game shares several key features with the classic Prisoner's Dilemma, most important the question of whether to trust under uncertainty.

6 P. J. Zak and S. Knack, "Trust and Growth," *Economic Journal,* vol. 111, no. 470 (April 2001): 295–321. Zak is a leader in the field of neuroeconomics, which looks at what happens in the brain as people make economic decisions. An interesting article for a lay audience about Zak's research, particularly the role of the neurotransmitter and hormone oxytocin and the relationship between trust and growth, is P. J. Zak, "The Neurobiology of Trust," *Scientific American,* vol. 298, no. 6 (June 2008): 88–95.

7 See T. Kiyonari, T. Yamagishi, K. S. Cook, and C. Cheshire, "Does Trust Beget Trustworthiness?: Trust and Trustworthiness in Two Games and Two Cultures: A Research Note," *Social Psychology Quarterly,* vol. 69, no. 3 (September 1, 2006): 270–83.

8 Family businesses can also run into the opposite problem: Junior knows the business well, so Dad trusts him completely—but Junior would rather pursue his own career, so lacks the motivation to run the family business. In both cases, Dad would be better off entrusting the business to someone else.

9 A. J. C. Cuddy et al., "When Professionals Become Mothers, Warmth Doesn't Cut the Ice," *Journal of Social Issues,* vol. 60, no. 4 (2004): 701–18.

10 Jennifer Aaker, Kathleen Vohs, and Cassie Mogilner, "Non-Profits Are Seen as Warm and For-Profits as Competent: Firm Stereotypes Matter" (working paper no. 69, Rock Center for Corporate Governance at Stanford University, forthcoming in *Journal of Consumer Research,* 2010).

11 This example comes from Jeffrey Pfeffer.

12 An excellent nontechnical discussion of cheap talk and the conditions under which it can be believed is J. Farrell and M. Rabin, "Cheap Talk," *Journal of Economic Perspectives*, vol. 10, no. 3 (Summer 1996): 103–18.

13 The notion of "truth bias" was introduced in S. McCornack and M. R. Parks, "Deception Detection and Relationship Development: The Other Side of Trust," in *Communication Yearbook 9*, ed. M. McLaughlin, pp. 377–89 (Beverly Hills, Calif.: Sage Publications, 1986). Subsequent experiments have confirmed this bias, as described in T. Kawagoe and H. Takizawa, "Why Lying Pays: Truth Bias in the Communication with Conflicting Interests," SSRN Electronic Paper Collection, 2005, ID: 691641.

14 Rachel Croson, Terry Boles, and J. Keith Murnighan, "Cheap Talk in Bargaining Experiments: Lying and Threats in Ultimatum Games," *Journal of Economic Behavior and Organization*, vol. 51, no. 2 (June 2003): 143–59.

15 An experiment on lying aversion is S. Hurkens and N. Kartik, "Would I Lie to You?: On Social Preferences and Lying Aversion," *Experimental Economics*, vol. 12, no. 2 (2009): 180–92.

16 Maurice E. Schweitzer and Rachel T. A. Croson, "Curtailing Deception: The Impact of Direct Questions on Lies and Omissions," *International Journal of Conflict Management*, vol. 10, no. 3 (July 1999): 225–48.

17 William P. Bottom, Kevin Gibson, Steven E. Daniels, and J. Keith Murnighan, "When Talk Is Not Cheap: Substantive Penance and Expressions of Intent in Rebuilding Cooperation," *Organization Science*, vol. 13, no. 5 (September 2002): 497–513.

18 The situation is more complicated than that: the experiments found that the effect of uncertainty depends on the cost of manufacturing. If manufacturing costs are high, then lower uncertainty (that is, less variability in demand) does indeed lead to less exaggeration and more trust. But if manufacturing costs are low, the buyer's exaggeration is the same regardless of the level of the buyer's certainty about demand; the low costs do lead the manufacturer to trust the buyer more, however, as we describe in the text.

19 Rachel Croson and Nancy Buchan, "Gender and Culture: International Experimental Evidence from Trust Games," *American Economic Review, Papers and Proceedings*, vol. 89, no. 2 (May 1999): 386–91.

20 Ibid.

21 M. Pillutla, D. Malhotra, and J. K. Murnighan, "Attributions of Trust and the Calculus of Reciprocity," *Journal of Experimental Social Psychology*, vol. 39, no. 5 (2003): 448–55.

22 P. J. Zak, K. Borja, W. T. Matzner, and R. Kurzban, "The Neuroeconomics of Distrust: Sex Differences in Behavior and Physiology," *American Economic Review*, vol. 95, no. 2 (2005): 360–63.

23 This argument is articulated in J. Mark Weber, Deepak Malhotra, and J. Keith Murnighan, "Normal Acts of Irrational Trust: Motivated Attributions and the Trust Development Process," *Research in Organizational Behavior*, vol. 26 (2005): 75–101.

24 These were the figures as of November 1, 2008, according to FGG's Web site, fggus.com.

25 I. Bohnet, F. Greig, B. Herrmann, and R. Zeckhauser, "Betrayal Aversion: Evidence from Brazil, China, Oman, Switzerland, Turkey, and the United States," *American Economic Review*, vol. 98, no. 1 (March 2008): 294–310.

26 J. Cox, "How to Identify Trust and Reciprocity," *Games and Economic Behavior*, vol. 46, no. 2 (2004): 260–81.

27 Jeffrey H. Dyer and Wujin Chu, "The Role of Trustworthiness in Reducing Transaction Costs and Improving Performance: Empirical Evidence from the United States,

Japan, and Korea," *Organization Science,* vol. 14, no. 1 (January–February 2003): 57–68.

28 Michael Spence, "Job Market Signaling," *Quarterly Journal of Economics,* vol. 87, no. 3 (August 1973): 353–74.

29 Another solution to the potential high costs of costly signaling is countersignaling—the risky strategy of trying to send a signal by not signaling. By not advertising on TV, for example, you might succeed in conveying the message that "my reputation speaks for itself." Similarly, by wearing slacker clothes and downplaying your degrees and titles, you can signal that you don't need conventional trappings. All such forms of false modesty work only if you're certain that your reputation does precede you.

30 Reliable communication doesn't have to involve costly spending. Anything that reveals information works. For example, a wholesaler asking for a forecast from a retailer might get an inaccurate one, since the retailer has no incentive for accuracy, but by offering the retailer a discount for placing an advance purchase order, the wholesaler in effect elicits an accurate forecast. The signal is quantity information in the order itself, and the reliability comes from the financial incentive to place the order early.

31 It probably makes sense for other reasons, too, such as giving the workers a place to let their hair down and speak frankly in a way that office protocol doesn't allow.

32 R. Sosis, "The Adaptive Value of Religious Ritual," *American Scientist,* vol. 92, no. 2 (March–April 2004): 166–72.

33 Bradley J. Ruffle and Richard Sosis, "Does It Pay to Pray? Costly Ritual and Cooperation," *B.E. Journal of Economic Analysis and Policy,* vol. 7, no. 1 (2007): Article 18.

34 Diego Gambetta, *Codes of the Underworld: How Criminals Communicate* (Princeton, N.J.: Princeton University Press, 2009).

35 This argument comes from Peter T. Leeson, *The Invisible Hook: The Hidden Economics of Pirates* (Princeton, N.J.: Princeton University Press, 2009).

36 The exploitation of trust within an identifiable ethnic or religious group, an example of affinity fraud, has also occurred at other times in other tight-knit communities, including Mormons and Baptists.

Chapter 7. Playing to the Rules of the Game

1 See Jane Costello, "Shopper Turns Lots of Pudding into Free Miles," *Wall Street Journal,* January 24, 2000, and James Bone, "Pudding Buyer Can Fly Free for a Lifetime," *The Times* (London), January 26, 2000. Other details of this story come from Kathleen Holder, "Engineer Finds Sweet Travel Deal in Cups of Pudding," *Dateline UC Davis,* February 4, 2000; "Roger and Out," *Airline Industry Information,* March 17, 2000; and Larry Jaffee, "Promoland," *Promo,* August 1, 2007.

2 For a study of the effect of physician report cards, see Timothy P. Hofer et al., "The Unreliability of Individual Physician 'Report Cards' for Assessing the Costs and Quality of Care of a Chronic Disease," *Journal of the American Medical Association,* vol. 281, no. 22 (June 9, 1999): 2098–105. The No Child Left Behind Act had many unintended consequences; this particular one is discussed in Sam Dillon, "States' Data Obscure How Few Finish High School," *New York Times,* March 20, 2008.

3 Steven Mufson, "Papermakers Dig Deep in Highway Bill to Hit Gold," *Washington Post,* March 28, 2009.

4 Melissa Morrison, "Arizona Taxpayers Fuming over $200 Million Boondoggle," *Washington Post,* December 11, 2000.

5   David Waldstein, "Nationals Sign Top Draft Pick, but Need Record $15 Million Bonus to Do So," *New York Times*, August 18, 2009.

6   Alvin E. Roth, J. Keith Murnighan, and Francoise Schoumaker, "The Deadline Effect in Bargaining: Some Experimental Evidence," *American Economic Review*, vol. 78, no. 4 (1988): 806–23.

7   Another economist, Muhamet Yildiz of MIT, offers an explanation. He reasons that if the two parties are too optimistic about the relative bargaining power, they will not compromise and strike a deal until the last minute, when further delays will cost both parties greatly.

8   Chico Harlan, "A Franchise, and a City, Pin Their Hopes on a Mighty Arm," *Washington Post*, August 19, 2009.

9   Ian Larkin, "The Cost of High-Powered Incentives: Employee Gaming in Enterprise Software Sales" (working paper, May 17, 2008), http://isites.harvard.edu.

10 Dan Ariely, Axel Ockenfels, and Alvin Roth, "An Experimental Analysis of Ending Rules in Internet Auctions," *RAND Journal of Economics*, vol. 36, no. 4 (Winter 2005): 890–907. See also Alvin E. Roth and Axel Ockenfels, "Last-Minute Bidding and the Rules for Ending Second-Price Auctions: Evidence from eBay and Amazon Auctions on the Internet," *American Economic Review*, vol. 92, no. 4 (September 2002): 1093–103.

11 When eBay changed its feedback mechanism, as described in chapter 5, on reputation, it made it a point to layer the new feedback on top of the old for precisely this reason: to minimize the shock to the system.

12 For example, see Ali Dasdan, Santanu Kolay, Panagiotis Papadimitriou, and Hector Garcia-Molina, "Output Bidding: A New Search Advertising Model Complementary to Keyword Bidding," Fifth Workshop on Ad Auctions (in conjunction with the ACM Conference on Electronic Commerce), July 6, 2009, Stanford, Calif.).

13 This distinction becomes murky with online retailers. Technically, the price shown next to an item on a Web site is considered the advertised price, not the real price; the real price doesn't appear until a customer looks in the shopping cart. Online merchants can display a MAP price in one place and a lower price elsewhere. For example, one vendor of MAP pricing software for e-commerce sites describes its product this way: "The Minimum Advertised Price extension helps you to escape the conflicts with the manufacturers and sell products at the prices you wish. Minimum Advertised Price adds a special Check Price button instead of the product price. Having clicked this button, you add an item to the shopping cart, and only then the required price becomes visible."

14 When record companies (including Time Warner, EMI, and Sony) tried to overstep the bounds of MAP by mandating a minimum advertised price on music CDs *even when retailers were using their own money to advertise discount prices*, the Federal Trade Commission slapped them with an antitrust case.

15 Gary Charness and Kay-Yut Chen, "Minimum Advertised-Price Policy Rules and Retailer Behavior: An Experiment by Hewlett-Packard," *Interfaces*, vol. 32, no. 5 (September–October 2002): 62–63.

Chapter 8. Predicting the Unpredictable

1   According to an HSX press release: "Traders Hit 88% of Oscar Awards," February 23, 2009.

2   Anita Elberse, "The Power of Stars: Do Star Actors Drive the Success of Movies?" *Journal of Marketing*, vol. 71, no. 4 (October 2007): 102–20.

3   William Goldman, *Adventures in the Screen Trade: A Personal View of Hollywood and Screenwriting* (New York: Warner Books, 1983).

4   James Surowiecki made a similar comment in one of his columns: "Nobody knows anything. But everybody, it turns out, may know something." "The Science of Success," *New Yorker,* July 9, 2007.

5   The $1.3 billion figure comes from an industry analyst quoted in "Wii Shortage Means $1.3bn Lost Sales for Nintendo This Christmas," *The Times* (London), December 18, 2007.

6   Nintendo of America president Reggie Fils-Aimé quoted in Cliff Edwards, "A Long, Long Wait for a Wii," *BusinessWeek,* December 17, 2007.

7   Malcolm Gladwell, *Blink: The Power of Thinking Without Thinking* (New York: Little, Brown and Company, 2005).

8   Another recent book along these lines, more focused on giving practical advice for taking a data-driven approach to decision making, is Thomas H. Davenport and Jeanne G. Harris, *Competing on Analytics: The New Science of Winning* (Boston: Harvard Business School Press, 2007), and its follow-up, Thomas H. Davenport, Jeanne G. Harris, and Robert Morison, *Analytics at Work: Smarter Decisions, Better Results* (Boston: Harvard Business School Press, 2010).

9   James Surowiecki, *The Wisdom of Crowds: Why the Many Are Smarter Than the Few and How Collective Wisdom Shapes Business, Economies, Societies, and Nations* (New York: Doubleday, 2004).

10 Quoted in Caren Chesler, "A Bettor World," *The American,* May–June 2007.

11 http://us.newsfutures.com/home/clients.html.

12 For a more detailed explanation of this process, see Scott E. Page, *The Difference: How the Power of Diversity Creates Better Groups, Firms, Schools, and Societies* (Princeton, N.J.: Princeton University Press, 2007).

13 Emile Servan-Schreiber, Justin Wolfers, David M. Pennock, and Brian Galebach, "Prediction Markets: Does Money Matter?" *Electronic Markets,* vol. 14, no. 3 (September 2004): 243–51.

14 Also, the market trading price of the team each market favored to win in each game closely mirrored the likelihood that it would win: the average pregame trading price of a favorite on TradeSports was 65.1 percent, and on SportsExchange it was 65.6 percent.

15 Chris Hanson, an economist at George Mason University, tells of having the idea for "ideas futures," a concept he came up with before he trained to become an economist.

16 Charles Plott and Shyam Sunder, "Rational Expectations and the Aggregation of Diverse Information in Laboratory Security Markets," *Econometrica,* vol. 56, no. 5 (September 1988): 1085–118. See also Charles Plott and Shyam Sunder, "Efficiency of Experimental Security Markets with Insider Information: An Application of Rational-Expectations Models," *The Journal of Political Economy,* vol. 94, no. 4 (August 1982): 663–698.

17 http://www.nhtsa.dot.gov/CARS/rules/CAFE/overview.htm.

18 Andy Serwer, "Making a Market in (Almost) Anything," *Fortune,* August 8, 2005.

19 Like all prediction markets, Intrade actually sells "futures contracts." Intrade calls these futures contracts "tickets," but other prediction markets might call them securities, shares, or assets. Because buying a ticket on TradeSports is equivalent to placing a bet, we'll call the tickets bought and sold on TradeSports *bets.*

20 Bo Cowgill, Justin Wolfers, and Eric Zitzewitz, "Using Prediction Markets to Track Information Flows: Evidence from Google" (working paper, 2008).

21 Jay W. Hopman, "Using Forecasting Markets to Manage Demand Risk," *Intel Technology Journal,* vol. 11, no. 2 (May 16, 2007): 127–36.

22 Short for Behaviorally Robust Aggregation of Information in Networks.

23 They don't get paid in direct proportion to the number of tickets in the correct bucket, but rather with diminishing returns. In other words, the first ticket bet on the correct outcome is worth more than the second ticket, the second is worth more than the third, and so on.

24 See these papers from HP Labs: http://www.hpl.hp.com/research/idl/papers/future/future.pdf and http://www.hpl.hp.com/research/idl/papers/public/publicinfo.pdf.

25 Interview with Martha Lyons, Distinguished Technologist in HP's Technology Transfer Office. For now, BRAIN is available on a case-by-case consulting basis to select customers, and HP is keeping clients' names confidential.

26 Even so, prediction markets are occasionally prone to a natural form of double counting, in the form of bubbles.

27 Quoted in Shailagh Murray, "Online Exchange Chooses Turmoil as a Commodity: In Bizarre U.S. Project, Traders to Bet on Events in Middle East," *Wall Street Journal,* July 29, 2003.

28 Interview with Joseph Segel, October 24, 2006.

Conclusion

1 This incident comes from Richard P. Feynman's delightful memoir, *"Surely You're Joking, Mr. Feynman!": Adventures of a Curious Character* (New York: W.W. Norton, 1985).

INDEX

· · · · · · · ·

Ability
  and reputation, 126–27
  and trustworthiness, 154–55
Academy Awards prediction, 187–90
Adverse selection
  and reputation, 126
  and uncertainty, 35–37
Akerlof, George, 64–66, 165–66
Alaska Airlines, 128–29
Altruism, and trustworthiness, 163
Amazon
  bidding extension rule, 181–83
  price discrimination, 52–54
  uncertainty, dealing with, 24, 26
Anchoring, 92
Apple, reputation, 118–19, 128, 141, 145
Ariely, Dan, 181
Attributions, Sinister Attribution Error, 153,
    161, 191
Automobile leasing, 16
AutONA (Automated One-to-one
    Negotiation Agent), 94–95

Babbling equilibrium, 157
Babcock, Linda, 51
Baby halo, 138
Bargaining
  and fairness. See Fairness
  process, components of, 41–42
Bearden, Neil, 98
Beer Game, 99–100

Beer on the Beach study, 54
Benjamin Hotel, 29
Bereby-Meyer, Yoella, 58
Berg, Joyce, 148
Bid sniping, 141–44
Bohnet, Iris, 163
Bolton, Gary, 142
BP refinery explosion, 130, 139
BRAIN method, 203–5
Brown, Jennifer, 133
Bubbles, prediction markets, 203
Bullwhip Effect, 99–100
Buyer-seller experiments, 81

Cachon, Gérard, 91–93
Cantor Fitzgerald, 190
Capital One, 4
Casanova, Giacomo, 11–12
Charitable giving
  as costly signal, 170
  and reciprocity, 76–79
Charness, Gary, 72, 184–85
Cheap talk, and trustworthiness,
    157–58, 164–65
Cheaters
  punishment of, 80–83
  retaliatory, rationale for, 130–31
Chen, Kay-Yut
  AutONA (Automated One-to-one
    Negotiation Agent), 94–95
  BRAIN method, 203–5

Chen, Kay-Yut (*cont.*)
  buyer-seller experiments, 81–82
  endgame effect, reducing, 186–87
  fairness and game procedures, 50–51
  forecasting, improving, 209–12
  freedom to decide, 103–10
  MAP violation penalties, 184–86
  optimizer's paradox, 101–5
  optimizing for demand, 97–98
  reputation, 129, 131–32
  risk attitudes, 16–17, 113–14
  starts HP Labs, 2–3
  trust, 156–57
Children
  Envy Game, 48–49
  and fairness, 58–59
Choice, paradox of, 101–7
Cialdini, Robert, 77
Coca-Cola, 54
Collective intelligence, forecasting with,
  194–99
Commitment devices, to predict sales,
  209–10
Competition, human competitive
  forces, 61
Conflict, escalation and reciprocity, 83–85
Consignment agreements, 30
Contamination of experiments, avoiding, 67
Contracts
  and fairness, 61
  for optimal results, 108–11
Cooperation, human cooperative forces, 61
Costly signaling, and trustworthiness,
  166–71
Croson, Rachel, 49–50, 161
Culture
  and sense of fairness, 55–56
  and trust/trustworthiness, 161
Curse of Knowledge, 124–25

Deadlines. *See* Timing rules
Dear Abby Dilemma, 212–13
Decision-making. *See* Rationality
Decision markets, 199–200
Demand
  forecasting for new products, 193–94
  stability and trustworthiness, 159–60
Dickhaut, John,
Dictator Game, 43–46, 59, 83–87
Domino's Pizza, 28–29
Down payment, as commitment device,
  210–11

EarthGrains, 164
eBay
  bid sniping, 141–44
  reputation issue, 119–20, 133,
    141–44
Economic experiments
  academic roots of, 6
  basic premise, 2–3
  companies utilizing, 4–6
  first and HP, 1–2
  thought experiments, 187
Elberse, Anita, 189
Emotions
  emotional appeals, 62
  impact on thoughts/actions, 62
Endgame effect, 132, 186–87
Envy Game, 48–49
Exploitation, of reputation, 131–35
Exxon Valdez, 138–39

Face-to-face communication, and fairness,
  56–58
Fairfield Greenwich Group (FGG), 162–63
Fairness, 39–62
  and children, 58–59
  cultural differences, 55–56
  Dictator Game, 43–46, 59
  Envy Game, 48–49
  and face-to-face communication, 56–58
  importance of concept, 60–62
  paying price for, 41–43
  in pricing, 46–48
  versus self-serving choices, 51–52
  Ultimatum Game, 41–43, 46, 55–59,
    62, 79
Faith Game, 151–52
Falk, Armin, 76–77
FDIC insurance, 139
FedEx, 69
Fehr, Ernst, 65, 80, 82
Feynman, Richard, 214–15
Fishman, Peter, 47
Fisk, Shelly, 58
Forecasting, 188–213
  accuracy, improving, 209–12
  collective intelligence, 194–99
  commitment devices, use of, 209–10
  guesstimation, 192
  incentive-based system, 211–12
  new product demand, 193–94
  number crunching, 192–93
  See also Prediction markets

Franklin Mint, 209–10
Free-riders, and reciprocity, 79–81
Future, predicting with reputation, 127–29

Gächter, Simon, 80, 82
Gambetta, Diego, 169
Gambler's Fallacy, 38
Gambling, martingale strategy, 11–12
Gates, Bill, 138
Gift Exchange Game, 65–72
Gneezy, Uri, 18, 67–71, 78
Goldman, William, 189
Goodnight, Jim, 63
Google, 4, 31, 203
Greenberg, Jerald, 82
Guarantees
    profitability of, 26–30
    and trustworthiness, 165
Guesstimation, 192
Güth, Werner, 41

Harrah's, 4
Hastings, Reed, 47
Hazing rituals, 168
Healthy Choice, miles for labels offer,
    172–75
Hedging, compared to risk pooling, 23–24
Hewlett-Packard
    HP Labs, origin of, 1–3
    HP Labs economic experiments, 107, 115
    prediction markets, 195, 201–2, 204–5
    See also Chen, Kay-Yut
Hogg, Tad, 113
Hollis, Martin, 149
Hollywood Stock Exchange (HSX.com),
    188–90
Holt, Charles, 13, 15, 17
Hot-Hand Fallacy, 38
Hurd, Mark, 8
Hussein, Saddam, capture, prediction
    market for, 200–201
Hyperfit USA, 129

IBM Valuepoint, 94
Incentives
    and forecasting, 211–12
    and prediction markets, 197–99
    and trustworthiness, 155–61, 165, 171
Insurance companies
    adverse selection, dealing with, 35–36
    moral hazard, dealing with, 33–34
    no-fault insurance, 33

risk pooling, use of, 23, 25
risk premiums, 25
Intentions
    instability of, 127
    and reciprocity, 72–75, 84–85
    and trustworthiness, 152–54
Iowa Electronic Health Market, 195
Iowa Electronic Market, 195, 202, 207

Jin, Ginger, 136
Jobs, Steve, 118–19, 141, 145
Johnson & Johnson, 138

Kahneman, Daniel, 4, 46, 91–92, 98
Kasparov, Garry, 94
Katok, Elena, 100
Kelleher, Herb, 6
Keysar, Boaz, 83
Kill fees, 34–35
Knack, Stephen, 151
Knetsch, Jack, 46
Kramer, Roderick, 153
Kube, Sebastian, 70

Larkin, Ian, 180
Laury, Susan, 13, 15
Law of Large Numbers
    and prediction markets, 195–96
    and uncertainty/risk, 12–13, 25
Lawyers, risk pooling, use of, 23
Lazear, Edward, 45
Leeson, Peter, 169–70
Lemon Problem, 122–23
Leslie, Phillip, 136
Levitt, Steven, 4
Likelihood, and trustworthiness, 154
List, John, 4, 18, 44, 67–71
Loch, Christopher, 73
Loewenstein, George, 51
Los Angeles Times, 130
Lying, aversion to, 157–59

McFadden, Daniel, 101
Madoff, Bernie, 132, 162–63, 170
Major League Baseball, first-year player draft
    deadline, 176–78
Market liquidity, and prediction markets,
    196, 201–2
Martingale betting strategy, 11–13
Mattel, lead-filled pigment problem,
    146–47, 152, 156, 171
Mencken, H. L., 49

Men's Warehouse, 26
MetLife Benefits Simplifier, 93
Microsoft, 138
Minimum Advertised Price (MAP), violation
    penalties, 184–86
Moral hazard
    and reputation, 126–27
    and uncertainty, 33–35
Morgan, John, 133
Murnighan, Keith, 176
Murphy, Ryan, 98

Negotiation
    and anchoring, 92
    AutONA (Automated One-to-One
        Negotiation Agent), 94–95
    and deadlines, 175–80
    face-to-face, 57–58
    and fairness, 39–41, 51–52, 57–58, 60
    and risk aversion, 32–33
    self-serving choices, 51–52
    Ultimatum Game, 41–44, 52
NetExchange, 206
Netflix
    decision-support tools, 88
    fairness and pricing, 47
    uncertainty, dealing with, 24
Nintendo Wii shortage, 191
No-fault insurance, 33
Number crunching, 192–93
NTT DoCoMo, 58

Ockenfels, Axel, 181
Orman, Suze, 139
Orthodox Jews, costly signals of, 168–69
Özer, Özalp, 156

Phelps, Michael, 117–18
Phillips, David, 172–74
Pierre Cardin licensing deals, 134–35
Plott, Charles, 7, 16, 199, 200
Poindexter, John, 207
Policy Analysis Market (PAM) failure,
    206–7
Polk, Charles, 206
Pooling, risk, 22–25
Pope, Devin, 47
Prediction. See Forecasting
Prediction markets, 194–203
    BRAIN method, 203–5
    bubbles, 203
    companies utilizing, 195

decision markets, 199–200
Hollywood Stock Exchange, 188–90
incentives, impact on, 197–99
information needs, 202–3
Law of Large Numbers, 195–96
liquidity, necessity of, 196, 201–2
pitfalls related to, 200–203
Policy Analysis Market (PAM) failure,
    206–7
Pricing
    Beer on the Beach study, 54–55
    fairness in, 46–48
    price discrimination, 52–55
Prisoner's Dilemma, 79, 81, 150, 158
Proctor & Gamble, 120–21
Prosper.com, 131
Public-goods games, 79–81
Punishment
    of cheaters, 80–83
    distrust penalty, 162–63

Quality, and reputation, 126–27

Rapoport, Amnon, 98
Rationality, 86–116
    Beer Game, 99–100
    Bullwhip Effect, 99–100
    contracts for optimal results, 108–11
    erratic demand problem, 89–91
    freedom to decide, 103–7
    manageability of problems project,
        107–8
    measurement of, 111–15
    paradox of choice, 101–7
    rationality index, 114
    Secretary Problem, 95–96
Reciprocity, 63–85
    on behalf of others, 79–83
    buyer-seller experiments, 81
    carrot first concept, 78
    charitable giving, 76–79
    conflict, escalation of, 83–85
    Dictator Game, 83–87
    eBay experiment, 119–20
    versus economic concepts, 64
    field testing, 67–72
    and free-riders, 79–81
    Gift Exchange Game, 65–72
    and intentions, 72–75, 84–85
    noncash gifts, effectiveness of,
        70–72, 76–78
    partial gift exchange, 64–65

public-goods game, 79–81
punishment of cheaters, 80–83
relative reciprocity, measurement of, 74
rewards to workers, 69–70
social relations, impact on, 72–75
thank-you gift, effects of, 78–79
Unscrupulous Diner's Dilemma,
   79–80
Religious groups, costly signals of, 168–69
Repeated Prisoner's Dilemma, 81
Reputation, 117–45
   about ability and quality, 126–27
   about intention or motivation,
      126–27
   and adverse selection, 126
   buying and selling of, 139–40
   definition, 125
   endgame effect, 132
   erosion, impact of, 129–31
   exploitation of, 131–35
   importance of, 118–21, 124–25
   Lemon Problem, 122–23
   markets reliance on, 121–23
   moral hazard problem, 126–27
   negative aspects of, 144–45
   past as driver of, 127–29, 133–34
   rubbing off, 138–39
   as self-fulfilling prophesy, 141
   strengthening, 141–44
   transparency effect, 136–38
   and trustworthiness, 164
   as unreality, 135–36
Restocking fees, 36–37
Retailers
   returns policies, 26–30, 33, 36–37
   risk aversion, profitability of, 27–29
   risk pooling, use of, 23
   risk premiums, 25–26
Returns policies, of retailers, 26–30, 33,
   36–37
Risk attitude, assessment of, 13–20
Risk aversion, 13–22
   profits generated from, 26–33
   reducing risk, methods, 22–26,
      30–32
   and uncertainty, 16–20, 38
   variance, considering in, 20–22
Risk loving, 15
Risk neutral, 15
Risk pooling
   adverse selection, 35–37
   compared to hedging, 23–24

moral hazard, 33–34
   and risk reduction, 22–25
Risk premiums, 25–26
Risk spreading, 23
Risk transfers, and risk reduction,
   25–26, 30–32
Roth, Al, 55–57, 176, 181
Ruffle, Bradley, 169
Rules
   gaming the system, 172–75
   Minimum Advertised Price (MAP)
      violation penalties, 184–86
   See also Timing rules

Sabotage, by employees, 82–83
Sales compensation
   commitment device, use of 209–12
   exploring with thought experiment, 187
   and moral hazard, 34
   nonlinear bonuses, 179–80
   and risk aversion, 30–31
   salary versus commission, 30–31, 34
SAS, 63–64
Schoumaker, Francoise, 176
Schweitzer, Maurice, 91–93
Sears, 140
Secretary Problem, 95–96
Segel, Joseph, 210
Self-fulfilling prophesy, reputation as, 141
Shang, Jen, 49–50
Sheffi, Yossi, 87
Simonsohn, Uri, 19–20
Sinister Attribution Error, 153, 161, 191
Smith, Vernon, 4
Social factors
   high status benefits of, 60
   relationships and reciprocity, 72–75
   social dilemmas, 79
   social preferences, 60–61
Sosis, Richard, 168–69
Southwest Airlines, 6
Spence, Michael, 165–66
Subprime mortgages, 133–34
Sunder, Shyam, 199

Taleb, Nassim Nicholas, 20
Thaler, Richard, 46, 54–55
Theft, employee, 82–83
Timing rules, 175–87
   bid sniping versus extension rule, 180–83
   close to deadline decisions, 175–80
   endgame effect, 186–87

Track records, and data-collection, 128–29
Trader Joe's, 26–27
Tragedy of the commons, 79
Transferring risk. *See* Risk transfers
Transparency effect, and reputation, 136–38
Trip-cancellation insurance, 35–36
Trust and trustworthiness, 146–71
  and ability, 154–55
  and betrayal aversion, 163
  bias toward, 157–59
  cheap talk, impact on, 157–58, 164–65
  costly signaling theory, 166–71
  cultural context, 161
  distrust and aggression, 162
  distrust penalty, 162–63
  Faith Game, 151–52
  incentives, impact on, 155–61, 165, 171
  increasing trustworthiness, 158, 160–61
  and intentions, 152–54
  and likelihoods, 154
  luck and outcome, 154–55
  and lying aversion, 157–59
  and reputation, 164
  and stability of future demand, 159–60
  Trust Game, 148–51, 153, 161–62
Truth, lying aversion, 157–59
Tversky, Amos, 91–92, 98

Ultimatum Game, 41–43, 46, 55–59, 62, 79, 157
Uncertainty, 11–38
  and adverse selection, 35–37
  managing, 24–25, 38
  martingale strategy, 11–13

  and moral hazard, 33–35
  returns policies, 26–30, 36–37
  risk aversion, 13–22, 16–20
  risk pooling, 22–25, 33–37
  risk spreading, 25–26
  risk transfers, 25–26, 30–32
  Uncertainty Effect, 19–20
University of Illinois, 130
Unscrupulous Diner's Dilemma, 79–80

Variance, negative aspects of, 20–22

Wars, 83
Washington Ballet, 39–41, 51, 60
Whitman, Meg, 8
Winfrey, Oprah, 140
Wolfers, Justin, 193–94
Woods, Tiger, 118, 145
Workforce
  employee theft and sabotage, 82–83
  employer/worker reciprocity. *See* Reciprocity
  risk transfer, use of, 30–32
Wu, Diana, 100–101, 103, 109–10, 114
Wu, George, 18
Wyden, Ron, 206–7

Yahoo! 4
Yamada, Ryuji, 58
Yellen, Janet, 66

Zak, Paul, 151, 162
Zappos.com, 28, 33–34
Zhang Shuhong, 146–47
Zimmer, George, 26